HERITAGE TREASURES

The historic homes of Ancaster, Burlington, Dundas, East Flamborough, Hamilton, Stoney Creek and Waterdown

Susan Evans Shaw

Photography by Jean Crankshaw

JAMES LORIMER & COMPANY LTD., PUBLISHERS

TORONTO

James Lorimer & Company Ltd. acknowledges the support of the Ontario Arts Council. We acknowledge the support of the Government of Canada through the Book Publishing Industry Development Program (BPIDP) for our publishing activities. We acknowledge the support of the Canada Council for the Arts for our publishing program. We acknowledge the support of the Government of Ontario through the Ontario Media Development Corporation's Ontario Book Initiative.

The Canada Council | Le Conseil des Arts
for the Arts | du Canada

ONTARIO ARTS COUNCIL
CONSEIL DES ARTS DE L'ONTARIO

Library and Archives Canada Cataloguing in Publication

Evans Shaw, Susan, 1944-
    Heritage treasures : the historic homes of Ancaster, Burlington, Dundas, East Flamborough, Hamilton, Stoney Creek and Waterdown / Susan Evans Shaw ; photographs by Jean Crankshaw.

Includes bibliographical references and index.
ISBN 1-55028-867-9

1. Historic buildings—Ontario—Hamilton. 2. Dwellings—Ontario—Hamilton. 3. Hamilton (Ont.)—History. I. Crankshaw, Jean II. Title.

FC3098.7.E92 2004   971.3'52   C2004-903935-0

James Lorimer & Company Ltd., Publishers
35 Britain Street
Toronto, Ontario
M5A 1R7
www. lorimer.ca

Printed and bound in China

Table of Contents

Introduction

The loveliness of the city of Hamilton is one of Ontario's best kept secrets. While Toronto's glass towers glisten like the City of Oz across the lake, dowdy Hamilton is seen to belch smoke from her mills and factories, unable to shake the blue-collar, lunch-bucket image perpetuated by the misinformed.

My colleague, Jean Crankshaw and I are not native Hamiltonians but we have chosen to live here and to live downtown. We are both fond of walking and, the one-way streets notwithstanding, Hamilton is a good city for walking; plenty of trees, parks, alleyways, neighbourhoods and architecture. Take a look from the escarpment or from the top of a tall building and you'll see from west to east how green the city is. Canopied by all those trees are houses, grand and humble, and so many of architectural merit.

Head-of-the-Lake, as the area was called originally, is an area full of history and crammed with event. James Elliott's book about the journeys of Robert Land *If Ponies Rode Men*, woke me to the complexity of happenings that began with the American Revolutionary War. After reading the book I walked up James Street South to have a look at the two pillars from Landholme, now fronting the driveway of what was the Leather home. Then I drove down to Barton Street and looked for traces of the house that Robert Land built, although I knew from

Elliott's book that it had been demolished in 1928.

In the autumn of 2000, a long struggle between a property owner and the Architectural Conservancy ended when the historic stone mansion, Bellevue, a landmark on the mountain brow and the mate to Whitehern, was pulled down. There was nothing to be done. The building had been derelict for years, the city couldn't or wouldn't contribute to restoration, and the cost was too high for most private purses.

How many other buildings are threatened? We know countless old places have been demolished. A project to make a record of the houses and publish something beautiful that would make Hamiltonians sit up and take note seemed a worthwhile enterprise. And so we started. As I drove around the city on errands I would make note of houses that looked like possibilities. Jean did the same and also checked web sites for heritage homes. The list grew rapidly, even with our cut-off date of 1914. While we were scurrying about, the city of Hamilton became the New City of Hamilton and Jim Lorimer (by then we had a publisher) pointed out that we would have to extend our boundaries.

Jean did most of the exploring in Ancaster, Dundas, Flamborough, and Aldershot, while I sifted through the files in the Local Architectural Conservancy Advisory Committee (known as LACAC) office in the former Stoney Creek City Hall and the Hamilton Public Library's Special Collections for material on each house. At this stage we began to winnow out houses for which there was insufficient information.

Choosing the houses for inclusion in the book was a tough job. There were so many and the list grew to more than 300. We mailed letters to all the homeowners, explaining our project and asking for their permission and cooperation. The response was very encouraging and of those who didn't respond, either I telephoned or Jean knocked on doors if we particularly hoped to include a place, or I moved the entry to a back list we kept. Only two householders refused to take part when approached and one house was excluded after the owners proudly reported they had completely remodelled the interior, its most interesting feature.

As Jean began the photography, she discovered that taking pictures out of doors using camera and a tripod is a magnet to neighbours and passers-by, permission having already been obtained from the householder. Every outing she returned with another story either about the house, former occupants or the neighbourhood, some of which we have included. We arranged visits to tour interiors, particularly of those houses with intact features inside like moulding, baseboards, stairways and so forth. Some of the visits we made together so that while I talked to the homeowner, Jean set up her tripod and snapped photos.

Before 1815 few settlers had the means and leisure to build a permanent home, so they started with log houses. As time passed, Ontario's farmers turned to stone and brick to construct more substantial houses to reflect their worth. Much of the material for building was to hand; white pine forests, stone found in fields and the escarpment, and good clay for brick in stream beds.

Today only the very rich can afford to construct a house of such style and quality. Few have the time or the skill to build for themselves and the cost of labour and materials would be prohibitive. Technology prevails over craftsmanship and much of the material used in building nowadays is synthetic. A consequence is an occupational hazard specific to firemen when these materials catch fire.

Fifty-nine houses are featured in *Heritage Treasures*. We have arranged them by date in the book, the oldest house first and the most recent last. Each is representative of a period and style and for every one

included there are dozens more out there. You have only to look around. Some, like 179 Mary Street, are hidden in a streetscape of tall houses, others stand in splendour, like 250 James Street South, on a busy corner, and still others, like 179 York Road or the Shaver Homestead, are still in a country setting.

Jean and I wore out a fair bit of shoe leather trekking around from house to house, but it would have been to no avail without the assistance of all those who became involved. We owe a thank you to everyone who gave us their time and let us make use of their expertise: Stephanie Barber and David Cuming at the City of Hamilton LACAC, Sylvia Wray of the Waterdown Historical Society, the staff in Special Collections at the Hamilton Public Library, and the LACAC in Dundas Public Library. To each and every homeowner who welcomed us we owe a special thank you. You kindly showed us around, allowed us to poke into kitchens and cupboards, and, when available, gave us copies of relevant documents or, in the case of George and Mary Lewis, loaned us their slides.

This has been a fascinating project from beginning to end, and instructive too. Neither of us had much more than a rudimentary knowledge of architecture when we started, although Jean has a good eye for detail. We learned as we went along. As a result, although we have tried to be as accurate as possible, any errors are entirely our own.

Erland Lee House, 1801

552 Ridge Road, Stoney Creek

A fine example of Ontario Gothic revival architecture. From the parking lot the first view of the house is of the west elevation.

In 1792, James and Hannah Lee, United Empire Loyalists from Maryland, arrived at Saltfleet Township, where James, in 1801, was granted 200 acres along the Niagara Escarpment. Their eldest son, John, married Mary, eldest daughter of Enoch Moore, Lee's next-door neighbour. Enoch owned land at what is now 552 Ridge Road, where he had been living from the time of the 1791 survey. About 1800, Enoch left his family and disappeared without a trace and without obtaining proper title to the land. It took forty-eight years, until 1844, before Mary at last got title, although she, John, and their family had been living on the property since 1808. In that year John built a small frame log house, where he and Mary raised eleven children.

In 1837, their youngest son, Abram D'Arcy Lee, added a front section to the already existing house. Abram married Jemima Pew, and their son Erland Lee, born in 1864, inherited the farm. Erland, a charter member of the Farmers' Institute, in 1897 invited Adelaide Hoodless to speak at the Ladies' Night of the Saltfleet Farmers' Institute. On February 19, 1897, the first Women's Institute in the world was organized at Squire's Hall, Stoney Creek, with original by-laws and charter drawn up by Janet Lee, with wording assistance from her husband Erland, Ernest Disraeli Smith, M.P., and Frank Metcalfe Carpenter, M.P.P.

Adelaide Hoodless became a crusader after her fourteen-month-old son died from drinking impure milk. Since her successful effort in their founding, the Women's Institutes have become the world's largest rural women's movement, numbering about 6 million members in First- and Third-world countries. The Institute taught food safety, pushed for pasteurization, and saw to it that bread was sold in bags and

Top: A round-arched Gothic window.
Above: Hand-carved bargeboards.

The summer kitchen, featuring remnants of the original 1808 cottage.

roads had yellow dividing lines.

The house is a well-preserved example of Ontario Gothic revival, a white board-and-batten structure with bay windows, green shutters, and, along the gables, hand-carved maple bargeboards, so called because the pattern resembles a paper chain of maple leaves. The steep side-gabled roof has a central Gothic gable surmounting a pair of round-arched windows with matching green shutters, and directly underneath them is a pair of rectangular windows with shutters. Between the upper and lower pairs of windows are paired carved medallions. The double front doors and Georgian lintel, arched sidelights, and plain pilasters are sheltered from the elements by an elaborately trimmed front porch.

From the parking area the first view of the house is the west elevation, which is topped by a gable with decorative bargeboards over two pairs of windows that echo those under the front gable. Farther south along the same elevation there is a large rectangular two-over-two sash window embellished with a shallow arch.

Typical of this style of house, there is a summer kitchen tail behind

The parlour in the 1837 addition to the front of the house.

the middle section, constructed around the original log cabin. Little is left of the 1808 cabin but the floorboards, a dresser, and a very plain door, free of moulding. In the front section of the house, the pur boasts a 9½-foot ceiling, but the medallion, valence, and rug all date from the 1940s. The fireplace is only a façade, and the house was heated by a coal stove, the vent for which remains in the hall.

Upstairs there are four bedrooms opening from a central hall. In what was once the boys' bedroom, there is a low door in the south wall that is the height of the original unheated loft — 45 inches — where the family slept in the days of the 1808 cabin. John and Mary Lee and their children would have been happy to snuggle together on bitter winter nights.

The recent popular movie *Calendar Girls* recounts the true story of a remote Yorkshire village where the Women's Institute embarked on a project to raise money for leukemia research. Eleven middle-aged members of the group posed discreetly nude for a calendar. The funds raised were in the millions of dollars and the calendar was a sensation. One wonders what Adelaide Hoodless would have said.

Top: Dining room and walnut table on which the first Women's Institute charter was written.
Above: The 1870s drive house has its original interior hand-hewn timbers.

Ingledale House, 1815

1489 Baseline Road, Stoney Creek

This property was originally owned by John Green and his wife, Mary Davis, both United Empire Loyalists, immigrants to Upper Canada in 1787. Green purchased Broken Front Concession, lot 1, Saltfleet Township in 1813 and sold it to John Inglehart in 1815. Inglehart had arrived in Upper Canada about 1798 with his wife, Magdalena, and several other Pennsylvania German settlers. Between 1815 and the early 1820s, Inglehart constructed a dwelling for himself and his family. When he died in 1835, his son Jacob built the south addition to the home after removing half the original building and retaining the rest to be used as a kitchen. Jacob died in 1853 and the property passed to his son Hiram Frew Inglehart, who sold it in 1870 to Henry Magill. In 1890, Jonathan Carpenter bought the property from Magill. He took down the east wing of the house. The property remained in the Carpenter family until 1971. It is now part of the Fifty Point Conservation Area.

Parts of the original house remain. The north end has two symmetrical six-over-six double-hung windows on the second floor. A third window with a nine-over-six sash is centred on the first floor. Extending east is a 2-metre addition with a trellised porch. The north addition presents a pleasingly harmonious vernacular neo-classical exterior with many of the details associated with the style: rectangular façade with a low-pitched roof, gable ends with short returning cornices, repeat-pattern mouldings in the roof cornice, and asymmetrically placed window openings.

A view from the west. The rear of the original house is now a kitchen.

The front façade has windows flanking the centre doorway instead of the usual sidelights. These windows are twelve-over-twelve sash and match the windows on either side. Simple unadorned pilasters flank the door and windows, and the door has a rectangular transom. This central arrangement is repeated above on the second storey with a door that opens onto the roof of a porch made into a verandah. A finely moulded cornice links the door with the windows on either side. The outer windows on both levels have louvred shutters and the edges of the clapboard have been treated with contrasting trim to match the shutters and trim around doors and windows.

On the exterior, the windows, shutters, doorways, roof, chimneys, and masonry foundation are all original. All the interior woodwork on the ground floor, including the baseboards, window mouldings and trim, panelling, doors, and flooring, is original. A panelled wall is located in the older wing of the house along with a built-in desk and cupboard, staircase, and closet. In true character of Loyalist architecture, Ingledale combines Georgian concepts of beauty and propriety with neo-classical treatment of details.

Above: Detail of the twelve-over-twelve sash windows on the front façade.
Right: Original neo-classical front doorway and porch.

Arlo House, 1816

206 Main Street West, Hess Village, Hamilton

The original land grant for Arlo House was given in December 1796 to Caleb Reynolds, a lieutenant in the British army. The grant consisted of land bounded by the present-day streets Main, Hess, York, and Queen, and the original building on the site remains as part of the western façade of the present building. Arlo House is the oldest occupied house within the original boundaries of the city of Hamilton. Between 1803 and 1835, the small house was owned at various times by Margaret Rousseaux, widow of Jean-Baptiste Rousseaux of Ancaster, by Peter Hess, and by George S. Tiffany.

The restrained Italianate villa with projected eaves and brackets was designed and built by an unknown architect. Its symmetrical centralized character with loggia and ornate console bracket catches the eye of passersby even to this day. Basement doors can be seen to match those of Dundurn Castle. Arlo House is one of many gracious homes in the city that used features of Sir Allan MacNab's grand Italianate villa as models.

George Tiffany still owned the house when its assessed value jumped from $100 in 1853 to $1,200 in 1855. His tenant in the enlarged house was Plummer Dewar, founding president of the

The stained-glass transom over the front door is reflected in an ornate mirror inside the entrance.

Landed Banking and Loan Company of Hamilton. A year after Tiffany's death in 1856, his widow sold the house. Ownership of the house changed a few times more until it was finally purchased by Mrs. Mabel Dalley, wife of Fenner Frederick Dalley, a prominent Hamilton businessman.

In 1909, Mrs. Dalley planned to hold a dance in the house, and as part of the preparations, she asked her architect brother, Julian Foster, to look it over. He discovered that the foundation beams were in a bad state and the result was extensive renovations to the interior. There had been a door between the dining room and drawing room, but Mrs. Dalley had it walled up. A china cabinet was built into the embrasure on the dining-room side. Some time before the renovations began, Mrs. Dalley had bought a fine large sideboard from Lady Gage, and the dining room was planned around this object as a focal point.

Mrs. Dalley also had a water-operated elevator between the first and second floors, the mechanism of which remains in the basement to this day, enclosed by drywall. The original kitchen had a large cauldron and was perhaps located behind the present kitchen. Like any grand home of its type, Arlo House had stables and a carriage house, which were converted into chauffeur's quarters in 1912.

The house is now used as dentists' offices and little remains of the original features in the interior. Original ceiling and woodwork are still visible in the entrance and an original fireplace remains in the waiting room, but most of the other ceilings have been ruined by renovation over the years. Only the fine stained-glass windows have been spared.

An exterior view of the stained glass window in the stairway landing.

The stained-glass window in the stairway landing.

Harmony Hall, 1816

335 Lima Court, Ancaster

Now situated in a suburban cul-de-sac, Harmony Hall was once an isolated rural farmhouse. A rare example of brick construction from the early nineteenth century, it is a substantial two-and-a-half-storey house with outer walls constructed of handmade bricks four wythes thick, a monumental

undertaking in such a remote area. Clay for the bricks is thought to have come from a stream running near Garner's Cemetery on Southcote Road. A kiln, constructed at the northwest corner of the property, served to fire the bricks. Just building the kiln required skilled labour — to make bricks and structure sound enough to withstand high temperatures.

Evidence exists to support the theory that the house was built in stages between 1816 and 1851. Four different styles of brickwork suggest the bricking was done at different periods. The house was

designed in the Georgian style as a 27 foot x 45 foot rectangle with a side-gabled roof, matching end chimneys, and a centre-hall plan. The five-bay façade features the original front door with sidelights, fanlight, and a radiating brick arch. In the hall, pine floorboards, ½-inch thick and secured by tongue-and-groove, are of widths up to 7¼ inches. A plain but elegant staircase rises from the entrance hall to the second floor and the bedrooms.

On either side of the hallway are two large rooms: a drawing room on the right and a dining

Above left: The remains of a stone cook oven under a brick arch in the rubble-stone half-basement.
Above: The semi-elliptical transom matches the porch roof.
Left: Original front door and wooden storm under a porch with a semi-elliptical roof supported on Doric columns.

Top: The half-moon window between the divided interior chimney flues.
Above: The end gable with decorative bargeboard.

room on the left. Each has its original coal-burning fireplace, but the mantels are replacements. The chimney flues were designed to be interior to give extra heat, but to comply with modern fire regulations, both had to be closed off and the east brick chimney was replaced about 1970 with an outside stone chimney. In the attic on the west side, the brick chimney divides into two flues with a half-moon window between. On the east side, a window in the same style is obscured by the outside chimney.

A rubble-stone half-basement contains the remains of a stone cook-oven under a brick arch. Because it was used for cooking, the basement is raised to allow light in through rectangular windows set in brick wells. The stairs to the half-basement under the left half of the house are probably original. A crawl space is all there is under the right half. A single 10-inch-thick beam runs east-west and supports the whole house; in turn, it is supported by three massive white oak pillars.

Harmony Hall was constructed by Israel Dawdy, a Loyalist of German ancestry. He was born in 1769 in New Jersey and came to Ontario in 1796. From 1805 to 1824 he served in the militia, during which time he was part of a mutinous 1,000-man battalion. The men were forced to march from St. Catherine's to Lundy's Lane (now Niagara Falls), and in retaliation, when they reached the battlefield, the men refused to fight. In the melee, the commanding officer was shot by one of his own men and Dawdy took off. He was caught and put under house arrest, to be court-martialled for deserting his regiment, but the court martial never took place. The Methodist community had come to resent the British high-handedness in matters of religion and administration, and the authorities deemed it unwise to proceed against the accused. Meanwhile, Dawdy used the hiatus of house arrest to build himself a new home, probably financed by the back pay all militia officers received in 1818.

For twenty years Dawdy and his wife, Anna Sneider, had lived in a log cabin on the property. When a section of the brick house was completed in 1818, they moved in and lived there for the next forty years, childless and quarrelling endlessly. In order to stay separate from each other they divided the house. The unique incorporation of side doors near the front is perhaps explained by this division. The brickwork around these doors is undifferentiated from the rest of the is oriented east-west and hers north-south.

The house remained in the possession of Dawdy's nephews until 1864, when it was sold to Samuel Nash Olmstead, reeve of Ancaster, and then to John Hostein, whose family continued to farm there until 1969. In the 1860s, a Gothic-style central gable containing a round-headed louvred attic vent was inserted in the plain Georgian roofline. Decorative bargeboard along the eaves was added during the same period. In 1882, a projecting rear addition to the house resulted in a T-shaped building plan.

The origin of the name "Harmony Hall" is the subject of much speculation. Possibly it was named for the town Harmony, New Jersey, the home of a builder friend of Dawdy's. Or the name could have been bestowed later in the nineteenth century in recognition of the Victorian values of faith and respect for persons, nature, and responsibility. Certainly Israel Dawdy's time there was not harmonious. Apart from the divided house, he lived as a man split between loyalty to his country and his belief in democracy and religious freedom, between Britain and America, and between sects of Methodism after the Church of England lost its hold on the community.

Above: Harmony Hall's dining room can be closed off with pocket doors.
Right: A centre window in the upstairs hall gives light into an area once used for sewing and schoolwork.

brickwork, suggesting the marital split occurred while the house was still unfinished. Dawdy died of natural causes in 1851 and in his will left his wife his "best set" of goods as well as "unfettered access to the outhouse." They are buried together in Garner's Cemetery, but his body

17

The Nash-Jackson House, 1818

77 King Street West, Stoney Creek

The Jackson farmland was originally a Crown grant in 1789 of 600 acres to Loyalist William Gage. William and his friend Samuel Nash from Norwich, Connecticut, arrived from the United States in the late eighteenth century to be among the first settlers of Saltfleet Township. Samuel married William's daughter Susanna. In 1809, her father ceded lot 28 in concession 3, the above-mentioned land at the corner of King Street and Nash Road. In 1813, the famous Battle of Stoney Creek was fought at the farm of William and Mary Gage, now Battlefield Park. A quarter mile away and a safe distance from gunfire, Susanna and Samuel's house became a hospital during and after the battle.

The Nash-Jackson home was built in 1818, up against the original 1794 log building, so that fireplaces and chimneys were shared. In 1909, the older part was pulled down. It is a two-storey wood frame structure with well-preserved original clapboard siding and an asphalt-shingled roof, built in the classical style with a five-bay symmetrical façade and end chimneys. The front doorway leading to a central hall has narrow, classically detailed sidelights framed by pilasters. There was once a verandah along the

1818 Georgian cupboard, typical of the Adam style.

front, but it was replaced in the 1940s by a gable porch with paired Ionic columns, modelled on a style of porch popular in the early nineteenth century. The one-and-a-half-storey kitchen and dining wing was added to the back of the house in 1856.

Leone Jackson (née Nash) was the great granddaughter of Samuel Nash and the fifth generation of the Nash family to occupy the house. When she died in 1997, her children deeded the house to Stoney Creek. In November 2000, to make way for a residential facility for the Thomas Health Care Corporation, the house was moved to Battlefield Park, where following restoration it will open to the public.

Billy Green House, 1820

30 Ridge Road, Stoney Creek

Billy Green was born February 4, 1794, purportedly the first white child born in the new settlement, son of Adam Green, a United Empire Loyalist who arrived in Saltfleet Township from New Jersey in 1790. According to popular local legend, Billy played a significant role in the Battle of Stoney Creek when, in June 1813, American troops camped in the vicinity of the Gage family home (now Battlefield House). By subterfuge, Billy's brother-in-law Isaac Corman learned the night's watchword, which he passed along to Billy. Immediately, Billy left on horseback to warn the British troops. Somehow, Billy stealthily crossed the American lines and delivered the message to General Vincent, commander of the troops camped at Burlington Heights. A swift overnight march to Stoney Creek took the American troops completely by surprise, and the ensuing battle resulted in a decisive victory for the British.

Adam Green willed the property to his son Billy in 1815, and about 1820 Billy built a home on Ridge Road, a red-brick one-and-a-half-storey Gothic revival cottage. Typical of the style is the symmetrical front elevation with central door and matching six-over-six sash windows on either side. There were once matching chimneys at the gable ends of the roof, but only one survives. Windows and door are ornamented with gently arched radiating bricks, and under a central gable is a rounded-arch Gothic window.

The original cottage consisted of just two rooms. In the room to the right, most of the original wide pine plank tongue-and-groove flooring survives. Over the fireplace, there is a wooden mantelpiece made by Billy, but the present owner's father took out the decorative fireplace and replaced it with one of angel stone. The angel stone has since been replaced with old brick, but without the decorative touches.

Ceilings in the two rooms are original, and portraits of Green ancestors, including one of Billy, hang on the walls. A breakfront hutch on the east wall and a wooden chest are thought to be Billy's handiwork. In the 1850s, a wing was added to the back of the house with a raised basement and rubble-stone foundation. A basement door found under the wing is thought to be the entrance to the cabin Billy inhabited while building his house.

The original front door remains in place but is no longer used. Outside, along the road in front of the house, a fence of twisted cedar

The centre gable and Gothic arched window are repeated on the north elevation.

Top: The wooden mantelpiece made by Billy Green.
Above: The rubble-stone foundation of Billy Green House.

stumps looks almost recent. In fact, the stumps were wrested from the soil in the 1790s by Adam Green with a team of horses. Elsewhere, four sturdy Rhode Island Greening apple trees survive from the same period. Until recently, the Ridge Road property was used for mixed farming, but now only the fruit trees are maintained.

Six generations of Adam Green's descendants have lived on and worked the Ridge Road property, leaving many artifacts. Adam also had brothers who settled in other parts of the area, two of whom were John Green of Greensville and Freeman Green of Progreston Road. The present owner of the Billy Green House will be the last of the family to live there.

George Rolph House, 1820

41 — 43 Cross Street, Dundas

Detail of the front entrance of George Rolph House.

George Rolph, a lieutenant in the war of 1812, moved to Dundas in 1816 and bought 300 acres, part of the former Ann Morden farm. Ann Morden, a widow, had come to Upper Canada in the 1780s after her husband Ralph was hanged by the American patriots for acting as a guide for Robert Land on his way to Fort Niagara. As a sort of reward, the Crown granted her considerable property in the area, which she sold off in lots.

Rolph put up a log house and added to it over the years in a haphazard fashion. The result is a home with peculiar room layouts. One of the oldest surviving houses in Dundas, only part of the original building remains and it is of highly unusual design without any distinct architectural style.

A wealthy man, Rolph had grand plans to build a home to rival Dundurn Castle, but only impressive gates and a high fence were constructed. One set of those gates now guards the York Street entrance to Dundurn. Rolph lived on Cross Street until his death in 1875, but he also had a home on Wilson Street for his second law practice in Ancaster. In the period 1826-1832, George Rolph and his brother, Dr.

John Rolph, with offices in Dundas, Ancaster and Vittoria (near Simcoe) had the largest legal practice west of York, today's Toronto. Rolph was always unpopular with the townspeople of Dundas and remained aloof from them, perhaps a factor in an incident in 1826, when a group of disguised men, Alexander Robertson, Sheriff Titus Simons, and Dr. James Hamilton, beat up Rolph then tarred and feathered him. Ostensibly, the reason was that Rolph, a married man, had a housekeeper, Mrs. Evans, living in his house on Cross Street, but in fact Rolph's most serious offence was being an ardent supporter of the Reform party.

All the same, Rolph was generous to the people of Dundas. He permitted the townspeople to avail themselves of the flat, open part of his property, now Dundas Driving Park, as a village common, and he donated stone for the building of St. Augustine's Roman Catholic Church. He also built Sydenham Road at his own expense, but he then secured a charter to make it a toll road.

Shaver Homestead, 1820

1166 Garner Road West, Ancaster

Wilhelm Schaeffer and his wife, Katrinka, were German Protestants who emigrated in 1765 from the Electorate of Hanover in the Rhineland. They settled in Oxford Township, Sussex County, New Jersey, but when the Revolutionary War broke out in 1776, three of the Schaeffer sons chose to fight with the loyal Britishers. After the war the Schaeffers were among the thousands who trekked into Canada, where they took up land granted to Loyalists in Ancaster Township. The sons — John, Frederick, and William — anglicized the family name, first to "Shafer" and later to "Shaver." John's son William married Mary Catherine Book in 1798. They settled on the Shaver Road property and raised a family of

Top: Original Loyalist door. This building is now used as a garage.
Above: The original tail and east verandah, with its simple supports, behind the 1856 brick house.

thirteen children, one of whom, William, was given lot 35 on concession 4, the present 1166 Garner Road West. Among the many family effects in the parlour is a daguerreotype photo of twelve of John and Mary Catherine's children.

Since 1820 the farm has been owned continuously by the Shaver family. At one time all the surrounding farms belonged to John Shaver's descendants, but now only a very few remain. The oldest of the several buildings on the Shaver Homestead property dates from about 1820. It is a post-and-beam frame house with shiplap siding. An eight-panel Loyalist door, still with the original brass keyhole, opened into a sitting room. The other two rooms would have been bedrooms in the original 1820 house. In the absence of walls, room divisions can be divined by the ceiling beams. The hand-split lath-and-plaster ceiling is still secured by hand-cut nails, and pine-board floors are still in place. An original dresser stands against the back wall. The house was built without a foundation, which was added in 1930. Curiously, the old windows on either side of the back door don't fit their frames. Along one side of the little house can be seen parts of both a snake fence and a stump fence.

The front section of the house was moved across the driveway on rollers in the 1850s. The old kitchen and woodshed were left in place, and in 1856 a two-storey Loyalist-style red-brick house with buff-coloured quoins was added onto the front. The post-and-beam woodshed remains much as it was, but the kitchen has been altered to more modern standards and includes, for example, a 1926 electric light that still has one original bulb working. Underneath, the basement is made of rubble stone and has a crossbeamed ceiling and 3-foot-thick support walls.

The main staircase rail is supported by narrow drum-shaped balusters terminating with a polygonal newel. Upstairs, the beds, with their high backboards and quilts, are original. One is noticeably shorter than the others because it has a feather tick; the other beds were lengthened to accommodate modern mattresses. A rail with hooks is fastened on the wall — closets were unknown in those days. The six-over-six sash windows were sufficiently sound that storms were never needed. All the woodwork, floorboards, and an inlaid blanket box are made of pine from the forest on the property. A centre window in the upper hall has a moulded frame and vertical bars

with an arch dividing the panes.

The front façade of the house is symmetrical with projecting eaves. Constructed of handmade bricks kilned in the field across the road, the building includes timber logged from the property's

Right: The centre window with its moulded frame, arched medallions, and date stone allows light into the upper hall sitting area.
Below: The decorative west verandah and entranceway to the kitchen.

Detail of a turned post and ornamental string the on west verandah.

The combination bake- and wash-house, built of leftover bricks.

virgin pine forest, while the foundation is built of stone from the local quarry. Rotted bargeboards on the front had to be taken down and were replaced by aluminum, but a piece of original bargeboard remains on the west porch. The east verandah belongs to the original house, as evidenced by the simple supports. The more decorative west verandah has turned posts and an ornament string along the posts and eaves as well as a square box enclosing the brick-cased well with its original bucket and pulley used by Shavers for generations.

The side-gabled roof has matching chimneys at each end and a front gable over the centre doorway. Near the top of the east wall is a pair of quarter-pie windows, which allows light into the attic. The western pair was covered by an outside chimney after inside chimneys were prohibited by fire regulations. Radiators were added in 1926, but prior to that date the house was heated with wood fires.

A cow barn built on a foundation of local stone has a timber beam with the inscription "W. Shaver 1837." There is also a bake oven–bath house, built in 1856 from brick leftover from the construction of the house.

The east elevation with an original inside chimney and quarter-pie windows.

Crown Farm: The King House, 1825

736 King Road, Burlington

Burlington's King Road traces the ancient route of an aboriginal trail from the north shore of Burlington Bay to native camps around Lake Medad. In 1793, Charles King crossed into Upper Canada as a Loyalist from Morris County, New Jersey. The Crown, in return, granted him a 563-acre parcel of farmland. In 1802, King put up a log house beside the aboriginal trail and began to clear the land. Charles had three sons, two of whom, James and George, fought in the Battle of Queenston Heights and the third, Charles, seems to have disappeared. When Charles King Sr. died in 1846, it was discovered that he had willed Crown Farm to his grandson Charles Henry, then only five years old.

The present house was built in two stages. What is now the kitchen wing was a bubble frame structure built in 1825 of open timber clad with broad shiplap and later reclad with common-bond double brick. There is some uncertainty as to when the front part of the house was added, but most probably it was in the late 1850s or early 1860s. It is of Flemish bond with walls two-and-a-half-bricks-thick over a rubble-stone foundation. The raised basement has wells of brick containing windows surmounted by radiating bricks. The side-gabled roof, originally with a chimney at each end, has a centre gable above a large arched window. Under the eaves there is a plain boxed cornice and frieze. The symmetrical façade features six-over-six wood-framed sash windows, all original and still in good working order. The front door and storm door are original, as is the vermiculated stone doorsill, but the rectangular transom light divided by three mullions and the long sidelights, all with tracery glass, were

The front door has been stripped to its original paint.

beautifully restored by the present owners. The elaborate porch on the front conceals the bricks over the downstairs window and might be a later addition.

The interior face of the front door has been stripped to the original paint, revealing mustard-coloured panels surrounded by rust-red mouldings. Even the upside-down latch hardware is original. All the interior doorways are original, and the bubble-flawed windowpanes are characteristic of old glass. The façade suggests a centre-hall plan, but the staircase does not belong with the house. It came from a demolished hotel of the same period, and the present owners are uncertain where the original staircase would have been located.

Possibly the log house had faced north. Like a Janus mask, the kitchen wing also has a symmetrical façade with two six-over-six large sash windows flanking a central doorway. There is a double row of bricks under the doorsill. A decorative porch similar to the one on the

front was added at some later time. The west wall, now the rear of the house, looks more recent and seems uncharacteristic of the period. The two-storey solid-brick elevation is broken only by a second-storey off-centre window. Another clue is the pointing of the bricks, which is different from the older part of the house. Furthermore, underneath this part of the house there is only a crawl space.

Four generations of the King family occupied Crown Farm. When Charles Henry died in 1919, the farm was purchased at auction by Ada, second wife of his son Wesley, a successful fruit grower in Port Nelson and a member of the Burlington Village Council. In 1941 the farm was sold to Leenart and Kathe Keyzer, who operated a market garden for many years. In 1990 the house was purchased and saved from demolition by its present owners.

Two verandahs, at the front and side entrances of the house, feature carefully restored ornate spool work, trim, and turned posts.

Detail of the ornate spool work and trim.

Enerals Griffin House, 1827

733 Mineral Springs Road, Ancaster

Originally built in 1827, this house and 50 acres were sold by John Lawrason to George Hogeboom and his wife, Henrietta Ryckman. In 1834, the couple sold the house to Enerals Griffin for £125.

This plain clapboard house is made up of four rooms and is built in a simple Loyalist style. The foundation is of rubble stone, and the basement is raised with windows visible on the south and west sides, suggesting a basement kitchen. There are two rooms on the ground floor and two bedrooms above. There is also a white-washed dry storage area in the basement. A large open hall at the top of the enclosed staircase may have been used as an extra sleeping area. All the rooms are lime-plastered, and the larger upper bedroom has the remains of pre-1850 wallpaper. There are two fireplaces, located in the main room downstairs and the larger bedroom upstairs. A single brick chimney on the west end of the side-gabled roof served both fireplaces and probably the basement kitchen.

The front façade is oddly asymmetrical. A centre door is flanked by matching six-over-six sash windows in three bays of unequal size. Above, to the left of the door, is an offset nine-pane casement. All the openings are framed in wood with plain lintels and no ornamentation. Apart from the front, the second-floor windows are located under the gables with their turned eaves. Double-hung, nine-pane casements provided illumination for the upstairs bedrooms. An outside entrance on the north side gave access to the storage area. The east façade matches the front with a door and pair of windows, but there is no window on the second floor.

Oral history in the Griffin family recounts how Enerals Griffin came to Canada by means of the Underground Railroad. Mr. Griffin was a slave of Virginian plantation owner Edward Lee and had been promised a letter of passage when Lee died. Lee, however, had not made any arrangements for guaranteeing the freedom of his slaves by the time he lay on his deathbed. Griffin decided to act to ensure his freedom and wrote his own letter of passage, then took a horse and began the long journey to Canada. When he reached Pennsylvania, he was interrogated by local officials, who believed neither his story nor the letter. When they discovered Griffin could read and write they became even more suspicious and accused him of writing the letter himself. They

Archaeological digs around the Griffin homestead have unearthed many artifacts including ceramics, glass, bone fragments, hardware, and jewellery.

demanded Griffin copy out the letter, but the fear of being caught changed the characteristics of his handwriting sufficiently that the officials let him go.

Griffin arrived in Upper Canada in either 1828 or 1829. He eventually settled in the Niagara area and married Priscilla (1795–1850). Not much is known of Priscilla except that she entered Canada around the same time as Griffin. Historians believe she was Caucasian, as their son James, born in 1833, was mulatto.

The young family signed the deed for the property in Ancaster on January 1, 1834. There are no records of hostilities towards the family. They attended St. Andrew's Presbyterian Church and were active in the community. Mr. Griffin lived in his home until he died in 1878. He is buried with Priscilla in St. Andrew's Churchyard in Ancaster. His descendants continued to live in the house until they ceded it to the Hamilton Region Conservation Authority in 1988.

Cherryhill, 1836

259 Eighth Concession East, East Flamborough

Cherryhill is something of a puzzle. The one-and-a-half-storey clapboard house was built on 400 acres acquired in 1827 by John Eaton for his family's future home. Eaton was one of the original settlers of Carlisle, and in 1836 he sold 62 of those acres to his third son, Levinus, a carpenter who erected a log house for himself and his new wife, Catherine Bournes. Levinus sold the property in 1845. By that time a neo-classical front portion had been added to the log house and the whole of the building was clad in narrow white clapboard. John Corrigan bought the property in 1871 and soon after demolished the 1836 log house. In 1875 he built a rear portion on the old foundation then replaced the narrow clapboard with perfectly matched pine clapboard siding covering both parts of the house. In the 1960s, a woodshed and summer kitchen on the west side of the house were pulled down. In keeping with changing times they were replaced by a garage and breezeway. Because they are the work of the well-known restoration architect Arthur Wallace, the modern replacements blend well.

The elegantly designed front doorway has sidelights and a rectangular transom with four vertical bars. The doorway is framed by wood pilasters and a projecting lintel. Matching six-over-six sash windows on either side complete the symmetrical façade. Remarkably, the shutters on all the windows are original. Overhanging eaves with an unusually wide underside and deep frieze enhance the charm of the front approach. Originally there were three chimneys, but only the one on the west gable end remains in place. The others were taken down and all the fireplaces were removed.

Pine plank floorboards, some as wide as 8 inches, and 12-inch baseboards are standard throughout much of the house. The centre-hall plan was changed in order to accommodate an enlarged parlour. To compensate for the loss of illumination, a long narrow window was cut out of the rear façade to throw light towards the front door, which would otherwise be in heavy shadow. When the 1875 section was added, the staircase was relocated to the back wall of the neo-classical portion. On the second floor over the staircase there is a narrow bridge that joins the two upper sections of the house. Up here the doors are simple two-panel leafs whereas in the 1875 addition, where the kitchen is located, the doors have four panels with a diamond-shaped design (◆) at eye level. All doors still operate with an old-fashioned latch rather than a door handle.

Fern Cottage, 1840

190 Hatt Street, Dundas

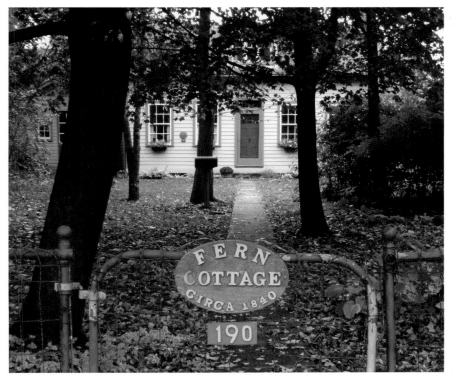

Fern Cottage is the only home on Hatt Street set so far back from the road.

Almost hidden from view under a canopy of trees is a pretty, pale green clapboard cottage, set well back from Hatt Street behind a gated fence with the name "Fern Cottage." In spite of the neighbouring houses, the place seems isolated. A path crosses an expanse of grass dotted with clumps of flowers to a simple yet classic doorway. On either side of the door are paired sash windows forming the three-bay façade of a centre-hall plan house in the Georgian style. The cottage was built in 1840 by Scotsman Alexander Watson, a boilermaker. It is a typical worker's cottage in a working-class district. All the houses along lower Hatt Street used to belong to the labourers and skilled tradesmen who worked in the thriving manufacturing businesses up the street.

The roof once had chimneys on each gable, but the east chimney has been removed, leaving a single chimney on the west gable. The doorway is surmounted by a rectangular transom with four vertical bars. Directly above are three casement windows in a dormer. An unusual placement of vertical bars separates the casements into two panes in the top half and a single pane below.

Two mirror-image rooms open off each side of the centre hallway: a living room to the left and a dining room to the right. However, like Linquenda (see pp. 68–69), the present front was once the back of the house. The house formerly faced onto a reservoir created by Ewart's Dam. The dam had been constructed by Richard Hatt on Spencer Creek in the early nineteenth century to provide power for his mills. On this façade the original door and glass storm are still in place but had been kept closed for years. To admit southern light into the hallway, the

A view of the north-facing dining room windows.

present owner has propped open the panelled door, but the storm remains fastened shut. The steps are long gone and the door frame looks badly rotted.

All the interior doors are constructed with six panels of heavy wood and most have their original latches, locks, and hinges. Even the big front-door key still exists and is treasured by the the present owner. All the windows are the original six-over-six sashes, and most still have their original glass panes. The living room has original six-inch baseboards and a chair rail, but the ceiling is modern. Pocket doors that once separated the east front room from a smaller room behind were removed so the doorway could be widened and a new doorframe installed. Steep stairs descend from the hallway into the rubble-stone basement, its mud floor recently concealed with cement tiles. Although the basement is raised, only one of the windows still opens — it must have been used as a coal chute. The rest have been blocked up.

The house's clapboard siding and front windows are original.

There are two large bedrooms upstairs with a bathroom between them in part of the former centre hall. The casement dormer mentioned earlier is now the window of the bathroom. In each bedroom a warming cupboard is situated against the heating pipe, and in each is a built-in wardrobe, unusual for the period.

A kitchen wing was added to the west side of the house about 100 years ago. Before that the kitchen was probably in the basement, but the only trace remaining is the chimney flue.

A dilapidated 1920s garage, due to be demolished, stands at the east side of the house. A three-part hinged door is an interesting feature. The door rolls sideways on a track around the garage wall and opens to the south, where there is still a narrow roadway.

In 1915 a heavy summer storm washed out the dam. By then maintaining the dam was costing more than it was worth, and it was never replaced. Spencer Creek returned to its old bed, but the property line remained at the shore of the vanished reservoir.

Keswick: the Crosthwaite Farm, 1840

1651 King Street East, Bartonville, Hamilton

As you drive east along King Street, just past Ottawa Street where the road curves, a flash of bright yellow on the north side catches your eye. A brightly painted 160-year-old dwelling is the original farmhouse of the Crosthwaite family from Keswick, Cumbria, the part of England known as the Lake District. The property belonged to Daniel Crosthwaite, listed in the Roll of Captain Durand's company in the War of 1812. Three Crosthwaite brothers fought in that war but none are listed on the memorial in Stoney Creek because none of them died in the war. The Crosthwaites were a United Empire Loyalist family and proud of it. Their history in Hamilton is long and interesting, particularly that of those who kept the family market farm and orchard. An 1870 Wentworth atlas shows the Crosthwaite property straddling King Street and extending from Ottawa Street to Kenilworth. Directly adjacent is the Gage land grant, from which the Crosthwaite farm may have been severed after 1814.

The present owners bought the farmhouse in 1987 from Vangie Crosthwaite and are the first non-Crosthwaites to live there. Vangie was a daughter of Frank Crosthwaite (1870–1957) and his wife, Nellie Jane Gage. Vangie never married and was in her late eighties at the time the house was sold. She claimed that she was the last Crosthwaite except for a branch of the family still in the United States. For reasons of her own, she refused to acknowledge Crosthwaite relatives living in the area.

The house was built in two stages. The original farmhouse was a

Above: The Crosthwaite farmhouse from King Street East.

Left: Detail of the carved bargeboard trim and rear kitchen chimney.

four-room box with a centre-hall plan and a tail, which might once have been the summer kitchen. A raised basement with a massive old chimney suggests that the original kitchen could have been in the basement. The rear kitchen had fallen into disrepair and the present owners had most of it pulled down and replaced. However, they left a portion of the original rubble-stone foundation, which has become a low garden wall. Nearby, a circle of flat stones marks the location of the old well, and under the kitchen are the remnants of a brick cistern.

Now covered in stucco and painted bright yellow, the house was originally board and batten, but the thickness of the outside walls, 12 to 15 inches, indicates there is insulating material, such

Above: The principal entrance to the house since the construction of the one-storey addition.
Right: The verandah running the length of the east-wing addition.

as stone or brick, underneath. A decorative bargeboard embellishes the end gable over the three-bay front façade. The house faces at a slight angle onto King Street, which at that point curves to the southeast. The centre door was blocked off and covered with a trellis at the time a one-storey wing was added on the east side. There is no trace of the doorway, and it is safe to assume the stucco was applied to both parts of the house at the time of the addition. Above the trellis on the second floor, a large centre window topped by a decorative triangle allows light into the loft area. The west wall of the house has a projecting three-sided bay window with brackets under the roof and decorative wood trim above the windows.

The doorway opening off the verandah became the principal entrance to the house. The verandah itself runs the full length of the

Above: The decorative bay on the east addition is identical to the one on the western side of the house.

east-wing addition. No bargeboard decorates it; instead, a plain frieze runs under the eaves from the east side of the old part around to the north side of the newer section. On the wall of the new wing is an east-facing bay window, decorated on the exterior to match the other on the west side, but seen from inside, there is no similarity in the moulding around the windowpanes.

The Levi Lewis Homestead, 1843

265 Lewis Road, Stoney Creek

Top: A sketch of the house in 1859 used to ornament a map of Wentworth County.
Above: The east façade. The attractive carpentry work was done by a master carpenter and one helper for £280.

This beautifully proportioned Georgian-style colonial house with its striking Palladian porticos was built by Levi Lewis in 1843–1845. The principal front of this two-storey brick structure faces south to the present Highway 8, which at the time the house was built, was the only road. Later, when Lewis Road opened, running north-south from Highway 8, a formal elevation was added on the east side to face the new entrance drive. Further along the east wall, the shed-roofed kitchen-wing made a tail to the main structure and had to be disguised by a level parapet forming a rectangular wall facing the road. Pine timbers used in the framework of the house were cut on the farm and the nearby mountain brow. The handmade red clay bricks were formed and fired in the field opposite the house. Evidence for the location has accumulated over the years as broken pieces of brick were brought to the surface by ploughing.

The two-level portico has two similar centre doorways on the ground and second floors. Each entrance has a six-panel door with transom, sidelights intricately divided into rectilinear patterns, and octagonal porch columns. The east elevation front also has a centre doorway and a porch similar to the front, but gabled. The six-panel door has false sidelights, which are made to resemble the front aspect.

The Lewis family left New Jersey as United Empire Loyalists in 1780, one of the first families to settle in the Grimsby-Winona district, taking up land that was later given them by Crown deed. Ties between the Lewises and the district have been strong from the beginning. Levi Lewis's

Top: The drawing room, where important callers would be received.
Above: The dining room.

The front entrance hall. The brass hardware on the door is original.

The cluttered and comfortable living room where the family would gather. The portrait on the left is of Levi Lewis. The one on the right depicts his wife, Mary.

grandfather and father were members of the first Municipal Council of Upper Canada in 1790, and Levi's father was elected a member of the Legislative Assembly in 1801. Both Levi and his son, George, were elected reeves of the township of Saltfleet. As for the house, apart from a twelve-year gap ending in 1970, it has never been out of the possession of the Lewis family.

The interior is that of a centre-hall plan home with a dining room to the left of the hall and a drawing room to the right. A staircase in the hall leads to the second floor. Continuing towards the back and down three steps, a back room is part of the kitchen wing tail, with 40-foot beams extending the width of the room. This is the original kitchen and much of it is intact. A long wooden mantelpiece stretches over the old-style fireplace and has the old hooks for cooking pots and a bake oven. Beside the fireplace are built-in cupboards for storage. The pine floors are made of boards that vary greatly in width to as much as 24 inches. The panes of the nine-over-nine working sash windows have the irregularities and flaws of old-fashioned glass, and all the hardware in the house is original. Tiny brass doorknobs are a curious feature of the large doors.

A door opens from the west side of the kitchen to what was once the buggy shed, which also contained an enclosed indoor privy, a Goldilockian three-holer with large, medium, and small openings. Sewage did not go into a hole in the ground but rather was disposed of by a removal system. The form of containment is uncertain, whether it was pails or a tray, but waste was collected and transported to a distant location.

Above left: Detail of the fireplace with its carved mantle and handmade bricks.

Above right: Forty-foot beams support the ceiling. The built-in cupboards are original.

Right: The original fireplace was used for cooking as well as for heat. To the left the framed 1859 sketch of the house is partly visible.

Platt Nash House, 1844

22 Cross Street, Dundas

Platt Nash purchased property from George Rolph and built this two-storey red-brick dwelling in 1844. Nash operated a hat and glove business, making use of the front window to display his goods. A public-spirited man, he also ran the Dundas branch of the Upper Canada Bible Society.

The building combines two styles that were popular in early Ontario: Georgian and neo-classical. A basic rectangular plan with the long sides forming the front and rear façades is very much the Georgian style. So too is the symmetrical three-bay front aspect presented to the street. The small scale of the house and its

Window detail.

low-pitched roof with return eaves is neo-classical. The two side gables with matching chimneys are neo-classical, although the chimneys themselves are recent but modelled on the Georgian style. A rear brick summer kitchen was added shortly after the construction of the house. It had no heat or insulation. Plaster was applied directly to the interior of the brick walls. The limestone doorsill from the main house, worn down by the passage of many feet, testifies to its heavy use.

A high brick garden wall with a wooden doorway joins the house and barn on the north side and encloses the property. It was built quite recently using period bricks after the rather flimsy 1950s wall was pulled down. When the rebuilding began, the workers discovered the base was only one brick wide. As for the style of the original fence, no one knows for certain whether it was picket, hedge, or rail.

Surviving front-door mouldings are simple, flat, and narrow in the Georgian style, while the first-storey windows have flared rusticated stone lintels and rusticated stone projecting sills. Unfortunately, the original six-over-six sashes were replaced by plain glass. However, the six-over-six

sash style can be seen on the second storey, where the windows are situated so close to the eaves that the radiating yellow brick arches are almost hidden. On the north wall there is evidence of a doorway, long since bricked up, that might have been the street entrance to Platt Nash's shop.

In the interest of keeping up appearances, the brickwork on the front and north façades that face Cross and Park Streets is Flemish bond, a refined style of bricklaying with alternating rows of headers and stretchers, whereas

The front hallway.

the obscured south and rear façades are of common bond. The deeply recessed front doorway, unusual for Dundas, was a 1950s modification. The sidelights and rectangular transom are original. They were moved with the door as one piece, although the lovely etched glass is recent. The basement walls are constructed from rough-hewn stone and are clearly visible above the ground, so the main floor of the house is above street level. The outside entrance to the storm cellar was blocked in recent times and replaced by an inside staircase.

The interior has been much altered, although the centre-hall plan is still in evidence. Not much remains of the original ceiling, nor is it known whether the staircase is original, although the simple newel and square balusters are typically Georgian. Uncharacteristically, the ground floor was not divided into four equal-sized rooms. The living room, on the right, is unusually long and the back room, behind it, was probably the shop. The chimneys are a bit of a mystery. From ground level they are solid brick to a height of about 8 feet, at which point they become hollow. In the wall, an opening of about 12 inches in diameter probably accommodated a stovepipe that opened into the chimney. There is no evidence of there ever having been a chimney in the basement. Consequently, unusual as it would be for the period, the house must have been heated by wood stoves.

Stewart Log Cabin, 1844

77 Campbellville Road, Mountsberg, East Flamborough

In the 1830s, Alexander Stewart, a widower from Perthshire, and his six grown children — four boys and two girls — came to Upper Canada. In time they took up a lot on the 13th Concession among a group of Scottish settlers and Alexander's oldest son, John, helped his father choose the site for their first home. In order to obtain clear title to the land, Alexander, in compliance with regulations, put up a log cabin 20 feet x 30 feet using 16-inch squared cedar logs. To minimize the number of 30-foot logs that had to be lifted, the walls were built just nine logs high. Ordinarily, such a cabin would have been built over or pulled down, but because it was built on high round with good drainage, it survived. Another factor contributing to its survival is that the Stewart family covered the logs with lath and stucco, which preserved the original log cabin underneath.

After John's death, two of his sons divided the property. Robert and his wife, Janet, received the northeast section, and William and his wife, Mary Jane, received the southwest 50 acres. Robert put up a frame house while William and Mary Jane continued to live in the log house, which by then had been enlarged and covered with rough-cast stucco. In 1906 Robert sold his portion of the property to William and moved away. William and Mary

The modern front doorway faces onto the driveway.

The original front of the house faces Campbellville Road.

Jane moved into the large frame house but preserved the log house as a first home for their children to use as they married. The property remained in continuous possession of the Stewarts until 1966. A subsequent owner chose to remove the stucco and restored the log house to its original state.

The doors and windows of the cabin were finished with a very plain trim. Over the former front door, the name "A. Stewart" is stencilled in the lintel. The front door was closed off and a dormer was later added to allow light into the second-floor sleeping area. A lean-to of clapboard and stone was attached at the back of the house and the main entrance is now on the east side. When it was built, the cabin design was a basic centre-hall plan.

Foxbar, 1845

7 Overfield Street, Dundas

The lovely two-storey stone home known as "Foxbar" was built by and was once the home of Alexander Robertson, son of Ross Robertson of Perthshire, Scotland. Perched on the top of a hill overlooking Spencer Creek, Foxbar was named for the town in Scotland where Alexander was born. The only clue to its age is an 1851 map of Dundas, on which Foxbar is featured along with the house adjacent, called "Orchard Hill," known to have been built in 1840. Further evidence comes from the building's square classic style, with central doorway and narrow sidelights. A second-storey pair of Gothic arched windows with

Above: Intricate detailing on the north verandah.
Right: The main entrance to Foxbar.

shutters is central to the three-bay façade, typical of the period. Matched clustered chimneys stand at each end of the low hip roof and a central gable with a small round window. Seen from in front, the house appears symmetrical: even a sun porch, added on the north side, has been balanced by a conservatory on the south.

The first owner, Alexander Robertson, came to Canada in 1819 and settled in Ancaster Township. At that time the dividing line between Dundas and Ancaster Townships was the Governors Road. As Foxbar was south of Governors Road, it was considered an Ancaster residence.

Alex Robertson seems to have led a quiet and exemplary life except for an incident in 1826 when, following a dinner party, he, Colonel Titus Simons, and Dr. James Hamilton tarred and feathered lawyer George Rolph for keeping in his Dundas house a Mrs. Evans — ostensibly a housekeeper for the married man. Rolph sued Robertson, Simons, and Hamilton for £1,000 each. The defendants were represented by a team that included the Solicitor General and MacNab.

Robertson was acquitted but Hamilton and Simons were found guilty and fined £20 each. Following the trial, it was MacNab who wrote to his friends and supporters asking for contributions toward paying the fines.

Earlier that same year, Robertson had married Titus Simons's daughter, Mathilda. Their son, the Honourable Thomas Robertson, born January 1, 1827, practised law in Dundas. Thomas and his wife, Frances Louisa Read, lived in Foxbar until 1878, when he was elected to parliament for the first of two terms. They moved to Hamilton so Thomas could be closer to his constituency. Thomas bought 95 Upper John Street (now Arkledun Drive), a house known as "Rock Castle" and renamed it "Rannoch Lodge" after his ancestral home in Scotland. Although he continued his ownership of Foxbar, he rented out the property.

Thomas Robertson sold Foxbar to Harvey Binkley in 1890. Frank Ernest Lennard, of Samuel Lennard & Sons Ltd., manufacturers of hosiery and knitted underwear, bought Foxbar in 1901. It passed to his son, Frank Exton Lennard, in 1936. Sometime in this period there was a fire in the house. Perhaps it was at the time of its repair that the Lennards made changes to the rest of the house, including some art deco finishes to the front rooms and the transom and sidelight glass. They also added the conservatory along the south side. Over the eastern doorway, traces of a roofline suggest it replaced an earlier verandah.

For many years, Frank Exton Lennard represented Dundas as a Conservative M.P., and was notably silent in Parliament. Nevertheless, John Diefenbaker came to stay at Foxbar in the 1950s, and Frank and his wife Gladys McLachlan attended the coronation of Queen Elizabeth in London's Westminster Abbey in June 1953.

After Frank and Gladys died, the house was sold to a foundation for severely handicapped children. To accommodate wheelchair access, exercise equipment, and safety devices, many changes were made to the interior. The northern verandah was enclosed and lengthened to form two glassed-in rooms along the side of the house. An elevator was installed and the kitchen enlarged. Rather than destroy the original floor of panga-panga wood (an African hardwood) and the oak-panelled walls, renovators chose to cover the floors with linoleum and the walls with plastic.

The present owners had their work cut out to restore Foxbar. Even so, many original features remain. The graceful staircase, with its long shallow rises, was left intact, and the present study, which was used as an office, retains the original classical mouldings and possibly period wallpaper. All the interior doors are original, but are not necessarily in their original location. They are unusual in having a single long panel

The fireplace in the music room.

The mirror above the fireplace in the music room.

surrounded by moulding. The doors to the enclosed verandah have nineteenth-century brass locks with the keys still in place.

Upstairs, the chimneys are still working; their massive brick foundations can be seen in the basement, and there are fireplaces in both front rooms. In the room above the former music room there is a narrow closet — unusual in a period when closets were not built in — on the north side of the chimney flue and a warming cupboard for linen on the other side. In the attic it is possible to see how the massive flues were turned so that the matching chimney clusters would stand perpendicular to the roofline.

The graceful staircase remained undamaged while the house served as a home for children.

The Griffin Stone Cottage, 1845

24 Griffin Street, Waterdown

This cottage became known as "Griffin Cottage" after Ebenezer Griffin opened a road to his industrial site across the front of it.

This Regency-style cottage is almost certainly the oldest unaltered domestic building in Waterdown. Built during the 1840s, the cottage has survived virtually intact as a single-storey box structure of squared local rubble stone resting on a rubble foundation. The doorway is notable for its semi-elliptical transom, now blind but once with radiating tracery, and its original six-panel single-leaf wooden door, commonly known as a "Loyalist door." Sidelights, glazed two-over-two, have moulded panels below that match the door. Excellent stonework is visible around the doorway, although it is partially concealed by climbing roses. Below the entry is a sawn-stone stoop. Symmetrically constructed to a centre-hall plan, three bays, large relative to the elevation, are typical of the style. The two double-hung six-over-six sash windows flanking the doorway have mostly original glazing. Moulded openings with radiating brick arches are footed by sawn-stone projecting sills, and the sides of the cottage contain identical sashes to those on the main façade.

The house is on a sizable lot, set fairly close to the sidewalk. Originally it was part of a large estate — about 155 acres in 1823, when it was sold to Ebenezer Culver Griffin — but by 1852, a half acre was all that was left. The property included Grindstone Creek above the Great Falls, and a small stretch of the valley below. Griffin built a saw mill and a grist mill, then cleared the land for a settlement he called Waterdown. Either Griffin or one of his relatives built the cottage and when Griffin died in 1847, according to local tradition the funeral was held there. However, as his home was on the opposite side of Griffin Street, it is unlikely. Thomas Dyke, a business partner of Griffin's, bought the cottage in 1849, and in 1852 he sold it to Thomas Fretwell, a village wagon-maker. The cottage remained with the Fretwell family for almost a century.

Raich House, 1845

179 Mary Street, Beasley, Hamilton

Raich House, refined and restrained with its Ionic doorway, top light, and classical architrave, is thought to be the best surviving remnant of Hamilton's classical revival.

The house was built in 1845 for and, possibly, by carpenters Thomas and Peter Kirkpatrick, on land bought from Mrs. Samuel Sylvester Mills (née Aurora Holton).

In 1865, Anthony Riche — or "Rèche" or "Raich", as the name was spelt variously on deeds — bought the place to use as a source of rental income. The last surviving Raich, Louisa, also known as Mary L. Rèche, sold the house in 1942 to George Shannon and his wife, Elizabeth, grandparents of the present owner, an individual who knows the house well.

Above: A rare surviving example of pre-Confederation wood construction in the classical revival style.
Right: Elegant detailing of the Ionic columns.

still in place. Originally coal-burning, after a chimney fire the opening was filled with a marble surround and a gas fire was installed. Its wooden mantel is a smaller version of the Ionic front doorway. To the left of the fireplace, an 1840s built-in cupboard made of many types of wood, such as pine, cherry and oak, combines attractiveness with frugal practicality. All the rooms have 12-inch pine baseboards and plain 9-foot ceilings. Ceilings like these make a fan sufficient for cooling during Ontario's hot summers.

At the left of the hall an angled staircase with a narrow landing rises to the second floor. A sash window over the landing affords light on the stairs. The present owner remembers vividly the absence of heat in the upper rooms and how essential plenty of

Raich House is typical of the style: centre-hall plan, symmetrical façade, medium-pitched side-gabled roof with returned eaves, prominent end-chimneys, and six-over-six double-hung sash windows. Simplicity of design is combined with elegance of detailing — for example, the repetitive staccato of dentils and square blocks, which project from the cornice. Built on a rubble-stone foundation, the house has a 40-inch raised basement with a 7-inch stone border between the foundation and the clapboard. Visible on the rear-west elevation are traces of paint; at one time the house was painted creamy white or beige with rose pink trim.

The dining room is to the left of the centre hall and the parlour is to the right. On the north wall of the parlour, the original fireplace is

bedclothes were. Another narrow staircase leads down to the basement. Until the 1940s, the basement housed a kitchen with a huge cooking fireplace, like that in Dundurn Castle, and a wooden floor. Eventually a kitchen wing was added onto the back, where the original back door was reinstalled.

But for the superbly crafted doorway, its original sill intact, and the classical sash windows, the house looks small and shabby from the street, the clapboard badly in need of repair and paint. Seen from the north, the house appears tall and imposing with its symmetrical second-storey façade and chimney above. Nestled as it is between massive late-Victorian houses, Raich House has a grace and charm unequalled in the streetscape.

Herberton House: The Wyatt-Reid House, 1847

164 Townsend Avenue, Burlington

Among the many settlers from England who arrived between 1840 and 1860 and purchased land in the lower concessions of East Flamborough was Henry Wyatt. Wyatt had emigrated in 1845 from Long Ditton, Surrey, England, with his wife, four sons, and seven daughters. Within a year he had purchased lot 5 on the Broken Front Concession. In the same year his eldest daughter, Emma, married Hugh Cossart Baker of Hamilton, who, in 1843, had become the first manager of the Hamilton branch of the Bank of Montreal. Later Baker became the founder of the first insurance company in Upper Canada.

In 1847, Henry Wyatt oversaw the construction of a large brick house set back from Plains Road, built in the style of an English country house and named "Herberton House" after a grandson. The very best of materials went into the construction of the house, and the window glass, since replaced, was said to have come from England.

The Wyatts were well-to-do, cultured, musical, and deeply involved in the Anglican Church. Regular attendance meant they had to travel either to Hamilton or to Burlington for services. By 1849 Mr. and Mrs. Wyatt had begun soliciting funds from friends to build an Anglican church in East Flamborough, and in 1861 they donated a piece of their property as its site. The wood and stone building was constructed for $158 plus the $2 it cost to put up the picket fence in front. St. Matthews Church opened on September 22, 1861.

Situated at the corner of Herberton Place and Townsend Avenue, Herberton House is a symmetrical one-and-a-half-storey Flemish-bond brick structure with two cross-gabled side wings and two small stilted and gabled dormers. The bricks were made on the property of clay and straw. Two chimneys surmount the wide-eaved roof, which is offset from each dormer. The entrance door is set in a semi-circular brick vestibule with windows on each side under a pyramidal roof. All the windows have flat-head, radiating brick arches and dressed-stone sills. In the interior, many original features have been retained, such as the 2½-inch-thick pine floorboards, hand-carved wood trim, and fireplaces in every room.

The Wyatt family left for England in 1869 but returned early in 1871, a few months before the death of Henry Wyatt. The property passed to George Wyatt and then to John Reid by 1875. The house is illustrated in *The Gardens of Canada* (1902) as "Herberton House, residence of Reid Bros., Aldershot." Harriet Reid sold the property in 1913. At some point the house was converted to a duplex, over the course of which the circular staircase was altered. It was reconverted to a single family residence by the present owners.

Top left: Herberton House is situated on a large lot with mature trees and a circular driveway.
Above: Detail of the vestibule. The Flemish-bond brickwork can be clearly seen.

Lakelet Vale Farm & Drive House, 1847

50 & 54 Sanders Boulevard, West Hamilton

The Binkleys were palatine German Protestants driven out of the Rhineland by religious intolerance in a predominantly Roman Catholic society. A major freeze in the winter of 1708–1709 caused the river Rhine to freeze, turned wine to ice, and killed cattle in their sheds. The Binkleys, along with many other Palatines, travelled down the frozen Rhine and crossed to London, where they camped in tents surrounding the city. A dispensation from Queen Anne permitted those who took oaths to the British government and professed themselves Protestant to be naturalized as Britons. Eventually, to relieve overcrowding, these naturalized citizens were removed to America, where the Binkleys chose to settle in Lancaster County, Pennsylvania.

Opposite: Great care and preparation was taken in the building of this house, constructed by the original settlers.
Below: The 1860 stone drive house, now a private residence.

In the 1790s, Marx Binkley, his wife, Magdalena, and their family of three boys and two girls decided to try their fortune in Canada and set out with all their belongings in Conestoga wagons, bound for Berlin, now known as Kitchener, Ontario. On reaching the mountain brow on the top of Horning Road, now Osler Drive, they were so taken with the beautiful valley lying below, that Mrs. Binkley persuaded her husband to go no further.

The Binkleys applied for and received a land grant of 900 acres from the Crown. The land stretched from the mountain top on Horning Road to Cootes' Paradise, and from the border of Dundas along the present-day Cootes' Drive to encompass the present-day University Gardens and Binkley Crescent subdivisions. Different members of the family chose lots within the granted land that best suited them.

Jacob Binkley settled on the south side of the old trail between Hamilton and Dundas-Ancaster and built his first home at the head of a small ravine. Later he replaced it with the stately stone house at the end of what is now Binkley Road, then a long avenue of trees. Some of these, such as the tulip tree and the magnolia, were rare in the district at the time. Stone was quarried locally and lumber came from the clearing of forests. Even the eaves were large mouldings milled from solid timbers. The house was completed in 1847.

In the 1860s, a stone building called the "Drive House" completed the cluster of farm buildings. The upper, or ground, storey housed the carriages, cutters, and implements and provided a carpenter and blacksmith shop. The cellar was a solid-brick arch for the whole length of the building and was used to make wine from grapes grown on the farm. The wine produced was designated "Invalid Wine" and it was sold as far east as Montreal and Halifax.

The large wooden barn, which stood about 100 yards west of the house, has long since disappeared. The farm was called "Lakelet Vale," as the property included a small lake called "The Pond" and the valley, now McMaster University's west parking lot. Children gathered here for swimming and fishing in the summer and skating in the winter. The old family cemetery is still in evidence, although the gravestones have been damaged by vandals and the ravages of time. The earliest marker bears the date 1803. Marx Binkley passed away in 1806.

Right: A stone stable behind the old house.

Linquenda, 1847

28 South Street, Kirkendall, Hamilton

Driving west along South Street, Linquenda is easy to miss. Set well back from the narrow curving road, large houses on either side overwhelm their small and homely neighbour. Linquenda began as a combination house and barn in the ancient Saxon style. Daniel Springer obtained, by Crown grant, land that extended from the mountain to King Street, bordered on the west by Dundurn Street and on the east by Queen Street. By 1841, John Ashbaugh, a yeoman of British origins, was farming the land. Later it passed into the hands of Thomas Bush, who owned the property from 1848 to 1881. The actual builder of the house has never been identified.

Linquenda was built in 1847 as a rectangular farmhouse made of dolomite rubble stone using chunks salvaged from the escarpment behind. It is a two-storey cottage that, probably because of its early double function, is asymmetrical, with two windows on the west side of the door and only one on the east. The door is thus off-centre. The second storey has three evenly spaced windows in the classic style, although they don't quite match. The roof, low-pitched along its length, has parapets at each end with a built-in chimney at the west end and a modern stovepipe on the east. Carved cornices indicate a builder who liked to take extra trouble.

At that time only a few houses stood on what were, for the most part, fields, orchards, and woods. In time the housing density increased as lots were sold off. The present façade on South Street is actually the back of the house. What is now the front door functioned originally as the stable door. The former front door was set between sidelights and faced onto a long driveway from Aberdeen Avenue.

In 1950 the house was purchased by Ane Verduijn, who filled in and levelled the grounds. He removed the front porch and added two large windows in the east wall and another in the north wall. The original roof with its 12-inch planks was shingled in two layers to sharpen its angle, and he designed a new front entrance facing the mountain. The old-time front door now opens onto a deck and a fenced back yard. Verduijn called his house "Linquenda," a Latin word meaning "something that must be left behind," to remind himself of life's temporal quality.

Above left : The original north-facing front doorway with sidelights and a mullioned transom.
Above right: One of the large windows added in 1950 by Ane Verduijn.
Below: The ground-floor window in the former stable. Until 1950 the stable had a dirt floor.

Rastrick House, 1847

46 Forest Avenue, Corktown, Hamilton

Rastrick House is one of history's mysteries, a stone house of architectural excellence, yet the date of construction and architect are unknown. Its first mention is in an 1847 assessment roll that lists the house at 46 Forest and names its occupant as Milton Davies. In 1858, Frederick Rastrick moved in with his wife, Anna Mary Biggs, and lived there until his death in 1897. Their son Edward took over occupancy, remaining until 1909. Rastrick Sr., a prominent architect, designed the Customs House and Amisfield, known locally as The Castle. He was also hired by Sir Allan MacNab, the new prime minister of Upper Canada, to supervise the addition of a suitable portico to Dundurn Castle.

The light fixtures on either side of the finely moulded front entrance are original.

This six-over-six sash window still has its original wooden storm.

Rastrick House is generally of Renaissance design with classical revival detailing. Square in plan and two storeys in height, the house is built of limestone and has an ashlar façade. Among the fine details are the mouldings over the ground-floor windows and front door, which form Greek frets at their ends. The front elevation is asymmetrical, with the door in the left-hand bay and two large six-over-six sash windows in the next bays balanced by three corresponding windows on the second floor. Four stone chimneys grace the hip roof, one on each corner.

A law firm has turned the house into sets of offices, but much of the original interior has been carefully preserved. A former dining room retains its original fireplace, and in the back hall there is a dumbwaiter, now used as a storage cupboard, which carried meals up

Above: The steeply curved staircase.
Right: An arched window set in a moulded alcove gives an air of spaciousness to the narrow staircase.

quite effectively. Again, the original doorways have been retained and one fireplace remains in one of the offices. Behind a small doorway off the hall, steep ladder-like stairs lead to the attic.

The exterior walls are 21 inches thick, good for holding heat in winter and keeping the house cool in summer. Stone quoins adorn each corner of the building, which stands on a rubble-stone foundation topped by a dressed stone border between the raised basement and the first floor. The lower windows on the front façade have detailed mouldings; the rest have substantial stone lintels and all have vermiculated stone sills. The rear façade echoes the front with windows in rows of three on each floor. To the east and west there are dormers with round-topped windows and fitted shutters.

Above: Sixteen-pane wooden storms on the French windows still have the original glass.
Inset: The original front door latch.

from the basement kitchen. A drawing room to the rear of the house features double French doors, which once led out to a terrace, and shutters with mirrored panels. All the doorways have been preserved, as have the 12-inch baseboards and moulding in the downstairs ceiling.

Upstairs there were four bedrooms, now offices, reached by a steep staircase that turns sharply near the top to accommodate the narrow allowance. Turned balusters and a curved banister disguise the flaw

Rock Castle, 1848

95 Arkledun Avenue, Corktown, Hamilton

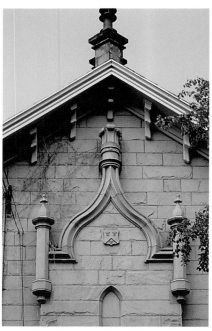

A first-time visitor stepping through the front door of Rock Castle can be excused for being transfixed by astonishment. The massive and gloomy Gothic exterior does not prepare one for the lofty entry, painted entirely in white with a moulded arch leading into the front hall, where a tall curving stairway beckons one to the second floor.

Rock Castle was built in 1848 in picturesque Gothic revival style, including elements such as elaborately carved bargeboards, eave brackets, clustered chimneys, and trefoil windows. Particularly notable is the stonework in the beautifully carved label moulds over the windows. These and the Tudor label terminated by two plain escutcheons surrounding the pointed arch of the doorway are obviously the work of a master stonemason. The motif of the pointed arch within a square head is repeated in the door panels and in the windows of the second storey. The outer walls of Rock Castle have the same style of dressed stone as St. Paul's Presbyterian Church, and it has been suggested the same stonecutter, George Worthington, did the work. A curious detail is the shield on the south wall, which bears three fleurs-de-lis. A thick stone fortress-like wall surrounded the house.

The thirty-room mansion is set at right angles to Arkledun Avenue and is irregular in the number of its levels. On the north side there are three storeys; on the mountain side two storeys; and on the south side, the former carriage house is entered directly from Arkledun Avenue. The carriage house is 40 feet long and comprises two levels, the lower level serving as kitchen and laundry. The stables were a separate building, with storage space on the lower level. A two-storey privy, once connected to the second-storey master bedroom by an open bridge, has long been an object of curiosity.

The original owner of the Rock Castle was Alexander Carpenter of the iron foundry company Gurney & Carpenter. A large household, the

Above: Detail of the west gable and a set of triple chimneys.
Opposite top right: South gable with the curious shield and fleur-de-lis.
Opposite bottom right: The west-facing front door.

The front door seen from the inside, illuminated by the huge arched transom and sidelights.

The main stairway to the second floor.

Above: Detail of a moulded arch.
Centre: The library fireplace, in what is now the kitchen, and original wrought-iron basket. The wood mantelpiece is made from an original beam.
Right: The marble fireplace in the drawing room.

Carpenters had seven children, two live-in servants, and several horses. Carpenter purchased the land from George Hamilton, whose family cemetery was once situated on the northeasterly side of the present building. Hamilton's first doctor, Dr. William Case, was buried in the small exclusive cemetery in 1848, for the reason that his special brand of agnosticism barred him from Christian cemeteries.

The main staircase and niche.

Subsequent owners included Judge Thomas Robertson, M.P., formerly of Foxbar in Dundas. Frank Anderson Merrick, an executive of Westinghouse, sold the house to Mr. and Mrs. Harold Patterson in 1949. Between September 1949 and July 1950, the Pattersons transformed the house into seven luxury apartments. Eighteen years ago, the present owners bought Rock Castle and set about restoration. First, they turned the main part into a single residence for themselves. Then they divided the coach house, the servants' quarters, and the basement into four apartments on three levels, each with a separate entrance. The original 10-foot ceilings with their decorative mouldings had been left intact, as had the doorways and tall recessed windows. There are eight fireplaces in the house, those in the front part entirely original. The dining room and present kitchen, formerly the library, have back-to-back fireplaces that share the same flue. Interestingly, the dining room fireplace has the original wrought iron grate and surround. All have marble mantels and surrounds. On the second floor, the two bedrooms over the kitchen and dining room have the same back-to-back fireplaces with wood mantels decorated in a Tudor rose motif.

All floors have marquetry border designs of geometrical patterns that vary from room to room. High ceilings and walls of stone as thick as 20 inches mean there is no need for air conditioning, even in the hottest Ontario summer, and the hot-water radiator system is more than adequate in the bitterest of winters.

Detail of the moulding around the drawing room ceiling.

An End-Gabled House, 1850

7 Melville Street, Dundas

Detail of the round-arched vent under the elaborate bargeboard and finial.

This end-gabled house, built in 1850, is a typical example of the vernacular Gothic revival style of architecture. Designed to give maximum display to the elaborate bargeboard, it is highlighted by a carved finial on the gable peak. The decorative effect is enhanced by the plain rough-cast wall behind and a little attic vent with its rounded lintel. Below the vent a pair of Gothic windows with carved half-moon lintels and two-over-two sash windows complete the Gothic façade.

End-gabled houses are unusual for the period. They didn't come into their own until the 1880s, when the original 60-foot x 120-foot survey lots were subdivided owing to increasing land values and diminishing supply of vacant lots.

The decorative front verandah has been restored by the present owners, but the double front doors and rectangular transom in their moulded frame are original. From the doorway and window openings, one can judge the thickness of the exterior walls at about 10 to 12 inches.

A large dining room serves as the home's focal point, from which five doorways lead out to five rooms: the living room, the hall, the kitchen, the sun room, and the den (used as a TV room). Two sets of original French doors open, one from the dining room into the living room and the second from the living room onto the verandah. The glass in the doors and tall windows contains the flaws and grains of sand inherent in nineteenth-century manufacture. Beautiful hardwood marquetry floors framed by substantial baseboards give the front rooms a very stylish air, while exposed beams add a homely touch. A plate rail around the dining room walls and a built-in cupboard allowed the family to make a modest display of their best crockery. Tall windows and 10½-foot ceilings lend light and airiness to a room meant for convivial dining and get-togethers.

The kitchen has been altered to meet the present-day needs of a young family, but the six-over-six sash window on the east side has been kept, and an original latch on the back door is still in use. A sun room with attractively painted floors and a den extend from the west side of the house. The present owners believe it dates from the original construction.

The house was owned by Walker Stock, but whether or not he built it is not recorded. Stock was employed by the town of Dundas as a tax collector until, in declining health, he, his wife, and their son, Thomas, moved to Waterdown. During their years in Waterdown, the Dundas house was rented. Upon Stock's death in 1900, his wife and son returned to live there.

Kennel Keeper's Cottage, 1850

9 Kinnel Street, Strathcona, Hamilton

The round attic window with its stone sill under the north-facing front gable.

Sir Allan MacNab's kennel keeper lived in this tiny 160-year-old cottage with his wife and eight children. Behind the house, handy to the keeper, were located the kennels, while the house was part of the Dundurn property. Today, only one stone wall of the kennel survives, almost invisible under a trellis with climbing hydrangeas.

The cottage exterior is of brick, the east and west walls done in a variant of English bond, every fourth row being brick headers. Paint conceals what might possibly have been contrasting brick arches over the windows and door. The south window on the west wall is a later addition, a change betrayed by the absence of an arch, although it has a stone sill. The north window on that side does have an arch, but the sill is made of header bricks. Over the front door, a small round window with stained glass darkened by time and weathering must have been the only source of light for the loft, where the children would have slept. The little window is under a gable in the steeply pitched hip roof.

An off-centre tail on the rear of the house could have been a summer kitchen. The raised foundation hints at a basement kitchen, but there is no way of telling if there was one once. No trace of a chimney can be seen, but how else would the dwelling have been heated and the food prepared? The foundation has been smoothed over with concrete, probably to beautify the original rubble stone.

The interior has been extensively renovated, but the original basement remains. There is also a pull-down ladder to give access to the loft.

Kinnel Street is named for a place in Scotland. Many streets in the area, and Dundurn itself, were named after Scottish locations.

Survey Office Cottage, 1850

50 Wood Street, North End, Hamilton

The front entrance of the survey office facing onto the bend on Wood Street.

This modest cottage was built about 1850 as a survey office for Sir Allan MacNab's estate and served as a residence for the surveyor as well. Originally designed as a centre-hall plan one-and-a-half-storey brick dwelling with the typical four rooms and hip roof of the Ontario-style cottage, it was meant to be a no-frills sort of place where business was done. A symmetrical three-bay front façade faces onto the curving street that once served as a wagon track to the wharves. The plain central doorway surmounted by a gentle brick arch is without transom or sidelights. On either side are two large windows with wooden sills and brick arches that match the doorway. Originally the windows were sash, but the cords have long been broken. A simple prop is used to keep them open in warm weather.

The interior has been completely altered, although traces remain of the walls that once divided the house into four. Original pine flooring, mostly top-nailed, has survived alterations, and there is evidence of tongue-and-groove flooring in the basement stairwell. Foundations of rubble stone can be seen in the basement of the 1870 addition, but there is no basement or crawl space under the 1850 section.

The low hip roof is new, replacing an older hip roof with dormers found by the present owners in the attic. They also discovered that the roof of the old section had been held on with pegs and still had its cedar shingles. From the way the attic is accessed, they speculate that it was once used as a sleeping loft. In 1870 a tail was added at the back of the house to accommodate proper bedrooms.

A black stain on the floor of the present kitchen suggests where a wood stove once stood. There is no trace of a fireplace or chimney. The master bedroom is situated in the 1870 addition, but the doorway and worn doorsill in the east wall are part of the original house. Standing in this doorway, it is possible to measure the thickness of the exterior walls on the old section at 15 inches. The ceilings, incidentally, are 11 feet high.

The cottage faces onto the bend in Wood Street West. Originally, the arm to the west was Wood Street, while that to the east was called Market Road. When the property was broken up, the lots were divided on a north-south axis at 45 degrees to the former Market Road, which left no. 50, at the bend, overhanging the lot diagonally.

Grove Cemetery Cottage, 1852

129 York Road, Dundas

You couldn't ask for quieter neighbours than those by Grove Cottage — except for the passing traffic on York Road. This modest stone dwelling was intended as an office and home for the superintendent of the new Grove Cemetery, which had opened three years before it was built. It is a typical vernacular building of the period 1840–1860, with a simple gable roof, originally wood-shingled, and two stone side-chimneys. The thick rubble-stone walls have rough-hewn corner quoins and the windows, dressed-stone lintels and sills.

Fortunately, most of the exterior features have been preserved, so the passer-by sees a charming Georgian stone cottage with a façade divided into three bays. The central doorway is characterized by a four-panel wood door with a rectangular transom and flanked by two asymmetrically placed double-hung windows. A raised basement features matching windows on either side of the front doorstep.

The design is that of a rectangular block with a centre-hall plan. The hallway extended from front to back with two rooms on either side and a front and back entrance. The walls are about 15 inches thick, and the windows were probably six-paned sashes like the one remaining six-paned upper sash in the living-room window.

Construction began in the fall of 1851 and was completed by June 1852, a relatively rare instance of a local stone dwelling. The identity of the builder has been lost, but the first superintendent was Richard Call, although it's not known if he ever lived in the cottage. He was dismissed in November 1855 after being sent to jail on a charge of felony. His successor, Stephen Johnson did live there until the 1860s, when he was succeeded by Thomas Caldwell. When Caldwell died about 1900, the superintendency was taken over by Stewart Watson and his son Herbert. They did not live in the cottage but used it as an office, shelter, and storage shed until the 1950s, when Herbert passed on. The last superintendent, Frank Dring and his wife, Sally, moved into the cottage in 1953 and remained until 1977.

After 130 years of ownership of the property, the town of Dundas sold the cottage to Ben and Mary Veldhuis in 1985, and the present owners bought it in the 1990s and set about its restoration.

There is no sign of a window on the south elevation, but modern mortar is evident in the lower half of the wall. The west façade, like the front, is divided into three equal bays, but the central doorway has been filled in and made into a window after the installation of a bathroom at the back of the hallway. On the north façade, a doorway has been cut, probably from a window opening, and has become the main entrance to the house and to the remodelled kitchen. A pot-bellied stove in the living room was removed after a proper basement was dug out of the old cellar and central heating was installed. The oak floors were in poor condition and have been covered with plywood and linoleum or carpet. Finally, the roof has been reshingled with asphalt.

The grounds are generous for such a small cottage. The north side is shaded by trees and one hears the cool chuckle of water cascading into a reflecting pond. In the sunny front garden an abundance of colourful wildflowers grow thick and tall.

Top right: The kitchen entrance in the north façade was probably cut from the matching right window. The reflecting pool in the foreground is part of a waterfall system designed by the present owners.

Ballinahinch, 1853

316 James Street South, Durand, Hamilton

With its dominating four-storey central tower, Ballinahinch exemplifies the monumental dwellings that began to appear in Hamilton after pioneer entrepreneurs in the city amassed their fortunes. The house was first built in 1848 for Aeneas Sage Kennedy, a Scottish dry-goods merchant who called his new home "The Wilderness." After a devastating fire in 1853, the house was rebuilt for Kennedy's widow to the plans of architect William Thomas.

Left: Italianate paired tower windows with pilasters in the Ionic style.
Right: A column capital on the porch to the right of the main entrance.

The house was meant to be impressive and substantial. Hamilton's manor houses of the period tended to cluster at the escarpment foot south of the Gore and were built of locally quarried limestone.

Ballinahinch is an outstanding example of the country villa style, with both Italianate and Gothic features. Anthony Adamson's inventory of architectural excellence gave the house a high rating. It is a rare survivor from a distinguished building period in the city during the 1840s and 1850s known as the "Stone Age."

The widowed Mrs. Kennedy married Robert Ferrie in 1858, but little changed until 1870. That year, the house was purchased by Edward Martin, grandson of Ireland's celebrated M.P. "Humanity Martin" and founder of the law firm Martin & Martin. He named it Ballinahinch after the Martin estate in Ireland. Exterior changes were introduced by the new owner's choice of renovations, such as the massive Italianate

Above: The room over the doorway was once a private family chapel.

Ceiling medallion in a first-floor room.

square central tower. Naturalistic flora carvings adorn classical capitals and Gothic mouldings alike, making an unusual study in contrasts.

Gothic battlements were included in the tower design — an odd choice when, at the time, the tower housed the family's private chapel. A Tudor arch entranceway and label mouldings over some of the arches further gentrified the already baronial mansion. Baronial attributes also included Martin's monogram over the front entrance. In the main entrance hall, a magnificent stairway confronts the visitor. The graceful curving banister is not only a proud ornament of the past, but also, on the authority of a former paper boy, excellent for sliding.

Ballinahinch housed the

Above: A doorway, now closed off, between the side porch and the front vestibule.

Left: The main staircase and carved newel.

Martin family for 46 years. In 1918 it served as an influenza hospital, then became the property of William J. Southam, publisher of the *Hamilton Spectator*. Southam did not occupy the place himself but rented it to Frederick I. Ker, who later succeeded him as publisher of the *Spectator*.

As time passed and taxes rose, Ballinahinch became too expensive to remain a single-family residence. After World War II it was divided into several small apartments, one of which was occupied by Evelyn Dick, and eventually fell into disrepair. Fortunately, the ceiling medallions, mouldings, and doorways mostly survived, as did the stairway banisters in spite of the paper boy's antics. In 1980 the house was purchased by a contractor who preserved the essential features of the house then divided the place into five spacious and elegant condominium apartments.

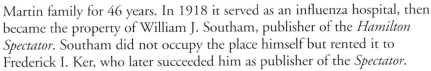

Top right: Stained glass with Edward Martin's monogram, EM, over the closed-off doorway.
Centre right: A leaded-glass window over the front doorway as seen from the inside.
Bottom right: The south entrance.

Roach House, 1854

55 Barton Street West, Central, Hamilton

Left: Classical revival window flanking the entrance.
Centre: The round-headed upper window can be traced to the Italianate style of Dundurn.
Right: The grand entranceway is prominent on this essentially modest dwelling.

Basically a modest dwelling but for the entryway, Roach House represents a transitional style from early Ontario architecture to Anglo-Italianate. The approach — through coupled pillars — is more appropriate to the entrance of a contemporary public building, and lends the house a pretentious air.

In the 1850s, stone was quarried from the escarpment in sufficient amounts to allow Scottish stonemasons to build many impressive buildings during what has been labelled Hamilton's "Stone Age." Roach House, on the south side of Barton and west of James, was built in 1854 for George Roach (1818–1904). The foundations are of rubble stone. Coarse stone was used for the side and back walls while good quality cut stone was reserved for the street aspect. The symmetrical three-bay front façade, with its projecting eaves and single brackets, are Italianate features and include a central belvedere, reminiscent of a Tuscan tower. On the other hand, classical revival elements are evidenced by the square porch pillars, the pediments surmounting windows with arch, and sculptured keystone on either side of the entrance. A rounded-arch window over the doorway could have been copied from Arlo House on Main Street West, built four years earlier. In both cases the architect is unknown but may have been common to the dwellings.

When Roach House was built there were extensive grounds behind with stables and a cottage. The raised basement suggests a kitchen, a common feature of the era. There is thought to have been a tunnel from the basement to the cottage and one can only speculate as to its purpose.

George Roach, as his house suggests, was a prominent individual as a Hamilton businessman, hotelier and restaurateur, and director of the Bank of Hamilton, among other directorships. He was also active in civic politics, being acclaimed alderman for St. Mary's ward three times and elected mayor by popular vote in 1875, then re-elected by acclamation in 1876. Members of his family continued to live in the house until after 1922. In subsequent years major alterations subdivided the house from its stables and cottage and later the house was broken up into apartments.

Kerr House, 1855

988 Concession Street, Sunninghill, Hamilton

This one-and-a half-storey stuccoed house overlooking the escarpment is set back from the roadway on a large treed lot with attractively landscaped grounds. Once upon a time the house stood at the northeast corner of an extensive 100-acre property that had frontage extending from Upper Gage to Upper Ottawa.

The house, originally known as Inkermann Cottage, was built in 1855. In 1858, John William Kerr and his wife, Mary Eliza Winslow, moved in with their four sons and five daughters. John developed the land into a productive mixed farm, and he and Mary lived in the house until their deaths in 1888 and 1907, respectively. Their five daughters, all unmarried, continued to run the farm, which was reduced to 34 acres after Kerr's death. The last surviving daughter, Louisa, died in 1930, and the remaining farm was divided among the heirs. The house was acquired by Charles Kerr and after Charles's death, by his son Albert; neither ever lived in the house. In 1946 the house and three-quarters of an acre were purchased by Reginald and Ruth Dodson, who remained until 1985.

The house is an unusual and possibly unique variation on the Ontario Regency cottage form, a one-storey structure of tall proportions, stuccoed, with tall chimneys and tall casement windows. It is atypical of the Regency cottage because of its L-shaped plan, contiguous roof form, and a rear summer kitchen wing with hip roof. Large wall-mounted brackets support the flared eaves. These brackets, sprung from supports and terminating in two pendants, are a distinctive and individual design feature. The doorway dates from 1855, including the four-panel wood door and rectangular transom. Four dormers with curved roofs and casement windows were added much later, but sometime before 1946. One major alteration to the front façade takes the form of a large horizontal window to the left of the front doorway, added sometime in the 1940s.

John William Kerr was a well-known fishing inspector and early conservationist, a leader in the early initiative to protect Canada's fish and game resources. He concerned himself with the declining fishing

The flared eaves and surrounding trees keep the house naturally cool in summer.

and game population in Hamilton Harbour, thus becoming a founding member of the Wentworth Society for the Protection of Game and Fish, which was established 1880. After his death in 1888, he was succeeded as fisheries overseer by his son Frederick, who died in 1902 to be succeeded by the next son, Charles, who held the position until his death in 1942.

The Wallace/Magill House, 1855

173 Main Street North, Waterdown

When it was built, the Magill House stood facing south at the end of a long lane that led north from Dundas Street. Over the years there has been some dispute over who built the house, but the matter of the lane helps settle the issue. Georgian and neo-classical features date the house to between 1850 and 1860, when the property belonged to one William Magill, who had purchased the land in 1846 from prominent businessmen Ebenezer Culver Griffin and his brother, Absalom, and put up a one-and-a-half-storey frame house. The enormous increase in the assessment of the property between 1851(£40) and 1861 ($2,200) suggests that this was the decade of construction.

In 1853, Ebenezer's son James Kent Griffin built Snake Road, the first toll road from Hamilton to Waterdown. A year later he extended the road to provide a north-south route to Carlisle along the eastern boundary of the Magill property, there being a definite curve in the road to accommodate the property line. After the toll road opened, all subsequent houses were built facing the laneway, now Main Street. In 1853 the property was sold to Hugh Creen, another prominent citizen, who in the 1860s bequeathed the house to his second daughter, Mary Patton, a widow.

In 1951 the renowned restoration architect Arthur Wallace, mentioned earlier in connection with Cherryhill, and his wife, Letitia, purchased the property. Wallace designed many buildings in the City of Hamilton, including the Federal Building at Main and Caroline.

Although one of the finest examples of late Georgian and neo-classical style, the building was designed as a saltbox, a shape common in New England but rare in Southern Ontario. Built of rough-cut limestone with massive stone quoins, the symmetrical three-bay façade has the restrained feel of the Georgian style. The large windows with six-over-six paned sashes, the simple cornice friezes, the gentle pitch of the roof, and the wide recessed doorway with its transom and sidelights, applied pilasters, and brackets are all neo-classical elements. Windows and shutters are original, as are the wooden stair banister and wood panelling in the living room.

Magill House is an example of the saltbox style of architecture. The house is named after its original owner, William Magill.

Hereford House, 1856

13 — 15 Bold Street, Durand, Hamilton

Top: The view from the east shows Hereford House's brick third floor. Above: A stained-glass transom ornamenting a back door.

Hereford House once stood in its own grounds, complete with gardens and a carriage house and all the other accoutrements of middle-class prosperity. When the house was built circa 1856–1857, there would have been a fine view towards the north, with a glimpse of Burlington Bay. Built in plain Italianate style with a low hip roof and central gable, it is an exemplar of beauty in simplicity. Peter Balfour, father of architect James, was likely the builder, and it is entirely possible he was working to a design by the architect William Thomas, as they were also constructing Ballinahinch during the same period.

Detail of the carved roof brackets.

Above: The remaining stone chimney.
Right: The trompe l'oeil *effect gives the impression of a projecting centre bay.*

Now hemmed in by surrounding buildings, Hereford House nevertheless encapsulates the dignity of a grander age. The beautifully symmetrical front façade is surmounted by overhanging eaves supported on carved roof brackets. On the top floor, the original windows and stone sills are in place, but the windows on the lower two floors have modern glass and frames set in the original openings.

The façade is made up of three bays, the central bay matching the width of the gable above. Each bay has a pair of matching windows at each level. The middle bay at ground level has paired doors to match the placement of the windows above. The limestone used on the street façade is as Peter Balfour intended; the outer bays are faced with ashlar and the centre bay of smooth sawn stone. The effect is *trompe l'oeil*: the centre bay appears to project but is in fact flush with the other two. Under the gable a blind half-circle niche with a keystone suggests a coat of arms that isn't there. The shingles on the roof are recent, but

the roof itself and the interior beams are original. The thickness of the walls is revealed in doorways, particularly in the interior. Every wall was built one-and-a-half-bricks wide, on both the interior and inside the exterior. On the exterior, each corner of the building is ornamented with large stone quoins.

The house was built as a single-family dwelling for Caleb Hopkins, who used it as a rental property. After he sold the property in 1874, it was subdivided into two dwellings. Isaac Baldwin McQuesten bought no. 1 (now no. 13), and Reverend Thomas Baker bought the other half, no. 3 (now no. 15). McQuesten married Baker's daughter, Mary, and the house remained in the possession of the McQuesten family until 1948.

In 1979 lawyer Herman Turkstra bought the building, which subsequently underwent exterior restoration, earning Turksta a conservancy award. The interior was in too bad a state to restore, and Turkstra converted it to modern office space. Only the private quarters on the top floor retain any original features. Turkstra donated the building to the Corporation of the City of Hamilton in 1980.

Veevers House, 1856

22 Veevers Drive, Vincent, Hamilton

The stone farmhouse known as Veevers House once crowned a hill surrounded by rolling pastures, woodland, and orchards. A stream fed by springs cuts though the fields to the west. The original 200-acre Crown grant was purchased in 1834 from John Thatcher by James Dean, who subsequently erected the present stone farmhouse between 1851 and 1861. The place changed hands once or twice after that until it was purchased in 1934 by Ronald, Bertram, Cyril, and Raymond Veevers, sons of a nonconformist clergyman from Manchester, England. All eight members of the family — father, mother, four sons, and two daughters — lived on the farm until the 1940s, when the two younger brothers and two sisters moved away after the parents died. At the time of the Veevers purchase, the land was badly neglected and considerable labour was involved in making it suitable for dairy and fruit farming. For ten years the family ran a successful dairy and fruit farm until the dairy was taken over by Silverwoods. Gradually the farm lands disappeared as cattle and land were sold off and the 35-acre cherry orchard was turned into a housing estate.

The one-and-a-half-storey house is built of rough-hewn stone

Top left: The front façade originally featured a wide doorway with a panelled wood door and sidelights. The present door and fanlight, like the dormers, is a 1968 modification.
Top right: The east wall and chimney with overhanging eaves.
Above: A front view of Veevers House showing the stone retaining wall around the upper garden.

quarried from the escarpment. The fine masonry work, wide horizontal proportions, and restrained ornamentation are characteristic of houses built by the early settlers from the 1820s to the 1850s. The well-proportioned five-bay front façade featured a wide central doorway with sidelights flanked by two pairs of sash windows with flat arched lintels and solid-stone sills. On the upper storey there was a somewhat unusual row of low square windows, but in 1968 they were replaced by higher and taller dormers. During the same period the doorway was modified.

The rough dressed-stone blocks of the front elevation put a best face forward, while the side and back outer walls are of rubble stone and undressed blocks. The panelled front door has a semi-circular mullioned window and fourteen-pane sidelights on either side. The dentillated lintel is surmounted by a stone arch. At each corner large stone quoins finish off the detailing. The side elevations are symmetrical, with two windows below and two on the second storey. Curiously, the sills of the lower windows are of wood while those of the upper windows are of stone. The side-gabled roof supports matching chimneys with dentillated trim under overhanging returned eaves. However, the chimney brickwork looks suspiciously modern.

The Bay South Terrace, 1857

210 — 218 Bay Street South, Durand, Hamilton

At the southwest corner of Bay South and Robinson stands a plain but handsome Georgian terrace. In 1857, William Crawford, a cashier at the Gore Bank, purchased lot 12 from the Kerr-Brown survey and constructed the three attached dwelling units. The front façade he clad with cut stone but left the other red-brick walls exposed. The tall windows on the upper storey, with their six-paned sash frames, stone sills, and lintels, are Crawford's handiwork. On the lower storey, one of the windows at no. 212 has been made into a door, subdividing a two-part dwelling into three parts. A raised basement reveals a rubble-stone foundation with original basement window openings, but only one is in use. In the basement of no. 210, the remains of a stone structure indicate the possible presence of a below-stairs kitchen.

Detail of the bay window at the front of 216 Bay Street.

In 1877, another dwelling was added at the south end of the terrace. This section is of brick, without the stone facing, but its charming bay window is listed as one of the most attractive in the city, although it and the porch are thought to be early twentieth century. The first owner and occupant of no. 216 was James Thornton, an organ maker, and his son Thomas. At that time the lot for the terrace was generous, bounded by Bowery (now Bay), Hannah (now Charlton), Caroline, and Robinson.

A later addition was added to the back of the two original dwellings to accommodate a kitchen. Above and extending along their length are modern decks with wooden stairs, giving back-door access. In the gap between the decks, a tall free-standing chimney rises like a monolith. Once it probably served as a shared kitchen chimney. In 1910, an ugly third floor, faced with brown brick, was added to nos. 210 and 212. It was meant to provide extra living space when the terrace houses were converted to apartments.

Over the years many changes were made to the interior of the homes. No. 210 has the original pine board floors in the front room and hall while no. 212 has the original carved banister. Most of the houses have original fireplaces, markedly shallow with unlined flues designed for burning coal. Fire safety codes allow the use of these fireplaces to burn only prefabricated fire-logs behind a glass screen.

The joined houses served as single-family dwellings until the beginning of the twentieth century, although they changed owners and tenants many times over the years. Among the tenants were some Hamiltonians who played a role in the growing community. James Turner was a wholesale grocer with branch stores from Montreal to Winnipeg. Thomas White and his brother Richard came to Hamilton in

The original shallow fireplace designed for burning coal.

Number 210 retains the original doorway with transom and sidelights. The steps to the door allow for the raised basement.

1864, and both worked as editors for the *Hamilton Spectator*. Later, Thomas was elected Member of Parliament for Cardwell and served under Sir John A. Macdonald. In 1895, another pair of brothers became tenants at 210 Bay South: William Osborne, a barrister, and Alexander Osborne, the city's first eye specialist. During World War I, Dr. Osborne travelled with his wife to England to offer his services and spent the war working in the military hospital at Taplow. In the spring of 1915, Mrs. Osborne decided to return to Canada. She was one of the few survivors when the oceanliner *Lusitania* was torpedoed.

The units were subdivided into smaller rental units, and by the 1960s the row had become derelict. Demolition seemed on the cards until an entrepreneur with foresight bought the terrace, restored and renovated the interior, and divided each unit into large, attractive rental apartments. In the 1980s the terrace was again sold, this time to individual purchasers as condominium apartments.

Sandyford Place, 1858

35 — 41 Duke Street, Durand, Hamilton

Built between 1858 and 1863, Sandyford Place is notable for being the best remaining example of stone terrace construction in the city of Hamilton. The land had been purchased in a sale of farmland by Peter Hunter Hamilton, half-brother to the city's founder, George Hamilton. Copied from Sandyford Terrace in Glasgow, Scotland, the four-unit limestone and sandstone terrace was originally built as attached single-family dwellings.

Along with 14 Duke Street, the terrace was built by Donald Nicholson, a stonemason who had arrived from Scotland in 1852 and bought up land.

The terrace was constructed pavilion-fashion, with the ends stepped forward to break the uniformity of such a long façade. Eave brackets and Renaissance lintels belong to the revival style. More distinctive are the three-sided dormers, with hip roof and sidelights peculiar to eighteenth-century buildings in Scotland and seen elsewhere in Canada only in the Maritimes. So reminiscent of architecture in Edinburgh and Glasgow are these and other stone buildings of the period. Other landmarks constructed during the decade of the 1850s include St. Paul's Presbyterian Church (1857), the Pump House (1859), the Customs House (1860), and the stone manse at 51 Herkimer Street (1857).

Sandyford Place was built for the city's wealthy merchants and became home to many famous and important citizens of Hamilton. Among them, Edward Martin, barrister, lived here until he purchased Ballinahinch in 1870. Adam Brown was such another. He brought the Pump House and a waterworks system to the city. One of his daughters, Elizabeth Ann, married the younger William Hendrie. At no. 35, the family of James Watson, a captain of Canadian industry, resided.

In more recent years the dwellings were divided into a multiple apartment units and as the building fell into a sorry state of neglect,

Left: The influence of Dundurn Castle on the builder, Nicholson, is discernible in the style of this window.
Above: The entryways are sufficiently diverse to lend character to each unit.

demolition became a distinct possibility. The end of the story is a happy one, however. A group of concerned Hamiltonians formed an association in 1977 known as Heritage Hamilton Ltd., which raised funds and successfully lobbied the city to purchase the terrace and arrange for its restoration. Eventually the terrace was made into twelve self-contained dwellings, and in 1982 the first owner-occupants moved into their spacious and elegant condominium residences.

The Tall House on Hess Street, 1858

172 Hess Street North, Strathcona, Hamilton

The Hess Street House, circa 1983.

When it was built in 1858, this was the northernmost residence on Hess Street. Built on a rise overlooking the bay by Thomas Peat, carpenter and builder, today its tall proportions and high end-chimneys continue to tower above the surrounding neighbourhood. Peat managed to complete the house just before the recession of 1858, which may account for the amount of detail over the front door and under the eaves, and for the decorative carved faces on the end brackets. Peat, also spelled "Peitt" or "Peit," occupied the house from 1858 until 1886.

The house next became associated with the early days of the iron and steel industry. From 1886 to 1911 it was occupied by Seth J. Whitehead and family. Born in England, Whitehead started out in the iron business in England before immigrating to America to continue in the business from 1858 to 1878. In 1878, he moved to Hamilton and became a leader in the metal industry as superintendent of the Hamilton Iron Forging Company, founded in 1879. In 1885, Whitehead established a rolling mill — an innovative improvement at the time — to produce sheets of iron for industry. From his house he could overlook the ironworks, which in those days were located on the block bounded by Hess, Barton, Queen, and Stuart streets.

One of the earliest and most distinguished houses in the area, 172 Hess reflects the growth of residential districts northwest of the city core towards industrial lands, railroad yards, and the waterfront. In the 1930s, the owners at the time had the house painted pink using a rubber-based paint from Portugal. Unfortunately, the paint is impossible to remove without damaging the brick.

Woodend, 1862

838 Mineral Springs Road, Ancaster

In the old days, Woodend took unwary visitors by surprise. Set back from the road on a knoll commanding a view in several directions, the house would be barely visible through trees until the main carriage sweep approached the ceremonial front door.

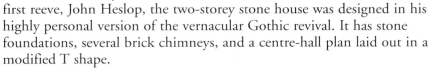

Built on Mineral Springs Road circa 1862 by Ancaster's first reeve, John Heslop, the two-storey stone house was designed in his highly personal version of the vernacular Gothic revival. It has stone foundations, several brick chimneys, and a centre-hall plan laid out in a modified T shape.

On either side of the main hall are two very large drawing rooms, each with an original marble-trimmed open fireplace. These rooms,

Top: A view of Woodend from the driveway.
Above: The kitchen wing. The servants' quarters are located behind.

Woodend's steep roof, delicate bargeboard, and sturdy brackets make for an imposing structure.

where visitors would have been entertained, have beautifully moulded doorways and ceilings. The pine floors are constructed of 4-inch planks and trimmed with 12-inch moulded baseboards. Graceful curves juxtapose adjoining walls over the front staircase, with its 11-inch-deep steps and shallow rises. Turned wood balusters, a newel with an octagonal base, and moulded panelling along the side of the staircase testify to the fine quality of workmanship. Upstairs, four bedrooms, each with moulded ceilings and doorways and an individual fireplace, open off the hallway.

The servants' quarters occupy a nearly separate stone building with its own stairs and doorways, and baseboards similar to those of the front of the house but, with an eye to economy, much simpler in design. The basement, which extends under most of the house, has joists supported by huge, heavy wood beams and massive stone columns.

Traces remain of the original picturesque landscaping by George Laing, who also landscaped Rock Castle, Auchmar, and possibly the Hermitage. The sweeping approach to the house was one of Laing's favourite touches.

Woodend was donated in 1970 to the Hamilton Region Conservation Authority by its last owner, George Donald, and is still the headquarters of

Left: The magnificent main staircase has a plainer, simpler replica in the servants' part of the house. Right: Woodend's marble mantelpiece is one of the few surviving originals.

the Conservation Authority. The present occupants have been careful not to alter original features unnecessarily, and the flavour of the house is still evident despite the ubiquitous filing cabinets and computer terminals, and an ugly addition on the west of the main house.

In 1891, Woodend was the scene of a murder, unsolved to this day. On a bitter January night, two masked men intent on robbery broke into the house. John Heslop confronted them and demanded to know what they were after. They shot him dead then ransacked the house, searching for town treasury funds they believed — incorrectly as it happened — were kept there. Failing to find what they were after, the men fled empty-handed. Four men were captured and charged with the murder, but a jury found them not guilty. John Heslop's unavenged spirit may still roam around the old attic, where thuds can be heard from time to time. As one Conservation Authority member said, "Is it just squirrels… or is it old John?"

Top left: The chimneys convey the house's spirit of solidarity and tradition.
Top right: A sense of medievalism is found in the heavy masonry of the façades and ashlar finish.
Bottom left: The stone lintels and painted arches on the second floor suggest the tower windows of an English manor.
Bottom right: View of Woodend circa 1970.

The Newell Farm, 1863

561 Seventh Concession Road, Carlisle, East Flamborough

One might call this a two-faced house. The front entrance faces northeast, but the property line is northwest-southeast. A little history of the area is needed to unravel the paradox. At the time of purchase the Newell property was a corner lot facing east to Millborough Line. On the south, concession 7 had been hacked out of the wilderness in 1842, but it was low-lying, swampy, and subject to flooding in spring. By 1907, a corduroy road packed with dirt and gravel made for a smoother and drier surface. Then, when a modern gravel road replaced the corduroy in 1965, the pond south of the house was created while the north pond was filled in.

The southeast façade.

The small gable and verandah on the southeast side of the house now appear to constitute the front façade.

William Newell, his wife, Agnes Magill, and their brood of eleven children came to Upper Canada from County Down, Ireland, in 1838. They travelled directly to the Head-of-the-Lake and settled on the seventh concession of East Flamborough Township. The lot was completely covered with thick bush and pine, which had to be cleared before a log house could be built. Ten years later, William's eldest son, Charles, was able to purchase 100 acres of lot 1 from the trustees for £100, and he walked all the way to the provincial capital, Newark (now Niagara-on-the-Lake), to register the deed.

A year later Charles married Emily Blagden, and they lived in a small log house built from trees felled as the land was cleared. By 1863 Charles was doing well enough to replace the log house with one of stone quarried from the Great Falls in Waterdown. It was built by the

An early photograph of the northwest façade and outside stone stairway to the attics.

Left: The real front façade, which faces northeast onto Millborough Line.

Below: Detail of the centre gable and Gothic window under an arched lintel.

local stonemason Thomas LeMesurier at a cost of $500.

The northeast-facing front of the house is finished with dressed stone in a checkerboard-like pattern and quoins at each corner. A central gable with a Gothic arched window complements the front doorway with its rectangular transom and sidelights. The two make up the middle bay of three to form a symmetrical façade. The north and south façades of this section of the house each have four windows, a pair on the first storey and another pair on the second. Above the end gables are matching chimneys. The rear section of the house, the kitchen tail, is made of rubble stone. The entire house is the same age although it looks like the rear portion is an addition because of the different stone used. The working front is now the door facing the barn on the north side, and the rear door faces the pond. An unusual outdoor stone staircase, built onto the rear wall to give access to the attics, is a reminder of the Newells' Irish origins. In the north yard a pump and well are still in working order.

By the beginning of the twentieth century the farm was a mixed operation with a variety of animals, a market garden, and an orchard. By the 1950s there was a change to cash crops, like corn; Sam Newell was one of the first to experiment with such a system.

The pyramid on the property was built by Sam in the early 1970s. A trip to the pyramids of Egypt inspired him to built one of his own, and he oriented the sides N-E-S-W by means of the North Star. Sam died in 1994 and left the farm to his wife, Dorothy. When she died in September 2003, the farm passed out of the family.

Top: A family gathering, circa 1920.
Above: The outside rubble-stone staircase is reminiscent of the steps to a church pulpit.

The barn, with Sam Newell's clock on the roof. The clock was rescued from the Canada Trust Building in downtown Hamilton.

Grant's Sail Loft, 1869

469 Bay Street North, North End, Hamilton

Above: The present day entrance.

Hamilton's North End used to be a two-fisted commercial empire of wharves, boathouses, shipyards, and warehouses. The Sail Loft at 469 Bay Street North is among the few remaining relics of that prosperous era. In its heyday the loft was a bustling waterfront business. It turned out better sails than any other manufacturer and employed a large force of men to ensure quality and prompt delivery.

The building was designed by William W. Grant, a sailmaker already in business on Zealand's wharf, now the site of the Royal Hamilton Yacht Club. Grant sited his new facility on the bluff above the wharves, giving it a one-storey gabled brick façade on Bay Street and a three-storey gabled rear portion of rubble stone that faced west towards Burlington Bay. Ballast from sail boats, mostly limestone quarried in Kingston, was used for the stone foundation. Completed in 1869, the Sail Loft was admirably situated and ideally specialized for the purpose of sailmaking, with interior dimensions of 27 feet x 77 feet and 9-foot ceilings free of supports. The rubble-stone walls of the two lower levels are 3 feet thick, while the walls of the upper level are three bricks wide. The long south wall holds the summer heat well into winter, spreading warmth into the interior. As well, it gets all the available winter sun, making it a fine example of energy-efficient construction.

White oak is light in weight, resistant to dry rot, durable and easy to fashion. The floor of the Sail Loft is of white oak, so hard that the present owner covered it with plywood so pins could be used to hold a sail in place. The attic is roofed with 12-inch white oak boards and oak beams. Fires have broken out up there but the wood is so hard it withstands flames. Only traces of black and charred spots on the beams are perceptible. Originally, the front doorway went straight into the loft from a short stairway, but over the years Bay Street has built up layer by layer until it threatened to collapse the east wall. The wall is now heavily reinforced with steel, leaving the entrance below street level. Double front doors with a transom are new and set in the original opening, as are the windows, except one that has been partially filled in. Only one original chimney survives, but traces in the attic indicate there was definitely another on the north side and likely two or three more on the south.

The top two floors were used for sailmaking until 1887, when the transition to steam-powered craft caused the industry to go into decline. By 1907, the Sail Loft had become Reid's Gasoline Engine Company, the first marine gas engine company in Canada. From 1923 to 1935, part of the building became a straw hat factory with another part used by the Calvin Presbyterian Sunday School. During both world wars the loft served as an ideal location for a dance hall and, in peacetime, headquarters for Hamilton's naval reserve and sea cadets. Its last incarnation was as a meeting hall for the Black community. By 1985 the building had fallen derelict. The present owner made an offer and purchased the building. One week later the building was condemned. A demolition company truck stopped in front one afternoon and the driver offered to pull the place down in exchange for all the oak beams. He was turned down flat and the owner set about restoration. The building is once more in use for sailmaking.

Left: The original latch and entrance to the sail loft in the south wall.

Top: The south wall showing the upper-level brick residential part of the house, and the lower rubble-stone wall of the sail-making floor.
Above: The stone lintel and voussoirs over the rear door at the lowest level.

The Herkimer Street Terrace, 1870

42 — 46 Herkimer Street, Durand, Hamilton

Here we have a lovely terrace designed in 1877 by James Balfour as a residential townhouse. Originally, it was designed as three separate units in the Second Empire style. In the 1960s, no. 42, the easterly unit, was torn down to make way for an apartment block.

The original owner of the terrace was Hugh Cossart Baker, who acted as an agent for the Hamilton Real Estate Association, which commissioned a Detroit firm to build the place. Baker lived at Burlington Terrace, at the corner of Herkimer and James, and lived on the rental income from the new terrace. With its mansard roof and graceful use of brick trimmed with wood, the terrace was intended to reflect the wealth and quality of the residents within. Such Second Empire features as dormers with heavy pediments, a roof cornice supported by carved brackets, a carved textured bay window, the decorative porches, and ornamental rounded windows speak of luxury, not practicality.

Intact, the eastern unit would have matched the western to make a façade of beautiful symmetry. Unfortunately, there are no early pictures or drawings to indicate what the terrace looked like in its heyday, so we can only imagine its impact on the streetscape.

The entrance to 44 Herkimer Street, the largest centre unit of the three. Opposite: The truncated terrace as it stands today.

Smith-Gooderman House, 1870

117 Wilson Street West, Ancaster

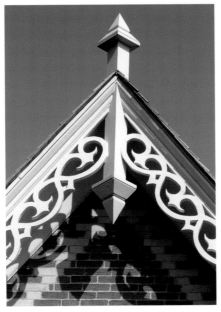

Detail of a gable, bargeboard and finial with decorative brickwork behind.

An arched window on the east-side ground level, the decorative theme is repeated in all but the bay windows.

When Jesse Smith built his house on lot 41, concession 3 in 1870, the property was outside Ancaster town limits. To this day, therefore, whenever historic houses of Ancaster are considered for tours or books, 117 Wilson Street West is sometimes passed over.

Jesse Smith was a descendant of one of the twenty-two original settlers in Ancaster Township. His father, James Smith, bought the north central 75 acres of the lot in an 1853 Sheriff's sale and gave the property to Jesse. In 1870, Jesse built a solid red-brick triple-gabled house in the Gothic revival style.

Stone corner quoins, contrasting brick arches over the rounded Gothic windows, and symmetrical projecting bay windows are the work of a master craftsman. Along the eaves, finely crafted gingerbread trim augments the impression of an owner's pride of place. The rear elevation also has a gabled roof line with the same corner quoins and gingerbread. Two massive chimneys are visible from behind, both built with flared contrasting brick around the tops. The roofline is interrupted by gables on every aspect: three on the front and rear and one each on the sides. The roof itself is of cedar shingle. Another fine touch, a brick carriage house is attached at the rear. In bad weather, passage from house to vehicle is conveniently sheltered.

Front bay window, between decorative quoins, semi-octagonal roof, and decorative brackets.

Working-Class Brick House, 1870

107 Inchbury Street, Strathcona, Hamilton

This sturdy red-brick house at 107 Inchbury was constructed by Hamilton shoemaker Edwin Hilder, and remained in the Hilder family for forty-one years. Henrietta Hilder, the last survivor of the family, sold the place in 1916 to Mrs. Alice Rodwell for $2,800.00. In 1921, Mrs. Rodwell sold it to railwayman Charles Alexander. The Alexander family occupied the house until 1972. By this time the house and property had fallen into disrepair, but unlike many Victorian homes, this one had not fallen victim to extensive structural alterations. That only the Hilder and Alexander families owned the house for nearly ninety years may account for its preservation. Its thick double-brick walls are another factor.

At one time, a late nineteenth century working-class cottage would not have been considered worthwhile for spending money on restoration. However, with the realization

Above: The house has a modest yet attractive front doorway.
Right: The north side of the house. The garden is faintly visible behind.

that these gems of another time are fast disappearing by the wrecker's ball, preservation and restoration have become a labour of love. The present owners moved into 107 Inchbury eight years ago and love it in spite of inconveniences like the absence of cupboards, kitchen cabinets, and drawers of any kind.

The front elevation is asymmetrical, with the doorway to the left and a pair of identical shuttered windows to the right. On the second

storey there are three windows, directly above the door and windows below. The current owner of the house believes the front door is original, and certainly the glass-transomed doorway with its gentle arch and radiating bricks matches the five surrounding windows. On the ground floor, the 6-inch-wide pine plank floors are original. So are the tin ceiling and wall mouldings in the living room. The house boasts five built-in chimneys, none of which works now, but four of them can be seen paired on the gables and the fifth, at the end of the tail, is located where a cooking hearth would have been.

A narrow staircase curves to the second floor, but the stairwell has been widened at the bend to allow passage for a large wardrobe. The second level has pine flooring, and there is evidence that the four rooms up there were probably once five. Three rooms at the front of the house, each with a window, make better sense than the uneven spacing of the windows in the present arrangement. A modern addition at the rear was once used as a greenhouse, but it was recently converted into a kitchen. In the original design, the dining room contained the kitchen.

In the fashion of the day, 107 stands close to the roadside, with only a narrow expanse of lawn. Behind the house there is a long back garden where children could play in safety and solitude.

Apple Villa: The William Dalton-J. C. Smith House, 1872

2201 Lakeshore Road, Burlington

For a number of years Apple Villa served as the Netherlands Consulate when the Dutch-born owner was appointed Consul. Window shutters painted with startling red, green, and white blazes proclaim the colours of the Dutch flag to the sedate neighbourhood.

According to Maud Smith, the house was built for William Dalton in 1872 and sold to her father, John Chamberlain "Apple Jack" Smith, in 1891. She, her sister, and their brother, Maxwell, who served three terms as mayor of Burlington, grew up in the house. In 1919, after his last term in office, Maxwell and his father broke up their 20-acre apple orchard and set about developing a housing survey, but they left Apple Villa with a fine corner lot on Lakeshore Road and what is now Smith Avenue.

The house is a two-and-a-half-

storey gabled brick Gothic box, 36 feet x 35 feet but with a 15-foot kitchen addition on the back, built at some uncertain time (although, judging from the brickwork and decorative features, it was not too long after the completion of the original building). The front façade is entirely symmetrical, with matching gabled towers on either side of a recessed doorway. Directly above the front porch there is a gabled arched window embellished by coloured squares of stained glass in the upper portion.

On the second storey, paired arched one-over-one sash windows and original wooden storms are set inside arched mouldings under radiating bricks and decorative keystones. On the ground level, bay windows, keystones, and decorative bands under mansard roofs are adorned with plain boxed cornices with frieze and brackets. The front door is double leaf with glass panels

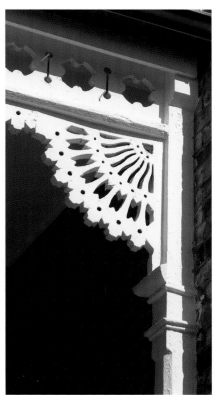

Top left: The front door transom, missing a panel.

Top right: A carved bracket under the bay-window roof.

Bottom left: Detail of the decorative brickwork and arches over an upper window.

Bottom right: Detail of the carved front porch.

surmounted by a three-section stained-glass transom. The varicoloured middle section should be flanked by matching glass panels engraved with blue flowers. Unfortunately, the panel on the west side met with a mishap involving a baseball and could not be replaced.

Ornate gingerbread once decorated all the gables and the entrance, but it has been removed. As well, the original wooden storm doors were replaced by painted aluminum, a replacement difficult to discern from the outside but visible from the interior. The original front steps were of wood, but by the 1950s they had rotted and become unsafe. They were replaced with brick, which eventually deteriorated and were replaced just recently.

The interior was altered in the 1960s by the addition of wainscotting along the lower part of the walls and stairwell. Jacobean-style ceiling beams were added in what would have been the drawing room. This Gothic box is perfectly symmetrical, made up of three sections: drawing room, hallway, and dining room, each 12 feet wide. A graceful staircase dominates the hall with its spindle balusters and curving banister. Long scratch

Above: The sewing area in the upper hall seen through the spindle balusters over the stairwell.

Right: The villa's stained-glass transom and eminently slidable banister, as seen from inside.

marks can be seen on the banister from the trouser zippers of small boys with a fondness for sliding.

The upper hall has a spacious area at the top of the stairs under the central window, perhaps once used for sewing and other light domestic duties. Along the walls can be seen the original baseboards, and in the bedrooms, the original hardwood floors. A door opens off the hall onto attic stairs, which are steep: 7 inches deep with a 10-inch rise. During the period of the consulate, the boys slept in the unheated attic.

In the rubble-stone basement, the 1870s cast-iron boiler continues to operate, although now it is fuelled by gas. In the past, the fuel was successively coal then oil.

In the east wall of the kitchen wing there is a curious anomaly: a doorway that, seen from the exterior, is topped with contrasting brick arches, indicating it might be original. However, it opens onto a straight drop into the basement stairwell. The door, needless to say, has long since been fixed shut.

In the west wall opposite the east door there is a window over the kitchen sink. The opening has been altered to remove an arch, but the arched bricks have been left in place with a mismatched keystone. Other mysteries about the addition, such as the absence of a servants' staircase, the out-of-period position of the basement stairs, and oddities in the brickwork, make this house something of a puzzle.

Eggshell Terrace, 1876

14 — 24 Charlton Street West, Durand, Hamilton

Architecturally distinguished, the terrace at 14–24 Charlton Street West graces the northwest corner of Charlton and James South. Built in the third quarter of the nineteenth century, all six units are still standing, with their pleasing proportions and detailing. No significant exterior alterations have spoiled the architectural integrity except for the two-storey porch added to 22–24 and dormer windows added sometime in the twentieth century. Bargeboards, rounded-arch doorways, and central gables are part of the attractive detail.

The Hamilton Real Estate Association, formed to bring together the many real estate dealers in the city, commissioned the building in 1876 as six attached single-family-dwelling units. The design is attributed to architect James Balfour, who also designed the Old City Hall, 42–46 Herkimer, and the ornate six-unit row house at 252–262 MacNab Street North.

Among the striking features are three central gables with round windows, jigsaw-cut vergeboard, and ornamental trim on eaves and window heads. Porches with slender Ionic columns decorate 14–16 and 18–20 and there is one remaining gabled and bargeboard-trimmed dormer with a tall sash window at no. 16. The façades of 14–20 are painted pale beige with black trim while the third pair at 22–24 has retained the original exposed red brick. The owners and occupants represented the middle class of the period: bank clerks, barristers, bookkeepers — also an artist and a freight agent.

Symmetry prevails from the round-arched doorway under the porch, to the arched windows above.

Conversion of the terrace to apartments began in 1914, except for no. 14, which remained a single-family dwelling until the 1970s. E. G. Payne bought the four eastern units of the terrace in the 1920s. He, his family, and their descendants lived there until the death in 2001 of Audrey Payne Carr, the last family survivor. She had a brother, but he had died a few months earlier in Australia. In any case, Audrey had cut him out of her will for converting to the Pentecostal faith. Audrey herself was a faithful Anglican and parishioner of the Church of the Ascension to the extent that she owned the second pew for Wednesday service. She was a lady who, even in her eighties, looked as if she modelled herself on Greta Garbo, sporting shoulder-length blond hair and bangs.

In 1993 she decided to sell and was offered $900,000 by a developer who planned to demolish the row houses and replace them with modern condos. Audrey ousted all her tenants, but when the deal fell through she left the place empty and used it for storage of her enormous collection of furniture, bought at flea markets and estate auctions. She made mention of the Church of the Ascension in her will. One can hope the proceeds of the sale were directed there.

According to the real estate agent who handled the sale of the four units, the row could not be sold as one piece. Units 22–24 are owned by someone else, a fortunate turn of events. If the row had been bought intact, these lovely buildings could have been demolished.

Detail of one of the gables.

The Cliff, 1879

6 Bull's Lane, Centremount, Hamilton

in 1877, Bull decided to move closer to the city and thus built The Cliff on the mountain brow. In 1886, Canon Bull moved to the Niagara Falls Village Rectory and, while there, founded the Mechanics Institute and the Lundy's Lane Historical Society. When he retired from Niagara Falls in 1902, Canon Bull, his wife, and daughters moved back to Hamilton, but not to Bull's Lane. His cousin George Bull Burland had bought 269 Bay Street South as a gift for Eleanor, Dorothea, Jemima, Mary, and Alice Bull. Canon Bull died there July 31, 1902.

The house on the mountain brow passed to his oldest surviving son. In 1924, William McPhie was hired to design an extension for the western side of the house. This he did with care and respect, matching the new section to the original.

Perched on the edge of the escarpment directly above John Street sits the substantial Georgian home known, appropriately enough, as "The Cliff." Built in 1879 of local limestone by Canon George Bull, the house remained the homestead of the Bull family until its sale in 1981. Alterations and additions were carried out over the years, but none disguises the classic symmetry particular to Georgian architecture. In fact, a Victorian porch on the cliff side was removed in the 1920s because it spoiled the symmetry. To add to its charms, the house has a panoramic view of the city while still allowing the family complete seclusion.

George Armstrong Bull was an Anglican clergyman, prominent in the diocese of Niagara. A great builder, he founded St. Paul's church in Mount Hope, St. George's in Hannon, and Holy Trinity in Hamilton. His first home was the Parsonage on West Fifth, designed by his brother-in-law William Farmer, and where Bull, and his wife, Eleanor, lived for twenty-one years and raised ten children. Although remote from Hamilton, the Parsonage was central to the many parishes Bull served. However, after he was made canon of Christ's Church Cathedral

Left: The division between the original house and the 1924 addition is to the left of the front door.
Above: East wall of The Cliff.

Detail of column capital.

A One-of-a-Kind Terrace, 1879

252 — 262 MacNab Street North, North End, Hamilton

In this late-nineteenth-/early-twentieth-century neighbourhood that surrounds St. Mary's Church, James Balfour designed a six-unit terrace that is one-of-a-kind in Hamilton. Of brick masonry construction, and built in 1879–1880, the gabled bays and segmental arched windows are characteristic of row houses of the period. The highly ornate square wooden bays are decorated with bracket cornices. The cornices separate the first- and second-floor windows, and pilasters frame the tall paired windows. The whole effect seems to have been inspired by the all-wood Italianate houses and row houses so common in San Francisco. With great skill, Balfour blended the forms and details of two quite different vernacular traditions. Two floors of wood bays in San Francisco Italianate are crowned by High Victorian Gothic steep-pitched gables decorated with bargeboard, and

Above: A picture of contrasts that nevertheless blend — two floors of San Francisco Italianate topped by High Victorian Gothic.

Left: A family group in the rear yard, likely during the 1940s.
Top centre: Winemaking in the rear yard, circa 1940s.
Bottom centre: One of a pair of eye-catching doorways.

the roofline is punctuated by steep gabled dormers. The original one-over-one sash windows mostly retain their original glass and wooden storms.

The entrance to each of the two buildings opens onto a side hall. Two rooms to the left, separated by French doors, serve as parlour and dining room. The dining room dimensions of no. 258 were 15 feet x 17 feet but the present occupant added a closet and built-in china cabinet along the north wall, which reduced the space to 15 feet x 15 feet. Great care was taken in the construction. The cabinetmaker altered his tools by using a piece of original moulding as a calibrator in order to make moulding that matched exactly. In the kitchen, the original wainscotting still borders the lower part of the walls. A lean-to summer kitchen on the back has been closed in for use as a bedroom. On the top floor, an arched casement window and a skylight look quite modern but are in fact part of Balfour's design.

Gradually, 252 – 262 MacNab North is being turned into short-

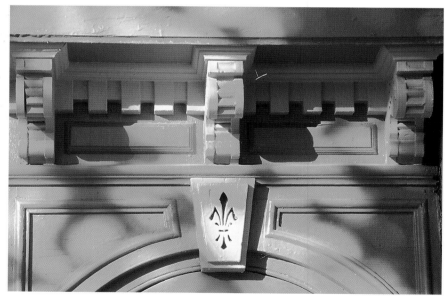

Top left: Detail of the elaborately decorated centre gable.
Top right: Detail of a cornice over a first-floor bay.
Above: Brackets and keystone over the first-floor bay.

Detail of the bay cornice.

term residences for guests in the city. None should ever have to complain of noisy neighbours here. Every wall, interior and exterior, is double brick.

The original owner of the terrace was Henry J. Larkin, a barrister and developer who built the Renaissance revival commercial block known as Treble Hall. It too was designed by James Balfour and erected in 1879. Real estate dealings were a highly popular pre–stock market form of investment in the nineteenth century, and the MacNab Street terrace remained in the Larkin family until 1889 and under single ownership until 1942.

Left: The drawing room overlooking MacNab Street.
Below: The drawing room fireplace.

Glover Cottage, 1881

198 Queen Street South, Kirkendall, Hamilton

Detail of the decorative verandah.

Glover Cottage sits unobtrusively on the west side of Queen Street South in a cluster of late-Victorian houses of varying styles. A typical Ontario worker's cottage, its modest size, low hip roof, and white clapboard siding seem dwarfed by taller, more substantial neighbours. Nevertheless, it catches the eye of passersby. A verandah stretches the width of the house overlooking the street; in summer its delicately carved treillage supports a climbing wild rose and in winter reminds one of frost patterns on windows.

The cottage was built about 1881 or 1882 by Walter Greenhill, a harness maker. In those days the cottage backed onto the Hamilton Street Railway horse barn, very convenient for Mr. Greenhill's profession. A raised rubble-stone foundation allows for the slope of the

Iroquois Bar, the ancient lakeshore on which the house is situated, with its front lawn sloping to street level. Like many cottages of its period, the original kitchen space was built as a tail on the back of the otherwise box-like house, but the kitchen interior has been modernized. Curiously, there is no sign of a chimney on the gently sloping hip roof, nor of a fireplace inside.

The centre-hall plan is reflected in the symmetrical façade of three bays, original two-over-two sash windows on either side of the door, whose upper panels are made of glass and lower two of wood. The verandah and its beautifully elaborate spindle work, carved cornices, and spindle frieze speak of a craftsman who aimed to please the eye while constructing a comfortable but practical home.

A Second Empire Townhouse, 1882

250 James Street South, Durand, Hamilton

This beauty, standing at the corner of James Street South and Herkimer Avenue, was built to a design by Hamilton-born architect James Balfour. The mansard roof, decorative contrasting brick exterior, balanced façade with arched windows, and George IV doorway with split fanlight make this house stand out among some outstanding houses.

The row of brass bells in the kitchen, each linked to a different room.

Detail of one of the bells.

In 120 years the house has changed hands only four times. The first occupant was Catherine Stuart Rutherford, who left the house to her seven children. In 1885, they went bankrupt and in 1886 sold the house to Imogene Waugh, wife of William John Waugh, a merchant. He died in 1931 and his wife remained in the house until her death in 1936, after which Dr. J. Frederick Houston bought the house and moved in with his wife and family. Dr. Houston added a doorway and vestibule on the south side near James Street as a separate entry to his basement surgery. He died in 1974 and the present owner bought the house from Mrs. Houston in 1975. Each successive owner has treated the house with the respect it merits. When Mr. Waugh's granddaughter visited recently from the United States, she said the house is just as she remembered it except for the space under the main staircase, which has been enclosed to make a closet. In the old days when parties were held, it had been the musician's corner.

One enters the house through two sets of double doors, the inner pair with glass panels ornamented with tracery that complements the tracery in the transom. A graceful curving staircase with carved banister, balustrades, and newel fills half the hallway. The stairs were battered by Mrs. Houston's walking stick and invalid chair and are now covered with thick red carpet. To the left of the hallway are two large and gracious drawing rooms that were once divided by pocket doors. The doors were taken out by Dr. Houston and moulding was substituted around the doorway. However, the original doors and wheels, full of rust, are stored in the basement. Beautiful ceiling medallions in the front rooms once held gas chandeliers, and a grand piano stood in the southwest corner. The western half of the drawing room has a magnificent Jacob Hayes mirror over the fireplace. There was a matching mirror in the eastern half, but it was taken by Mrs. Houston when she moved out and has now vanished.

Every major room has a porcelain-and-brass bell handle for the purpose of summoning a servant. The matching bells, made of brass with copper springs and buttons fashioned like moulded flowers, are fastened high on a wall in the kitchen. Each bell has a different tone to designate a particular room.

The housekeeper had a room over the kitchen at the top of the back stairs. It is an attractive and comfortable room, with paired arched windows overlooking Herkimer Street and a moulded light fixture in the centre of the ceiling. The kitchen was drab as a prison cell with grey walls, institutional-green ceiling, and little light. Oilcloth covered all the

Opposite top right: Stairwell window with typical decorative brickwork and windowpanes.
Opposite bottom right: Mr. Waugh's daughter outside his home, circa 1912, showing the south side before the surgery addition.

Above: Detail of elaborate carving on the top of Jacob Hayes' mirror.
Centre: Detail of Jacob Hayes' mirror frame.
Right: The drawing room fireplace with the mirror reflecting a ceiling medallion.

counters and there were no cupboards for dishes and condiments. Many of those deficiencies have been remedied for contemporary use. The square room also had large linen closets next to a long narrow pantry on the north side. An old-fashioned butler's pantry remains between the kitchen and dining room, complete with a copper sink and working water taps.

A nineteenth-century bathroom on the second floor has a claw-footed tub and old-style porcelain and brass taps. In the fashion of the time, the toilet is located in a separate small room. The third floor once housed the servants. Not long ago the house was being rewired, and a hidden room without an entrance was discovered. It has a cathedral ceiling, board-and-batten siding, and hardwood floors. It appeared as if nobody had ever been in there, and the present owners don't know where the entrance was. Legend has it that Petie Houston, Dr. Houston's daughter, was being courted by a young air force officer. At Christmas in 1942 he presented Petie with a ring and proposed marriage. She turned him down. He went up to the third floor and hanged himself from a beam in the room next to the hidden one.

All the windows once had shutters, but they were taken down in the 1980s. There were thirty-two shutters, those on the ground floor were made of glass and doubled as storm windows. Dr. Houston painted them grey so that the present owners weren't aware they were glass until they came down. Unfortunately, there is no present plan to restore them.

Two hundred fifty James South is a classical Second Empire townhouse. Many such houses were copied from imported builders' manuals and suffered in the translation. Architect James Balfour trained in Scotland and therefore had first-hand knowledge of the style.

The double windows of the living room overlooking Herkimer Street.

Stairwell window, north side.

Ferguson Avenue Terrace, 1886

207 — 215 Ferguson Avenue South, Corktown, Hamilton

In the 1870s, the Hamilton and Lake Erie Railway Company amalgamated with the Hamilton and Northwestern Railway to complete the line between Hamilton and Port Dover. As a consequence, there was a proliferation of brick row-housing in downtown neighbourhoods. The vernacular brick terrace at nos. 207 to 215 is one of the few surviving examples in the Corktown neighbourhood.

Built as an investment property in 1886–1887 for Margaret McIntyre, the terrace is an integral component of the streetscape. Each unit features a parapet end-dividing wall with a built-in chimney. The two off-centre upper windows and single bay window below in a hexagonal form are typical of 1880s row-housing. The front façades, stepped slightly to accommodate the slope to the escarpment, are dominated by five large bay windows (originally with sashes), colonnettes, and bracketed eaves. The brick masonry reveals original segmental arches over the front doorways and second-floor windows with a contrasting brick keystone and cornerstones.

Many changes have happened to the units over the years, but no. 213 retains arched transom lights and wood lintels with rope moulding and fretwork. On the eaves' undersurface are decorative dentil bands, which can be seen intact on two of the units. Decorated brackets support the eaves over some of the bay windows. Other original features include the west façades, the south façade of no. 215 and the north façade of no. 207.

Top left: The bay window on the south wall of no. 215.
Top centre: A bay window with its decorative brackets.
Top right: Detail of bay window of no. 209.
Bottom: South wall of no. 215 showing chimney and parapet.

Wooden Queen Anne, 1888

316 Herkimer Street, Kirkendall, Hamilton

Pale yellow clapboard trimmed with dark green and adorned by a two-storey gabled bay with frothy bargeboard and a spindle-work porch, this late-Victorian confection is a dwelling that is very easy on the eyes. The house was built in the late 1880s for Louis Duplessis, a patternmaker for iron casting. Its horizontal design emphasis, irregular planes, and elevations are typical Queen Anne, unusual only in that it is executed entirely of wood. The wood, moreover, is said to have come from France.

A well-preserved façade retains all the original wooden cladding and decorative trim, excellent examples of Queen Anne and Eastlake. Charles Eastlake, incidentally, was an English architect whose interior-design book *Hints on Household Taste* (1878) showing furniture with knobs, spindles, and latticework, later translated into decoration on late-nineteenth-century picturesque houses. The front porch, with its elaborate spindlework, is a typical example, whereas the fish-scale shingles on the second storey, the small stained-glass windows, and the bargeboard decoration under the eaves are all typical Queen Anne. The leaded windows and the shutters are a more recent addition.

Two sets of front doors, the first with bevelled glass and the second with tracery-patterned glass, open from the porch onto a graceful hallway and curving staircase. The stair railings were made from 2½-foot-wide boards ornately carved with a lacey design punched out of the wood. This has to be the work of a carpenter who wanted to add an outstanding detail to the otherwise modest house. Around the corner from the top of the stairs there is a small room now used as a study; it could originally have been a nursery or a maid's room. From the upper hall, another carved oak staircase leads to the loft, formerly a sleeping area.

Lacy stair railing and carved newel in the Eastlake style. Cone-shaped detail is just visible on the baseboard.

The living room opens to the right of the entrance hall; its red pine floors are noticeable in many parts of the house. All the baseboards have cone-shaped detail work in each corner. The same cone-shaped design appears on the handrail of the loft stairs. In the living room, an oak fireplace and iron screen marked "March 1850 New York" predate the house, but its provenance is unknown. Pocket doors, still in working order, can be used to close off the dining area from the living room.

Unfortunately, no dated photos of the house are available. There is a small extension on the back of the house, but no record of when it was added has been found. A 1986 survey shows the extension and a small garage on the back alley. The garage is no longer there.

The oak fireplace with its iron fire screen could be an early example of antique scavenging.

Chateau on Claremont, 1890

63 Claremont Drive, Southam, Hamilton

The original house at 63 Claremont was built in 1890 by Watson G. Walton, the person responsible for building the James Street Incline Railway. Understandably, he wanted to live nearby his technological masterwork, so he put up a house on the mountain brow near Upper James Street. Huge quantities of limestone had been brought from Kingston to build the handsome row of townhouses on James Street South, and Walton used the same limestone to build his own house on the mountain brow.

A wealthy man and fond of gadgetry, Walton owned the first electric car in the city, and on account of it the garage floor is a revolving table. Electric cars at the time could not operate in reverse, and the turntable solved the problem of backing out of the garage. The estate had its own hard-water well and a soft-water cistern for laundry. There was also a windmill and a magnificent cast-iron fountain on the front lawn that appears to have been modelled on the fountain in Gore Park.

In the 1930s, James Morrow bought and transformed the Victorian mansion into a Norman chateau. Morrow was obsessed with replicating a stately French home known as Chateau de Rochers. He brought over European architects and French artisans to ensure authenticity, so the original dwelling is now completely concealed. The fountain and the garage remain, as does a black walnut tree in the garden, said to be 350 years old.

In 1950, a man, who as a boy living in the neighbourhood had been entranced by the 1933 renovation, became the home's third owner.

Leaf-like moulding on the porch roof is an imitation of the French style.

The cast-iron fountain on the front lawn.

A casement window, blind-arched transom and fleurs-de-lis motif in the shutters, all typical French details.

Paisley Farmhouse, 1890

984 Main Street West, Westdale, Hamilton

This eye-catching stone farmhouse, hidden from view by trees and surrounded by post–World War II bungalows, was once the Paisley family home. In 1867, James Paisley bought the house and property, north of Main Street from Joseph Cline. This piece of a property, which originally stretched from Cootes Drive on the west to Beasley's Hollow on the east, had been part of the 400-acre 1802 purchase by James Forsyth from Robert Hamilton. The Cline home, at the corner of Cline Avenue and Main West, was a well-built structure with walls three stones thick and inside trim of chestnut grown on the farm. James Paisley, originally from Scotland, settled there with his son Robert, who gave up teaching to take up farming. As recently as 1956 the property was still farmed by a Paisley descendant.

Carved double doors set in a very plain moulded frame.

Second-floor windows set in stone walls 14 to 16 inches thick.

Right: The eastern front window's decorative woodwork is a charming touch for a plain farmhouse.

The house is of an unusual shape and may have had a wraparound porch on the south and west sides. The present porch is modern, and the section on the west side has been filled in as an unattractive pantry off the kitchen. The many-sloped roof with four gables has wide overhanging eaves and once supported two chimneys, of which only the west one survives. Radiating stones arch gently over windows, which also have stone sills. On the east side there is a single window topped with decorative woodwork on each floor. On the west façade the windows on each floor are paired. The carved double front doors have a rectangular transom; transoms over the first-floor front windows match. Unfortunately, the original outer front doors have disappeared.

Many changes have been made to the interior. All the fireplaces have been removed, but a chimney remains in the kitchen. Under the back porch there used to be a root cellar with an exit to the garage. The stairway to the second floor is original, with its sturdy banister and carved balusters. Upstairs, the pine floors and door mouldings have survived, but little else of what was probably a space with four bedrooms and a hallway remains.

Hendrie House, 1891

252 James Street South, Durand, Hamilton

This overwrought decoration on the central tower is typical of Richardson Romanesque style.

Henry Hobson Richardson, considered one of America's greatest architects, created a version of the Romanesque style that was distinctive enough to be called "Richardson Romanesque." The building style is characterized by a chunky shape, often with a tower, high roofs with broad planes, windows with transoms, and Byzantine leafwork ornamentation. The entryways are usually round-arched and deep set, and cladding is rock-faced ashlar, sometimes with red brick.

Hendrie House is an outstanding example of Richardson Romanesque–style architecture, the finest in Hamilton since the old City Hall and the Birks Building were demolished. Built in 1891–1892 for Tunis B. Griffith, manager of the Hamilton Street Railway, the architect was William A. Edwards, who had been practising some ten years in Hamilton. The house exemplifies the bold and flamboyant character of late-Victorian architecture with its wide rounded arches, projecting round and square towers, and steeply pitched slate roofs. The spacious entrance hall and stairway, marred by an unfortunate pillared canopy, are now part of the entry into a spa and salon. Some of the elaborately carved woodwork and colourful stained-glass panels are preserved in the interior, but most of the remaining original decorative features are to be seen on the exterior, particularly the east, north, and south façades. The hip roof with cross gables and patterned chimneys lift the exterior embellishments to a great height.

T. B. Griffith was managing director and secretary treasurer of the HSR from 1885 until his death in 1893. Under his management, the HSR was built up from a small horse-car service to one of the best electric streetcar systems in Canada. After Griffith's death, his house was purchased by John Strathearne Hendrie, a prominent businessman, politician, and president of the Bank of Hamilton. Hendrie also served as mayor of Hamilton from 1901–1902 and as Lieutenant Governor of Ontario from 1914–1919, being knighted in 1915. Sir John and Lady Lena died respectively in 1923 and 1928, and the house was subsequently occupied by their son Major Wm. Ian S. Hendrie, a recipient of the Distinguished Service Order in World War I and later a prominent businessman as director of Hamilton Bridge Works Company. Major Hendrie sold the house in 1937 to Samuel Henson, who converted it into apartments but, as was his custom, retained the best of the original features.

The Moorings, 1891

913 Beach Boulevard, Hamilton Beach, Hamilton

The Moorings was built in 1891 as a summer residence for Francis Edwin Kilvert, noted Hamilton lawyer and politician, and first cousin of Robert Francis Kilvert, a popular Victorian diarist. The house is one of Hamilton's best examples of late-nineteenth-century resort structures, and witness to a time when the Hamilton Beach flourished as a fashionable summer resort area in the Victorian and Edwardian eras.

The house is Queen Anne in style but instead of being covered in brickwork, the exterior is entirely shingled. The roof is done in conventional rectangular shingles whereas the upper reaches are finished with fish-scale shingles in the east-coast style. Typical of Queen Anne–style architecture, The Moorings has an ornate one-storey verandah stretching around the front and one side of the house. Nowhere is there symmetry in the structure. The roofline is irregular, the front gables are on different planes and at different heights, and the front doorway is set at the east side of the verandah while the front steps are placed centrally. The first-floor façade is divided into three bays, with the doorway on the left and matching windows centre and right. On the second level, gables project in all directions.

Elements of the west and south façades and the verandah are all original. Long gone are the croquet lawn and the rose garden at the front of the house.

Top right: A vaguely oriental east window adds an exotic touch.

Bottom left: The paired dormers face out over the lake.

Bottom centre: A tiny leaded south-facing window overlooks the driveway.

Bottom right: The offset door was incorporated into the front façade, date unknown. The original door faced the front steps.

The Pump House, 1892

188 Markland Avenue, Durand, Hamilton

This Second Empire–style brick cottage was built in 1892 by the Government of Ontario as a residence for the engineer in charge of the Queen Street Pumping Station. At the time the actual pumping station was located in a building next door, while the meters and dials were housed in the engineer's residence. Of the original three buildings, 188 is the only one to survive. The other two were pulled down after the government sold the properties. Two huge ceramic reservoirs are still buried under the next-door garden.

This dormer, with its arched cap, seems to grow out of the mansard roof.

The pumping station was built to supply drinking water to the Asylum for the Insane (now the Hamilton Psychiatric Hospital) on the mountain brow. By 1920 the city water mains had extended to the mountain, and a separate pumping station was no longer necessary.

A slate mansard roof, the dormer, bay window, and arched doorway are all characteristic of the Second Empire style. So too are the asymmetrical façade with a side entrance and centre bay window. Considerable care went into patterning the slate roof shingles in bands of different shapes. Directly above the front dormer stands a tall brick chimney. Very little of the original interior survives, but the chimney flue passes down through the remaining section of wall between the two upper rooms, traversing what was probably a dining room and living room on the main floor, and on into the basement. It's possible the fireplaces opened into the rooms on either side of the wall.

The staircase is the only interior structure that remains mostly as it was. Upstairs there were once two or three small bedrooms, but the walls have been removed except for the chimney flue, which separates the sleeping area from the studio.

Detail of the patterned slate roof tiles.

The moulded front door under a modern awning.

105 Aberdeen, 1893

105 Aberdeen Avenue, Durand, Hamilton

Left: The massive round tower loomed over the original main entrance.

Right: A side door became the front door after the verandah was dismantled.

At the southeast corner of Aberdeen Avenue and Bay Street stands a massive and stately home constructed in 1893–1894 for Hamilton lawyer Patrick M. Bankier. Situated near the foot of the escarpment, this imposing late-Victorian brick mansion overlooks the residential neighbourhood of Durand South, noted for its tree-lined streets and fine array of large, fashionable late-nineteenth-/early-twentieth-century homes. One hundred five Aberdeen Avenue has a particularly commanding presence, attributable to the tower-like round bay of the front façade, accentuated by the steep slope of the site.

The house represents a grand version of the restrained Queen Anne style adopted for the larger homes built in Hamilton around the turn of the century. Characteristic of this style are the solid and massive form; the asymmetrical composition with projecting bays and wings; the complex slate roof silhouette featuring dormers, gables, and tall chimneys; and the restrained classical ornamentation. Originally, a deep verandah with coupled columns and a bracketed cornice extended the full width of the Aberdeen façade. The verandah and long, broken flight of stairs leading to the front entrance were removed in 1964, at which time the main entrance was relocated to the Bay Street façade and the original doorway blocked up.

Nevertheless, the dominant feature is still the tall, projecting round bay on the Aberdeen façade, with its conical roof, tall double-hung sash windows with single curved-glass panes, and a horizontal band of windows beneath the bracketed cornice. On the north and west façades are several rounded-arch windows. All have matching sandstone sills and lintels.

The house has been owned and occupied by the families of three prominent Hamiltonians. The Glasgow-born original owner, Patrick MacIndoe Bankier, occupied the house for only four years. He was a partner in the well-known firm of Hamilton lawyers Crerar, Crerar and Bankier from 1886 until his sudden death in 1899 at the age of thirty-nine. In 1886 he had married a Miss Stuart, the only daughter of John Stuart, president of the Bank of Hamilton, and his death left her a widow with four young children.

Robert R. Moodie, vice-president of the J. R. Moodie Company (formerly the Eagle Knitting Company) purchased the house in 1919 and sold it in 1935 to Mark Holton, president of the Chipman-Holton Knitting Company. The house remained in the family until Mrs. Rhoda Holton died in 1988.

An enormous house such as 105 Aberdeen Avenue requires a lot of maintenance. After Mrs. Holton's death, the house stood empty and was threatened with demolition until the present owners purchased it and made a family home.

A Post-Victorian Townhouse, 1905

83 Pearl Street South, Kirkendall, Hamilton

Built in 1905 at the same time as four neighbouring houses, this imposing red-brick Victorian-style townhouse occupies a choice corner lot. Nothing is known of the builder, but the house was occupied by John S. Harker, merchant, who sold it in 1910 to Archibald Foulis, a lithographer and engraver. Foulis lived there until his death on July 14, 1953. The house was passed to his children Jean Isabel (1904-1977), and Bruce Frederick (1904-1978). In 1976, Bruce became too frail to manage alone in the house and put it up for sale. Two offers were made on the house and he accepted the lower one because the buyer wanted to restore rather than renovate. Hence, the house remains a lovely period piece, with many of its best features intact.

The front door and steps on the left are balanced by a large window on the right. Note the window's decorative border and stained-glass squares in each corner. The semi-circular upper part of the window features patterned glass with what appears to be bull's eyes at each end separated by hexagonal strips of glue-stick glass, giving the impression of winter frost. Radiating brick arches complete the ensemble. The symmetry of the façade appears to be vertical rather than the usual horizontal. The rounded window on the first storey is repeated directly above on the second. Again, the square door opening is echoed in a squared window above. Full-width porches adorn both levels on the front. A triangular gable with projecting eaves has a round window and paired square windows below, surrounded by fish-scale tiles. A projecting half-hexagon bay runs the full height of the south elevation, which is

Top right: Detail of the front window from outside.

Bottom right: The same window seen from inside the house.

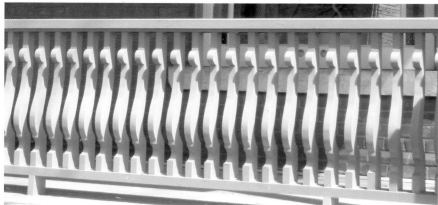

The front gable and balcony railing. The balusters are modern, but made to period design.

The front façade.

Above: Marquetry in the hall floor.

Right: The living room fireplace.

surmounted by a similar triangular gable. Windows on both floors are placed on the sides of the bay but not on the front.

Two entrance doorways are separated by a small vestibule before opening onto a hallway. The outer door, with its plain glass panel, is a period replacement, but the inner door and stained-glass panel are original. The present owners have worked hard to preserve what was original and to restore what has been lost or damaged, thus the interior is mostly intact, with a few modern changes in places like the kitchen. Some rooms still have their original wallpaper. The narrow drawing room to the right of the hall has a fireplace in the south wall. Pocket doors once closed off the dining room, but they were removed some time in the past.

Upstairs there are three bedrooms. A tiny room at the top of the back staircase was probably a maid's room. The master bedroom includes a charming bay with large two-over-two sash windows. Visible distortions indicate original glass.

The owners have a 1905 photograph of the house showing the family standing in the garden. A small tree grows at the edge of the sidewalk. That same tree has grown past the height of the roof and now blocks the front of the house. Its falling branches in high winds endanger this house and the one house next door. A low hedge bordered by rocks extends from the corner of the front porch to the corner of the sidewalk. An original feature, it hinders shortcuts across the garden.

Bank of Montreal House, 1911

6 Ravenscliffe Avenue, Durand, Hamilton

The imposing front entrance looms over visitors.

This imposing structure was built in 1911–1912 as a residence for the manager of the Bank of Montreal in the days when Hamilton was a major financial centre in Canada. The original property belonging to Ravenscliffe House was divided into lots in 1903 and 1909 to be used for the building of residences for the elite. The bank bought three adjoining lots then hired the architectural firm Stewart & Witton to build to their specifications using mainly local materials.

Built in the Greco-Roman style with classical columns and entablature, the house is a model of symmetry, proportion, and balance. Two colonnaded wings flank the main façade. Two double columns with capitals support an entablature, which in turn supports a California low-riding roof of red tiles with corners sloping outwards. A single dormer window projects from the roof, while windows on the ground floor are of Venetian type, long and round-headed, and match the central entrance in form. The columns contribute a strong vertical element, heightening the house and evoking the monumental qualities of strength, power, and security.

The symmetry of the façade continues in the interior. A wide central hall lit by two Waterford chandeliers has two rooms on either side, each doorway echoing the columns and entablature of the exterior. The first room to the left was once a book-lined study, while the one on the right was a

music room. In its heyday, the custom was for men to gather in the study for port and cigars while the ladies retired to the music room. The massive doors to each room are made of mahogany from Honduras and Cuba, and every room in the house is sound-proofed with cork so that business secrets could not be overheard. At the end of the hall a wide curving stairway leads to the second floor.

The next room on the left served as a dining room and has a magnificent Bohemian glass chandelier suspended over the dining table. French doors and a marble fireplace complement the elegant ambience. A pantry between the dining room and kitchen area boasts a marble bar, which was famously used as a gambling table. Across the hall the equally elegant drawing room has an Italian chandelier and French doors opening onto a sun room.

The rear portion of the house was originally the gatehouse to Ravenscliffe House and faced onto Aberdeen. The present house was simply added, facing Ravenscliffe Avenue. In the basement there was the kitchen, a laundry, and a bathroom. The rooms above on the main floor served as a breakfast room and morning room.

Above: Interior columns and entablature.

Top centre: A Waterford glass chandelier in the hallway.

Bottom centre: Detail of the ceiling and door moulding in the hall.

Far right: Capitals on the outside columns.

The second floor contains four bedrooms, each with its own bathroom. Two bedrooms for servants over the kitchen are reached by the back stairs, as is a full-sized linen room. The third floor had two more bedrooms and bathrooms for servants. In all, the house consists of fourteen large rooms, five bathrooms, eight fireplaces, and a swimming pool.

The house was owned by the bank from 1912–1958. When the first bank manager lived in the house it was being rebuilt and, without permission from the bank, had a bathroom installed in each bedroom. The six or seven extra bathrooms cost dearly and the bank made the manager pay out of his own pocket. Previously there had been only two, one for residents and one for the servants.

In 1958 the house was sold to Dr. Kenneth Colling, part owner of the Brant Inn. He used his home to entertain stars who performed at the inn. Louis Armstrong, Tommy and Jimmy Dorsey, Glen Miller and Zsa Zsa Gabor took advantage of the hospitality offered and the company of other famous people. It was during this era that the marble bar became a gambling table and the private ensuite bedrooms became very popular.

Left: Marble fireplace in the dining room.
Above: Corner light and ceiling moulding in the dining room.

Bibliography

Adamson, Anthony, MacRae, Marion, *The Ancestral Roof: Domestic Architecture in Upper Canada.* Toronto: Clarke Irwin & Company Limited, 1963.

Adamson, Anthony, Willard, Tom, *The Gaiety of Gables: Ontario's Architectural Folk Art.* Toronto: McClelland and Stewart Limited, 1974.

Anderson, A., Buttrum, Grace, eds., *Other Days, Other Ways; Historical Sketches of the Binkley School District*, October 12, 1965.

Arthur, Eric, *The Early Buildings of Ontario.* Toronto: University of Toronto Press, 1938.

Arthur, Eric, Witney, Dudley, *The Barn: A Vanishing Landmark in North America.* Toronto: McClelland and Stewart Limited, 1972.

Bailey, T. Melville, Editor-in-Chief, *Dictionary of Hamilton Biography, 1981-.*

Boyle, Terry, *Under This Roof: Family Homes in Southern Ontario.* Toronto: Doubleday Canada Ltd, 1980.

Brooksbank, Jack, *Old Relics.* Cheltenham, Ontario: The Boston Mills Press, 1976.

Byers, Mary, McBurney, Margaret, *The Governor's Road.* Toronto: University of Toronto Press, 1982.

Craig, Martha, "The Garden of Canada" Burlington, Oakville and District, Toronto: William Briggs, 1902. The 1973 imprint is a presentation of Joseph Brant Museum and Burlington Historical Society, 1973.

Dundas Heritage Association, *William Lyon Mackenzie Slept Here: Heritage Buildings of Dundas*, produced by the Executive of the Dundas Heritage Association to mark Ontario's Bicentennial Year, 1984.

Dundas Historical Museum, "Picturesque Dundas Update" 1981.

Elman, Russell, *Durand: A Neighbourhood Reclaimed.* Hamilton: NA Group, ca. 2000, 2001.

Feldman, Ilona, "The Notman House 1846," thesis submitted at Sheridan College, Interior Design IV, June, 1993.

Fram, Mark, *Well Preserved: The Ontario Heritage Foundation's Manual of Principles and Practice for Architectural Conservation.* Erin, Ontario: The Boston Mills Press, 1988.

Freeman, Bill, *Hamilton: A People's History.* Toronto: James Lorimer & Company Ltd., 2001.

Greenhill, Ralph, McPherson, Ken, Richardson, Douglas, *Ontario Towns.* Ottawa: Oberon Press, 1974.

Hamilton & Region Conservation Authority Web Site: <http://www.hpl.hamilton.on.ca/Collections/landmark/Hrca.shtml>.

Hamilton Mountain Heritage Society, *Mountain Memories: A Pictorial History of the Hamilton Mountain.* Hamilton: Hamilton Mountain Heritage Society, 2000.

Manson, Ann, Manson, Bill, *Up and Down Locke Street.* Hamilton: North Shore Publishing Inc., 1999.

McHugh, Patricia, *Toronto Architecture: A City Guide.* Toronto: Mercury Books, 1985.

McKay, A.G., *Victorian Architecture in Hamilton.* Hamilton: The Hamilton-Niagara Branch, Architectural Conservancy of Hamilton, 1967.

Milson, Terry Naylor, "6 Ravenscliffe" 4th year thesis (submitted at McMaster university, Hamilton, 1978).

Newcombe, Olive, *Picturesque Dundas Revisited.* Dundas Historical Society Museum, 1997.

Norris, Darrel A., Helson, Linda, ed., *Beyond Paradise: Building Dundas, 1793-1950.* Dundas, Ontario: LACAC Advisory Committee of the Town of Dundas, 1996.

Turcotte, Dorothy, *Burlington: Memories of Pioneer Days.* Cheltenham, Ontario: The Boston Mills Press, 1989.

Index

*Designated Heritage Property under the *Ontario Heritage Act*

YOUCAT
for
Kids

A Catholic Catechism
for Children and Parents

With a Foreword by
Pope Francis

Translated by Beata Vale

Ignatius Press   San Francisco

The original German edition, *YOUCAT for Kids: Katholischer Katechismus für Kinder und Eltern*, was published by the Austrian Council of Bishops, © 2018 by YOUCAT Foundation GmbH, Königstein im Taunus, Germany. All rights reserved. YOUCAT®, an internationally registered and protected brand name and logo filed under GM: 011929131, is used by permission of the YOUCAT Foundation, the sole shareholder of which is the International Pontifical Foundation Aid to the Church in Need, Königstein im Taunus, Germany.

The text was approved by the Pontifical Council for the New Evangelization on May 24, 2018, feast of Mary, Help of Christians, and produced by Martin Barta, Michaela von Heereman, Bernhard Meuser, Michael Scharf, Clara Steber, and Christoph Weiss, with the help of Barbara Cremer, Marietheres Hoch, and Isabel Meuser.

Design, layout, and illustrations by Alexander von Lengerke, Cologne, Germany.

Instructions for Use

The *YOUCAT for Kids: A Catholic Catechism for Children and Parents* explains the Catholic faith in language suitable for children. It follows the *Catechism of the Catholic Church* in a question-and-answer format. Each numbered question and answer (printed in bold) is a child-friendly presentation of the Catholic faith authorized by the Church. Explanatory text follows the passages in bold.

The bottom part of each page—with a colored background—serves as background information for parents and teachers. This section also contains quotes from faith leaders, the Bible, and the YOUCAT.

Symbols Key

 Quote Read Out Loud Quote from the Bible

 Info Joke Quote from *YOUCAT: Youth Catechism of the Catholic Church*

Ignatius Press English Edition

Unless otherwise indicated, Scripture quotations are from the Revised Standard Version of the Bible—Second Catholic Edition (Ignatius Edition) copyright © 2006 by the National Council of the Churches of Christ in the United States of America. Used by permission. All rights reserved worldwide. Quotations from papal documents are taken from the Vatican webside © by Libreria Editrice Vaticana. All rights reserved.

Nihil Obstat: Jeffrey Froula, Ph.D.
Imprimatur: + Most Reverend Salvatore Cordileone
　　　　　　 Archbishop of San Francisco
　　　　　　 April 10, 2019

© 2019 by Ignatius Press, San Francisco. All rights reserved.
ISBN 978-1-62164-285-5
Library of Congress Control Number 2018957305
Printed in the United States of America

www.youcat.org. From the proceeds of its publications and from donations, the not-for-profit YOUCAT Foundation supports worldwide projects that encourage young people to discover the Christian faith as the foundation of their lives. You can help further the work of the YOUCAT Foundation with your donations, which can be made through: Deutsche Bank AG, Routing Number: 720 700 24, Account Number: 031 888 100, IBAN: DE13 7207 0024 0031 8881 00, BIC: DEUTDEDB720.

20 19 18 17 16 15 14 13 12 11 10 9 8 7 6 5 4 3 2 1

Contents

Your little guides through YOUCAT for Kids:

Bob   Lilly

Foreword

by Pope Francis

Dear Children and Parents,

An eight-year-old boy from Canada once asked me: "What did God do before he created the world?" I thought about it and then said: "Before God created anything, he loved. That is what he did: he loved. God always loves. That is why, when he created the world, he wasn't doing anything but loving."

Thumbing through the *YOUCAT for Kids*, I encounter the questions that children ask their parents and catechists millions of times. That is why I think it is just as useful as the great *Catechism*, where we can find answers to the most important questions in life: Where does this world come from? Why do I exist? How and what should we live for here in this world? What happens after death? The *YOUCAT for Kids* is a catechism that is very different from the one I used. It is suitable for children and parents to spend time together in order discover the love of God more and more.

Dear parents, keep this catechism on hand and find the time to look at it with your children—page by page, mystery of the faith by mystery of the faith, question by question. Help your children to discover the love of Jesus! It will make them strong and courageous. I entrust the *YOUCAT for Kids* to you. Do not grow tired of asking questions and of telling children about your faith. Do not remain silent when you are pressed by your children's questions; instead, always have the strength to be a mediator of the faith, which you, too, have received from your parents. Be a living chain that makes it possible for the Gospel to be present in our families, communities, and in the Church from generation to generation.

I bless you from the bottom of my heart. Please pray for me.

Franciscus

Preface

Dear Parents, Grandparents, Godparents, and Teachers,

Parents and catechists have repeatedly asked us for a catechism for children. Catechisms have existed in the Church for a long time. A catechism is a kind of manual that contains everything children and adults need to know in order to deepen their knowledge of the Christian faith, step by step, and in order to develop a living relationship with Jesus Christ. A catechism is always authorized by the Church. The Church vouches for the accuracy of its content. Next to Holy Scripture, the catechism is the Church's most important medium.

In the fall of 2013, parents, teachers, priests, and leaders of children's groups from Austria, Slovakia, and Germany set out together to write this catechism for children. It was supposed to be cheerful and modern and to appeal to children between the ages of nine and thirteen. We did not want to develop this book as an armchair enterprise, and we agreed right at the beginning to test our results with groups of children. We realized soon that nothing is more difficult than saying something great in a simple and clear way.

And something else became clear to us: a book about the faith can only ever be an aid. It is not enough to thrust the *YOUCAT for Kids* at a child with the comment, "Read this sometime", and then hope that surely the child will find his way to God or deepen his faith on his own. We realized that we would have to write a book for children and their parents. Books can help—but ultimately, sharing the faith cannot be delegated to books or media. Faith can be awakened only by the oldest means in the world: from heart to heart, from person to person. The best books, the coolest movies cannot substitute for parents or grandparents who say, "I believe in Jesus. May I show you how wonderful that is?" Or, "Come, let's set out together and learn more about our loving God."

We are convinced that the decisive space for sharing the faith is not the classroom, and not even always the church building. Perhaps it is a corner in the nursery, a beach chair by the sea, a bench in the yard, or the edge of a bed. Nothing can substitute for the conversation between people who love and trust each other. Only in a space of loving closeness can the treasure of the faith be shared, passed on, or discovered together. One can ask questions and learn from and with another person. An exciting guide can be part of this endeavor—the *YOUCAT for Kids*.

Children have lots of questions, for example: "Why do I exist?" "How do we know that God exists?" "Why was Jesus nailed to the Cross?" These are wonderful starting points for using the *YOUCAT for Kids*. You can look for answers together. The bedtime ritual is the best opportunity for browsing through the *YOUCAT for Kids*. Of course, you can also select one question or another. It makes most sense to follow the proposed order of questions, because the Church's understanding of the faith has grown over a period of two thousand years. That is why actually no part of it can be left out without running the risk of leaving out or misunderstanding something important. Sunday, for example, can be understood only on the basis of the Resurrection. If you know something about the Resurrection of Jesus, you can explain Easter. If you have understood Easter, you will be able to tell what happens after we die. This way, one thing leads to another. It is fun to set out and discover God. And it is not only the children who learn something. How often have parents said, "It was only when I explained it to my child that it really made sense to me."

How to use the YOUCAT for Kids

We recommend following these steps:

- If you want to prepare, read the page you would like to look at with your child. First, what is it about? Do you understand what is meant by it? Do you have your own understanding of it? Do you need further information? Is there a passage in the Bible you should look up? Consider the illustrations—your child is going to discover them first. The texts with the colored background along the bottom of the page have information for you. You will be able to convey some of it to your child in your conversation.

- When you are with your child, first just look at the page that has a question written on it. There is a lot to discover there, and often there is something to laugh at, too. The two cheeky little kids, Lilly and Bob, make sure there is something to laugh at.

- Now turn to the question. Often, the illustrations will provide a good starting point for a conversation between you and your child.

- Perhaps at this point you will even close the YOUCAT for Kids. Your child has ideas. It is important that your child be allowed first to formulate initial understanding or knowledge about a topic. It is okay if you are uncertain about certain points. It will actually impress your child if you embark on this exploration together.

- After these steps, you can check the YOUCAT for Kids for answers. It is the Church's common answer, as it has been acquired from the Bible and from two thousand years of the history of the faith. Thus, this answer has a certain weight. Sometimes, the answer you find with

your child will not exactly match the experience of the Church. Not everything has to be clarified right away. Turn to the next question. Some things will become clearer as you go along.

- If at the end of your exchange you say a prayer with your child that brings the contents of your conversation before God, you have accomplished something wonderful!

- And there is something else: Pray to the Holy Spirit for the time that you spend in conversation with your child. Even if it seems strange to you initially, you will experience a deepening of your faith.

By the way, we, the authors of this book, did the same thing: we shared our faith. We projected a question onto a wall; and then we tried to find a common answer to it, in accordance with the Bible and the teachings of the Church. We called our method "community writing". Thus, the answers in the YOUCAT for Kids, are not from one, but from all of its authors.

And we did something else: throughout all these years, we prayed that we might accomplish something that truly helps children, their parents, and their other teachers of the faith to discover Jesus' message for their lives.

—The authors of the *YOUCAT for Kids*

1 Where does the world and everything
that is come from?

Everything
that is
comes from
God.

2 Why do I exist?

**You are here
because God wants you.**

He knows you.
He loves you beyond measure,
and he wants to make you happy.

 God who is love
Jesus appeared to St. Teresa of Avila in a vision and said to her: "I would create the universe again just to hear you say that you love me." That's how important we are to God.

Vision
We speak of a vision (from Latin *videre* = to see) when God shows himself to a person in a wonderful and miraculous way.

" It is a Christian duty ... for everyone to be as happy as he can.
C. S. Lewis (1898–1963), British author and literary scholar

3   *How do we know that God exists?*

**We know
that God exists
because we see his traces
everywhere.**

Look at everything:
the sun in the sky,
the stars at night,
the forests, the mountains, the seas, and the rivers,
the big animals and the small,
the people on all the continents.
God has made all that.

As **St. Paul** said, "In him we live and move and have our being."
Acts 17:28

The fish in the sea said to one another, "They say that our entire life depends on water. But what is water? We have never seen it." So they asked a wise old fish to show them water. The old fish said, "Oh, you foolish fish! You live in water, and you don't notice it?" Just as fish live in water, so man lives in God. He cannot live without his Creator and sustainer. And still man asks, "Where is God?" One needs to know two things: first, God is everywhere, and nothing exists without him. Second, God is not everything, but the cause of everything. He is infinitely greater than the things he has made.
Source unknown

4   *Can we know God?*

**Yes, but not without his help.
God is greater
than all of our images and
all of our thoughts.
God is a great mystery.**

God wants us to
know and love him.
That is why he shows himself to us.
That is called "revelation".

Revelation is what God has shown us about himself. In the YOUCAT, it says: "Just as in human love one can know something about the beloved person only if he opens his heart to us, so too we know something about God's inmost thoughts only because the eternal and mysterious God has opened himself to us out of love."

See **Question 7:** Why did God have to show himself in order for us to be able to know what he is like?

Too big
There is a story about **St. Augustine** (354–430) going for a walk by the seashore in order to think about God. A child had dug

a hole in the sand and was running back and forth with a shell to fill the hole with water.

"What are you doing?" Augustine asked. "I'm pouring the ocean into this hole!" the child said. "That is not going to work," said the saint. "The sea is far too big!" To which the child replied, "And you, Augustine, won't be able to fit the greatness of God into your little head!"

5 Can I talk to God?

Yes.
Talk to him!
Ask him to make himself known
in your heart.

Not only can you talk to God,
God is already waiting for you.
It does not matter if you are
riding your bike or waiting for a bus.
Just talk to him.

Does God really make himself known?

Whoever opens himself to God in silence and in prayer discovers how God speaks to us, how he guides us, directs us, consoles us, raises us up, heals us, and gives us the gift of his love. God is not some impersonal energy behind the universe, but someone who hears us and responds. Read Question 140: How can I hear God?

A wonderful prayer

LORD, you have searched me and known me! You know when I sit down and when I rise up; you discern my thoughts from afar. You search out my path and my lying down, and are acquainted with all my ways. ... Your eyes beheld my unformed substance; in your book were written, every one of them, the days that were formed for me, when as yet there was none of them.
Ps 139:1–3, 16

St. Faustina (1905–1938) lived in Poland. She had a vision of Jesus, who said to her: "Before I made the world, I loved you with the love that your heart is experiencing today, and, throughout the centuries, my love will never change."

6 *Believing in God—how does that work?*

**Believing in God means:
I put all my trust
in him who loves me most.
I accept what God reveals about himself.
I try to do what he tells me.**

Believing in God means
being safe and secure with him.
God loves us.
We do not need to be afraid.
With him, we can bring out the best in ourselves!

Your faith has made you well!
After Jesus cured people, he often said, "Your faith has made you well." He said it after healing a sick woman (**Mt 9:22**), a blind man (**Lk 18:42**), and a leper (**Lk 17:19**).

A man who trusted God
During World War II, the Lutheran pastor Dietrich Bonhoeffer was arrested and sentenced to death by the Nazis. In prison, in mortal fear, he wrote an amazing song:

By good powers wonderfully sheltered,
confident and comforted, we await whatever may come.
God is with us in the evening and in the morning,
and very certainly with every new day.

7   *Can we believe whatever we want?*

Yes, but only the truth is worth believing.
Christians do not invent the faith;
they trust in Jesus Christ.
He has brought us the truth about God.
It is written in the Bible
and in the living Tradition of the Church.

In the Church, together we live out
what we have learned from Jesus.
We should bring this faith
to all people.
Even though God is close to
everyone, he asks us to share our
faith with each other.

Read
Question 8: How is knowledge
about God passed on?
Question 9: Why do some people
not believe in God?
Question 10: What is the Bible?
Question 50: What does the word
"Church" mean?

Paths to God
Once, before he became
Pope Benedict XVI, Cardinal Joseph
Ratzinger was asked by a journalist:
"How many pathways to God are
there?" He replied, "As many as
there are people."

What Christians believe is written
in the Creed (see also **Question 13**).
This shared faith is so important that
it is said or sung by everyone together
at Mass, Sunday after Sunday, after the
homily.

8 How is knowledge about God passed on?

**Among God's people, from the beginning, knowledge of God
was passed on through stories about him,
which were written down in the Bible.
They are celebrated at Mass
and proclaimed by the** ➔ **Church.**

The Church is the community
where experiences with the living God
are correctly understood and
passed on from generation to generation.
Every ➔ Christian who lives by his faith
has a story to tell.
Christian parents and grandparents
try to pass on their faith
to their children and grandchildren.

➔ **Church:** When people hear the word "Church", many of them think only of a building or an institution. In **Questions 50–52**, you can find more information about the Church.

➔ A **Christian** is a person who is baptized and for that reason belongs to Christ. **Question 66** explains what Baptism is and what it does for us.

The witness of faith given by family members or friends is often more important than wordy explanations. Children need to see the example of faithful Christians and to hear about their personal experiences of God.

Knowledge about the faith
Two mothers were talking about their children's First Communion classes. "They haven't got a clue!" said the first mother. "The teacher asked them the names of the four evangelists, and they said Caspar, Melchior, and Balthasar!" The second mother said, "You should be glad they know at least three of them!"

Sometimes we learn about God
from the experiences of others.
When Christians recount the ways
God has showed himself to them,
guided them in their lives,
or healed them,
they give witness
to their faith.

A community of storytelling

We can think of God's people, to whom God revealed himself more and more over the course of thousands of years, as a community of storytelling. By the shepherds' fire, at the well, under a shady tree, on a rooftop, at the Temple—the sacred stories about God were told everywhere. They were written down later, and that is how the Sacred Scriptures of the people of Israel came to be. For a while, the early Christians passed along an oral tradition, before the Gospels and the other texts by the first Christians were written down.

9 Why do some people not believe in God?

**Some people have not yet heard
about God.
Some have → false images of God,
which stop them from believing in him.
After experiencing something evil,
some people refuse to believe in God.
Others do not try to believe
and do not want to know about God at all.
But God loves all people and
wants everyone to find him.**

Sometimes it takes a long time
for a person to believe
that it is God
who is knocking at his heart.
Some people grow old
before they believe and
trust in God.

Difficulties with faith
We must not believe that people who have difficulties believing and trusting in God are unworthy of his love. God is the Creator of all. He loves everyone without exception.

False images of God
Some people think that God

👎 wants to catch us making mistakes,

👎 needs our applause,

👎 isn't interested in the world anymore,

👎 is constantly offended,

👎 and punishes mercilessly.

FALSE **IMAGES OF GOD** MAKE US **SICK**

But God does none of these things. He is slow to anger and rich in mercy. With love and patience, we can reflect the true image of God.

10 *What is the Bible?*

**The → Bible is the most important book
in the world.
We also call it Sacred Scripture.
In it is written what we know about God.
The Bible tells us
how much God loves us.
Through the words of Sacred Scripture,
God speaks to us directly.**

Sacred Scripture
is not a bunch of old fairy tales.
When I read the Bible, God himself
is speaking to me.
For example, the words
"You are the light of the world" (Mt 5:14)
are meant for me, too.
God trusts me
to make the world
bright and beautiful.

" What would happen
were we to treat the Bible
as we treat our mobile phone?...
were we to turn back when we
forget it ... were we to open it
several times a day;
were we to read God's messages
contained in the Bible
as we read telephone messages?
Pope Francis

→ **Bible:** Greek
biblos = book

Two Christians are
talking to each other.
One of them says, "I can fall
asleep peacefully only if I
have read the Bible for ten
minutes in the evening."

"That is strange," the other
one says. "It's exactly the
other way round for me: if I
read the Bible for ten minutes
in the evening, I can't fall
asleep at all!"

Challenge
Go to a good library and
ask to see all the wonderful
children's Bibles!

11 *Is what the Bible says true?*

**Everything in the Bible
that we should know about God
and our path to him
is true.**

With → God's help,
the authors of the Bible wrote
what they learned about God
from what God's people
had experienced with him.
They wrote in their language
and with the cultural expressions of their times.

→ The Church uses the word **"inspiration"** to mean that the authors of Sacred Scripture wrote with the help of God. The Holy Spirit led them to the truth about God and us. An example: in the story of creation, the authors of the Bible did not write a scientific depiction of the beginning of the world. What mattered to them was not how God had created the world, but the fact that

● he *created* it,
● created it *from nothing*,
● and created it *for us* and entrusted it to our care.

**The most important book
in the world**
The atheist playwright **Bertold Brecht** (1898–1956) was once asked what the most important book in the world is. He replied, "You're going to laugh: the Bible!"

12 *What does the Bible tell us?*

**The Bible has two big parts,
the Old and the New Testaments.
It starts with the creation of the world,
tells the story of how man came to know God,
and ends with the coming
of the new heaven and the new earth.**

The Old Testament tells us
that God created heaven and earth.
It also tells us that he created man and woman,
who → turned away from God and lost paradise.
People began lying and killing each other.
But God did not abandon them.
He led the people of Israel from slavery to freedom.
He gave them the → Ten Commandments.
He sent them → prophets
to call them back to God.
The prophets spoke of the Messiah,
the Savior of the world.

→ To **turn away from God** is to sin. St. Teresa of Avila said that whoever prays does not continue in sin. He will either give up prayer or renounce sin, because "prayer and sin cannot exist together."

→ On sin and forgiveness of sin: **Question 55**: What is sin? and **Question 56**: What does sin do to us?

→ **The Ten Commandments:** see **Part 3**, p. 162 onward.

→ **Prophets:** The word "prophet" comes from Greek and refers to a messenger, speaker, or someone who tells the future. In the Old Testament, God calls prophets to speak to his people on his behalf. Some of the prophets were reluctant to reveal God's plans to others.

Jesus Christ is this Messiah.
The New Testament tells us about him
from beginning to end:

how he became man,
how he healed the sick,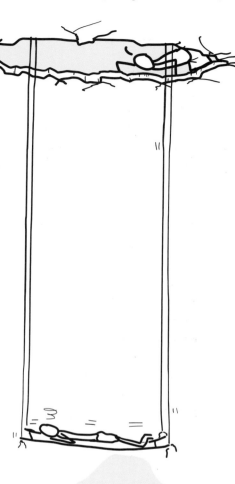
how he forgave sins,
how he raised the dead,
how he taught us
to love even our enemies,
how he suffered and died for us,
how he conquered death and rose again,
how he sent us his → Holy Spirit,
how he is the Lord of his Church
and will return at the end of time.

All this he did and does for me, too.
That is why I can also say
that he is my Lord.

→ **Holy Spirit:** read further
Question 47: Who is the Holy
Spirit?

Read to your child an astonishing story from the Gospel
of Mark **(Mk 2:1–12)**. Try to imagine it
vividly: people do everything to come
to Jesus and to experience his healing
power. There is a sick person who has
such great friends that they even remove the roof and break through the
ceiling to lower the man who is lying
on a stretcher down to Jesus.

Part 1

SEEING REALITY

THE CREED

12 Facts about God

Who God,
the Lord of the World, is.
How it is that we know
about him.
Why knowing him is the most
important thing
in the whole world.

Questions
13–63

13   *How does the → Creed go?*

1   **I believe in God, the Father almighty,**
     Creator of heaven and earth,
2   **and in Jesus Christ, his only Son,**
     our Lord,
3   **who was conceived by the Holy Spirit,**
     born of the Virgin Mary,
4   **suffered under Pontius Pilate,**
     was crucified, died, and was buried;
5   **he descended into hell;**
     on the third day he rose again from the dead;
6   **he ascended into heaven,**
     and is seated at the right hand of God
     the Father almighty;
7   **from there he will come**
     to judge the living and the dead.
8   **I believe in the Holy Spirit,**
9   **the holy catholic Church,**
     the communion of saints,
10 **the forgiveness of sins,**
11 **the resurrection of the body,**
12 **and life everlasting. Amen.**

→ This **creed** is the Apostles' Creed. It is so named because parts of it date back to the apostles. It summarizes the important facts of the faith in twelve key points. Christians should know this creed by heart. Somewhat later, in the fourth century, the Nicene Creed was written by bishops who met together in Nicaea and Constantinople, which is Istanbul today. Various versions of these two creeds are professed by Catholics, Orthodox, and Protestants. They show that Christianity is unified at its core.

I believe in God,
the Father almighty,
Creator of heaven
and earth . . .

God is.
God is almighty.
God is the Creator of heaven and earth.
God is also our Father.

14 Who is God?

God is God. He is everywhere, above and below.
He is without beginning and without end.
God was there before all else.
He will still be there when
this world comes to an end.
God is the one from whom
all good things come.
"God is love" (1 Jn 4:8).

A young man went to a scholar and said, "I'll give you 100 dollars if you tell me where God lives!" The scholar answered, "And I'll give you 200 dollars if you tell me where he cannot be found."

Before the mountains were brought forth, or ever you had formed the earth and the world, from everlasting to everlasting you are God.
Ps 90:2

The word "God"

The famous Jewish philosopher **Martin Buber** (1878–1965) said about the word "God": "Yes, it is the most loaded of human words. No other has been so besmirched and torn to pieces. That is exactly why I must not give it up. Generations of men have unloaded the burden of their worried lives on this word and have pressed it to the ground; it lies in the dirt and carries all their burdens.... Where could I find a word that would resemble it, to name the Highest! If I took the purest, most sparkling term from the innermost treasury of philosophy, I could only capture a tentative mental image, but not the presence of him whom I mean.... We cannot wash the word 'God' clean, and we cannot make it whole; but we can, besmirched and torn up as it is, pick it up from the ground and raise it up over an hour of great sorrow."

15 *What can God do? How powerful is he?*

God has power over everything.

Everything that is, exists
because God wants it, creates it,
and → sustains it:
time and space,
heaven and earth,
the universe and the stars,
→ angels, people, and animals ...
God has ordered everything wonderfully,
so that man can live on earth.

→ **Angels** are invisible, spiritual beings. God sends them to us as messengers, comforters, and helpers. Every person has a guardian angel.

→ See also **Question 20**: Does God still care about us and his world?

i "Naturally, what we would like would be a divine mightiness that fitted our own mindset and wishes: an 'omnipotent' God who solves problems, who intervenes to prevent us from encountering difficulties, who overcomes adverse powers, changes the course of events and eliminates suffering.... Nevertheless faith in almighty God impels us to have a very different approach: to learn to know that God's thought is different from our own, that God's ways are different from ours (cf. Is 55:8) and that his omnipotence is also different. ... His omnipotence is not expressed in violence, it is not expressed in the destruction of every adverse power as we might like; rather it is expressed in love, in mercy, in forgiveness, in accepting our freedom and in the tireless call for conversion of heart, in an attitude only seemingly weak—God seems weak if we think of Jesus Christ who prays, who lets himself be killed. This apparently weak attitude consists of patience, meekness and love; it shows that this is the real way to be powerful! This is God's power! And this power will win!"
Pope Benedict XVI, January 30, 2013

Question 40: Can God do anything? Is he almighty?

16 *How did the world come into being?*

Before all time,
when there was nothing yet,
not even darkness,
not even time,
there was only God.
God spoke: "Let there be …"
That's why God
is the Creator of everything
that is.

The Bible tells the story
of the six days of creation,
to say that God created the world.
For many millions of years until today,
the world, which he holds in his hands,
has been ➔ developing.

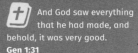 And God saw everything
that he had made, and
behold, it was very good.
Gen 1:31

➔ The **theory of evolution** does not contradict faith in God, the Creator. **Pope Francis** said, "The Big Bang theory, which is proposed today as the beginning of the world, does not contradict the intervention of a divine creator but depends on it. Evolution in nature does not conflict with the notion of Creation."

Question 42: Can someone accept the theory of evolution and still believe in the Creator?

The astronaut said, "I've been out in space many times but I've never seen God or angels." The brain surgeon said, "And I've operated on many clever brains but I've never seen a single thought."

Jostein Gaarder (*1952), Norwegian author

17   How is man different from all the other creatures God made?

**God loves everything he has made—
animals, too. But God made man, male and female,
in his own image, with mind and will.
He entrusted the earth to man,
so that he might cultivate and protect it.**

(see Gen 2:15)

Animals follow their instincts;
they do not choose their actions
the way people do.
Man thinks.
Man is also free:
he can choose
to do good or evil.
Man can even choose
to be the friend of God.

What is man that you are mindful of him,
and the son of man that you care for him?
Yet you have made him little less than the angels,
and you have crowned him with glory and honor.
You have given him dominion
over the works of your hands;
you have put all things under his feet.
Ps 8:4–6

We are not some casual
and meaningless product
of evolution. Each of us is the
result of a thought of God. Each of
us is willed, each of
us is loved, each of
us is necessary.
Pope Benedict XVI,
April 24, 2005

Then God said, "Let
us make man. ... So
God created man in his own
image, in the image of God
he created him; male and
female he created them.
Gen 1:26–27

18 *Why did God make me?*

"I am created
to do something or to be something
for which no one else is created;
I have a place in God's counsels,
in God's world,
which no one else has;
whether I be rich or poor,
despised or esteemed by man,
God knows me
and calls me by my name."
(→ John Henry Newman)

 → Blessed **John Henry Newman** (1801–1890) was a great English scholar, convert, and cardinal.

I know the plans I have for you, says the LORD, plans for welfare and not for evil, to give you a future and a hope.
Jer 29:11

One day at home, at table, I was asked: what do you want to be when you grow up? Do you know what I said? "A butcher". Why? Because the butcher at the market—there were three or four stalls for meat—took the knife, cut pieces.... It is an art, and I liked seeing him, watching him.
Pope Francis, December 31, 2015

19   *Why do we call God "Father"?*

**We call God "Father"
because through Baptism
we have become his children.
And Jesus, the Son of God,
has taught us
to call God
"Father".**

Human fathers can be courageous,
fair, loving, and generous.
Sometimes, however,
they are rarely there or not at all.
Sometimes fathers can be impatient,
selfish, or cruel.
When children feel sad about their father
they can know that they, too, have
the best father in the world:
our Father in heaven. 📖

A mother's love
In the Bible sometimes God's love for us is compared to a mother's love for her child: "As one whom his mother comforts, so I will comfort you" (Is 66:13) and "Can a woman forget her sucking child, that she should have no compassion on the son of her womb? Even these may forget, yet I will not forget you" (Is 49:15).

A story about trust
High above the market, a tightrope walker was performing the most daring tricks. Eventually, he asked the marveling crowd, "Who may I cart across the abyss in a wheelbarrow?" No one dared to raise his hand. Then a little boy volunteered. He climbed up quickly to the tightrope walker and sat down in the wheelbarrow, and the tightrope walker pushed him across the gaping deep. "Weren't you afraid?" the people asked afterward. "No," the boy said with a laugh, "the tightrope walker is my father!"
Source unknown

20 *Does God still care about us and the world?*

**Every second
God makes sure that the world
does not fall back into nothingness.
From the smallest ants
to the greatest galaxies,
nothing exists without God.**

God is not like a watchmaker
who built a big clock
and then left it alone.
On the contrary,
he even came into the world himself:
God became man.
He is close to me.
He sees me and hears me
when I call to him.

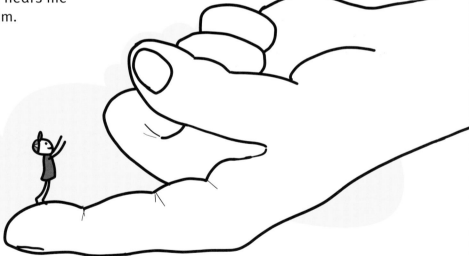

For thus said the
LORD ... he who
touches you touches the apple
of his eye.
Zec 2:8

God personally looks after me,
after us, after all mankind. I am not
abandoned, adrift in the universe and in a
society which leaves me ever more lost and
 bewildered. God looks after
me. He is not a distant God,
for whom my life is worthless.
Pope Benedict XVI, June 11,
2010

Keep me as the apple of
the eye; hide me in the
shadow of your wings.
Ps 17:8

21 *Does God direct my life?*

**Yes, God shows you the way
and helps you to walk it.
But you are free!
God does not direct you
like a remote-controlled robot.**

God has given you freedom
so that you can choose to love
by choosing to do good.
In order to make it easier for you,
he makes himself known in your life.
He speaks through your → conscience.
He shows himself to you
through people who help you,
beautiful moments,
and even painful experiences.

→ **Conscience**
See also **Question 113:** How do I know
if I am doing something good or bad?

Why doesn't God do anything?
When we are experiencing
something difficult, perhaps even an
injustice, we often ask: Why is God
allowing this to happen? We don't
always find an answer. Sometimes,
however, we discover later that the
difficulty led to something good.
In the Old Testament story about
Joseph (Gen 37–50), for example,
Joseph's jealous brothers sell
him into slavery. Only years
later, in Egypt, does he realize
that God used the evil done by
his brothers to save them and
God's entire people from famine.
There is a saying: "God can write
straight with crooked lines".

22 *Why is the world no longer as good
as God made it?*

**The world is in great disorder
because we choose to do evil.
We call that sinning.
We can't stop sinning just by saying,
"Starting today, we'll only be good!"
We are too weak to save ourselves.
We have been this way since → Adam and Eve.
We call that → original sin.**

→ **Adam and Eve**
The word "Adam" occurs in many languages, meaning "man"; in the Bible, it becomes the proper name of the first human being. The word "Eve" means "life" or "mother of everything that lives". Like the creation story, the story of Adam and Eve doesn't aim to provide a scientific explanation, but it says something about the relationship between God and man: we all are made by God, but we have fallen away from our original closeness to him (paradise).

→ The term **"original sin"** does not refer to our own sin or our own fault, but the broken condition we all inherit: the wounded state of mankind, into which we are born before we sin by our own free decision. The good news is that Jesus has overcome the power of sin.

FACT 2 ... and in Jesus Christ, his only Son, our Lord ...

Jesus Christ
is the Son of God
and our Lord.

Jesus'
PROFILE

Name: Jesus of Nazareth

Mother: Mary

Foster Father: Joseph, the carpenter

Birthday: The first Christmas

Place of birth Bethlehem in Judea

Profession: Carpenter

Languages: mother tongue: Aramaic; first foreign language: Hebrew

Outdoor-Activities: hiking, sailing, mountaineering

Things I like: being with my friends, celebrating feasts, being alone occasionally, healing illnesses and forgiving sins, talking to my Father in heaven, speaking with people about God, children

Things that annoy me: when my people turn against each other and when they refuse to live the way God wants them to

My greatest experience: I have had many great experiences. For instance, when my mother asked me to change water into wine at a wedding feast so that the bride and the groom would not be embarrassed. My Resurrection was the absolute highlight. I'm alive!

My Motto: "Change your lives now, because God is very close!"

What I like about you: that you exist and that you are spending time getting to know me!

23 Who is Jesus Christ?

**Jesus Christ
is the Son of God.
More than 2,000 years ago
he was born as a baby in Bethlehem.
God himself became man.
This is the greatest miracle.**

Jesus was really a man.
After his birth he was swaddled
like other newborns.
He cried when he was hungry
as other babies do.
He shivered when he was cold
and sweated when he was hot.
Yet Jesus was different
from all other men: he was also God.

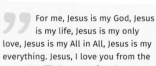

> For me, Jesus is my God, Jesus is my life, Jesus is my only love, Jesus is my All in All, Jesus is my everything. Jesus, I love you from the bottom of my heart, with my whole being.
> **St. Teresa of Calcutta** (1910–1997)

In the last book of Sacred Scripture, the Revelation to John, Jesus is described as the divine Lord over history and the world. The Lord says here about himself:

✝ I am the Alpha and the Omega, the first and the last, the beginning and the end.
Rev 22:13

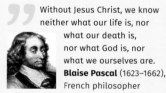

> Without Jesus Christ, we know neither what our life is, nor what our death is, nor what God is, nor what we ourselves are.
> **Blaise Pascal** (1623–1662), French philosopher

24 *What does the word "Christ" mean?*

**The word "Christ"
means "anointed one",
in Hebrew: Messiah.**

When someone became a ruler in ancient Israel,
he was anointed king with holy oil.
Jesus is the Christ, the "anointed one",
because he is the Messiah,
the Savior of the world,
whom the people of Israel awaited.
He is the King of kings and the Lord of lords.
Christ is therefore not
Jesus' family name
or the second part of a double name
as in John Henry or Laura Jane.

> Alexander, Caesar, Charlemagne, and I, we established empires. But on what did we build our creations? On power. Jesus Christ built his kingdom on love alone; and now, at this hour, millions of people are ready to die for him.
> **Napoleon Bonaparte** (1769–1821)

When Jesus came into the district of Caesarea Philippi, he asked his disciples, "Who do men say that the Son of man is?" And they said, "Some say John the Baptist, others say Elijah, and others Jeremiah or one of the prophets." He said to them, "But who do you say that I am?" Simon Peter replied, "You are the Christ, the Son of the living God."
Mt 16:13–16

"Christ the Savior is born."
This is a line in the most well-known Christmas song in the world: "Silent Night". Parish priest **Joseph Mohr** (1792–1848) first performed it on December 24, 1818, in Austria.

25   *Is Jesus Christ really God?*

Yes.

When Jesus was young,
almost everyone thought that he
was an ordinary man.
But when he began teaching,
when he healed the lame, the blind,
and the deaf,
when he raised the dead—
then people began believing that the power of God
was working through him.
But even Jesus' friends were puzzled.
Only after the Resurrection did they
really understand that Jesus is the Son of God.

The divinity of Jesus?

The famous English author C.S. Lewis (*The Chronicles of Narnia*) was an atheist who became a Christian. He realized that Jesus wasn't a founder of a religion or one of many wisdom teachers. Rather, the much higher claim that Jesus made for himself placed Lewis before an alternative: "Either this man was, and is, the Son of God, or else a madman or something worse."

> I have lost my heart to this Jesus of Nazareth, who was crucified 1,900 years ago, and I spend my life trying to imitate him.
>
> **Blessed Charles de Foucauld** (1858–1916)

26 **_What does it mean that Jesus Christ is the Lord?_**

**It means that everything
is in his hands:
space and time,
heaven and earth.
Everything and everyone are his.**

Jesus Christ, the Lord,
is more powerful than any president
and more important than any celebrity.
He is the Lord of your life, too.

Doubts about the faith

Many people have doubts when they take the daring step of accepting Jesus as the Lord of their lives. Jesus understands. When the apostle Thomas doubted the Resurrection, Jesus invited him to touch his wounds so that he would believe Jesus had really risen from the dead. **Pope**

Benedict XVI (September 27, 2006) said, "Thomas reacts with the most splendid profession of faith in the whole of the New Testament: 'My Lord and my God!' (Jn 20:28)."

We have no other Lord but him: Jesus, the humble King of justice, mercy and peace.
Pope Francis, April 9, 2017

27 *What is the Trinity?*

**There is only one God,
but he is three Persons.
God is a community within himself:
an eternal exchange of love
between Father, Son, and Holy Spirit.
We call this mystery
the Trinity.**

Jesus showed us that God is three Persons.
Jesus said he is the Son of God made man.
He spoke with God, the Father, and did his will.
He promised us the Holy Spirit,
who is God, just like the Father and the Son.

One in three?!?

The **Trinity** is the deepest mystery of the faith. People have tried to explain it with elements found in nature, such as an egg with shell, white, and yolk or an atom with proton, neutron, and electron. The image of three candles burning with a single flame is almost 2,000 years old. All these images fall short in describing God, who is one and yet a community of love between three Persons.

FACT 3 ... conceived by the Holy Spirit, born of the Virgin Mary ...

God became man:
the Holy Spirit filled
the Virgin Mary;
she became pregnant
and gave birth to Jesus Christ
in Bethlehem.

28   Who is Mary?

**Mary was a young woman from Nazareth.
She gave birth to Jesus.
She became the most astonishing thing
a woman could ever become:**
→ **Mother of God.**

A young woman in Nazareth,
in what is Israel today,
experienced something amazing:
God asked her, through an angel,
to become the Mother of his Son.
Mary said Yes, and the Son of God
became man and was born.
Mary swaddled and fed baby Jesus
and watched him grow like any other child.
But Mary knew that Jesus was different.
When Jesus began his mission,
Mary heard his preaching and saw his miracles.
Mary was there when Jesus was beaten,
mocked, and killed like a criminal.
Yet she never stopped trusting God.
After his Resurrection and Ascension,
Jesus prepared for us a place in heaven,
which Mary entered at the end of her earthly life.
Jesus made her our Queen and Mother.
Whenever we pray to her,
she takes our needs to Jesus.

→ **Worshipping Mary?**
Only God may be worshipped. Thus the Catholic Church does not worship Mary or any other creature God has made. The Church honors Mary as the **Mother of God**, the one who bore the Son of God in her womb, as she herself foretold: "Henceforth all generations will call me blessed" (Lk 1:48). From the Cross, Jesus gave us Mary to be our Mother (Jn 19:27). We can therefore turn to her with our needs.

Question 149: May we worship Mary?

29 *What happened in Nazareth?*

**The Annunciation:
Mary received
a message
that changed
the whole world.**

The angel Gabriel
went to Mary and said,
"Hail, full of grace, the Lord is with you."
Mary was troubled by this,
so the angel said, "Don't be afraid, Mary.
God has chosen you to be the Mother
of the Savior. You will give
birth to a son and name him Jesus."

Mary said, "How will this happen?"
The angel said, "The Holy Spirit will come upon you,
for the child will be the Son of God."
Then Mary said, "I am the servant of the Lord.
Let it be to me as you say."
(see Lk 1:26–36)

Message from heaven
Discuss with your child a time when the Lord asked something difficult of you. Were you afraid? Did you trust the Lord anyway? What was the outcome?

Nazareth was a small, insignificant village in Galilee, in northern Israel. Jesus and his disciples came from this region, which in their day was part of the Roman Empire.

30 What role did Joseph play?

Joseph was Mary's betrothed,
meaning her fiancé.
He was a just man
who listened to God.
When Mary was expecting a child,
who was from God and not from Joseph,
he didn't leave her,
but took her as his wife.
He trusted ➞ God's voice in a dream
and cared for Jesus and Mary.

Joseph was a carpenter.
He built things out of wood.
Joseph taught Jesus his trade,
and Jesus later worked with him.
Joseph is a great saint.
He will always help you
whenever you call on him.

Each Christian family can first of all—as Mary and Joseph did—welcome Jesus, listen to Him, speak with Him, guard Him, protect Him, grow with Him; and in this way improve the world. Let us make room in our heart and in our day for the Lord. As Mary and Joseph also did, and it was not easy.
Pope Francis December 17, 2014

➞ As [Joseph] considered this, behold, an angel of the Lord appeared to him in a dream, saying, "Joseph, son of David, do not fear to take Mary your wife, for that which is conceived in her is of the Holy Spirit."
Mt 1:20

31 *What took place in Bethlehem?*

**In Bethlehem, the first Christmas
took place when Jesus was born.**

The Roman emperor gave an order:

> I want to know how many people there are in my empire! → **PRONTO!**

For this reason, when Jesus was soon to be born,
Mary and Joseph traveled to Bethlehem to be counted.
It was very crowded when they arrived,
and night was falling,
but there was no room for them at the inn.

> When Jesus was born, there was no army of doctors and midwives as at a queen mother's bedside. There were no horns sounding from the castle balustrades. God made himself small to come to the small, became man in the everyday life of the poor, born in a shelter for animals and men. The little king lay on straw and cried for milk. And the poor came to look at the baby.
> **Luc Serafin** (*1953), German journalist

→ **Pronto:** quick, right now
(Why isn't it done already?!?)

Joseph and Mary found shelter
in a stable, and there in the straw Jesus was born.
Mary swaddled her baby to keep him warm
and laid him in a manger.
As shepherds were watching their sheep nearby,
an angel appeared to them,
and they were frightened.

The angel said,
"Don't be afraid. I bring you good news.
Today, the Savior is born."
Then a choir of angels sang, "Glory to God in the highest!"
The shepherds went in search of the child,
and they found the stable with Mary and Joseph
and baby Jesus.

Holy Scripture tells us about the first Christmas like this:

The Nativity (Lk 2:1–20)

In those days a decree went out from Caesar Augustus that all the world should be enrolled. This was the first enrollment, when Quirinius was governor of Syria. And all went to be enrolled, each to his own city. And Joseph also went up from Galilee, from the city of Nazareth, to Judea, to the city of David, which is called Bethlehem, because he was of the house and lineage of David, to be enrolled with Mary his betrothed, who was with child.

And while they were there, the time came for her to be delivered. And she gave birth to her first-born son and wrapped him in swaddling cloths, and laid him in a manger, because there was no place for them in the inn.

And in that region there were shepherds out in the field, keeping watch over their flock by night. And an angel of the Lord appeared to them, and the glory of the Lord shone around them, and they were filled with fear. And the angel said to them, Be not afraid; for behold, I bring you good news of a great joy which will come to all the people, for to you is born this day in the city of David a Savior, which is Christ the Lord. And this will be a sign for you: you will find a baby wrapped in swaddling cloths and lying in a manger. And suddenly there was with the angel a multitude of the heavenly host praising God and saying, "Glory to God in the highest, and on earth peace among men with whom he is pleased!"

When the angels went away from them into heaven, the shepherds said to one another, "Let us go over to Bethlehem and see this thing that has happened, which the Lord has made known to us." And they went with haste, and found Mary and Joseph, and the baby lying in a manger. And when they saw it they made known the saying which had been told them concerning this child; and all who heard it wondered at what the shepherds told them.

But Mary kept all these things, pondering them in her heart. And the shepherds returned, glorifying and praising God for all they had heard and seen, as it had been told them.

Important Events in the Life of Jesus

Young Jesus is found in the Temple

"How is it that you sought me? Did you not know that I must be in my Father's house?" (Lk 2:49)

Jesus is baptized

The Holy Spirit descended upon him in bodily form, as a dove, and a voice came from heaven, "You are my beloved Son; with you I am well pleased." (Lk 3:22)

Jesus calls his disciples

"Do not be afraid; henceforth you will be catching men." (Lk 5:10)

Jesus multiplies the loaves

So they gathered them up and filled twelve baskets with fragments from the five barley loaves, left by those who had eaten. (Jn 6:13)

Jesus changes water into wine
"Fill the jars with water." And they filled them up to the brim. (Jn 2:7)

Jesus teaches the multitude
Seeing the crowds, he went up on the mountain, and when he sat down his disciples came to him. And he opened his mouth and taught them. (Mt 5:1–2)

Jesus visits the house of Zacchaeus
"For the Son of man came to seek and to save the lost." (Lk 19:10)

Jesus blesses the children
"Let the children come to me, do not hinder them; for to such belongs the kingdom of God." (Mk 10:14)

Jesus heals a lame man

"I say to you, rise, take up your pallet and go home." (Mk 2:11)

Jesus is transfigured on the mountain

And he was transfigured before them, and his face shone like the sun, and his garments became white as light. (Mt 17:2)

Jesus walks on the sea

In the fourth watch of the night he came to them, walking on the sea. (Mt 14:25)

Jesus enters Jerusalem

So they took branches of palm trees and went out to meet him, crying, "Hosanna! Blessed is he who comes in the name of the Lord, even the King of Israel!" (Jn 12:13)

FACT 4 ... suffered under Pontius Pilate, was crucified, died, and was buried ...

Under Pontius Pilate,
Jesus was beaten
and sentenced to death.
He died on the Cross for us
and was buried.

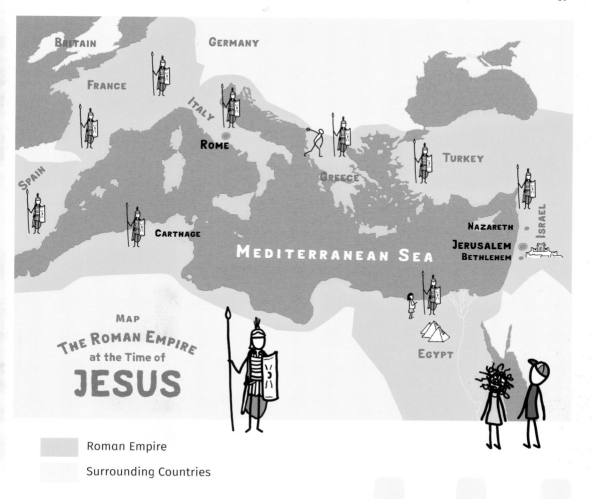

MAP

THE ROMAN EMPIRE
at the Time of
JESUS

BRITAIN GERMANY FRANCE SPAIN ITALY ROME GREECE TURKEY CARTHAGE MEDITERRANEAN SEA NAZARETH JERUSALEM BETHLEHEM ISRAEL EGYPT

Roman Empire

Surrounding Countries

32 *Who was Pontius Pilate?*

**Pontius Pilate was the
Roman governor in Jerusalem.
He sentenced Jesus to death,
even though he knew that Jesus was innocent.**

Who was responsible for Jesus' death? Often in history, Jews have been blamed for the death of Jesus. This is a terrible slander. The truth is, we all are to blame for the death of Jesus because he came into the world to die for our sins and to reconcile us to God. Jesus was a Jew, and some of his people accepted him as the promised Savior while others did not. Some of those who did not tried him and found him guilty of blasphemy. Then they turned him over to Pontius Pilate, the Roman governor, who sentenced him to death.

Pilate seems to have given in to the pressure exerted on him by others; thus, the evangelist Matthew describes how in a symbolic act, he had water brought to him to wash his hands of the guilt (see Mt 27:24).

33 *What crimes was Jesus accused of?*

**Jesus was accused of
→ blasphemy. People said
he disobeyed the laws of God.
Some thought he would lead
a revolution against the Romans,
who were occupying their country.**

The accusations were false.
Jesus was not a blasphemer;
he really was the Son of God.
Jesus also perfectly obeyed
all of God's commandments.
He showed the people
how to understand them.
Jesus wasn't thinking of revolution and violence;
he wanted to bring God's real power
into the world: love.

→ **Blasphemy** is showing irreverence toward God. In ancient Israel, murder was the only offense considered as serious as blasphemy.

" Jesus' love consists precisely in the fact that he would rather let himself be nailed to the Cross by us human beings than to use force to make people do anything.
Cardinal Kurt Koch (*1950)

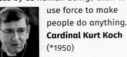

" There is really only one place in the world where we see no darkness. That is the person of Jesus Christ.
Albert Einstein (1879–1955), German physicist

34 *Why did Jesus let himself be killed?*

**Jesus died for us. He said,
"Greater love has no man than this,
that a man lay down his life
for his friends"** (Jn 15:13).

If you walk the way of love,
you often have to take on difficulties.
If you decide against violence,
you often seem to belong with the losers;
you are excluded and laughed at,
sometimes even bullied.
Yet it is the right way.
Love that takes on suffering
is God's way
of making the world whole again.

Friendliness will be victorious, compassion will triumph, laughter will triumph, love, caring, sharing will triumph. For we are made for the Good. We are made for love.
Desmond Tutu (*1931), Nobel laureate

How often we wish that God would ... show himself stronger, that he would strike decisively, defeating evil and creating a better world. All ideologies of power justify themselves in exactly this way, they justify the destruction of whatever would stand in the way of progress and the liberation of humanity. We suffer on account of God's patience. And yet, we need his patience. God, who became a lamb, tells us that the world is saved by the Crucified One, not by those who crucified him. The world is redeemed by the patience of God. It is destroyed by the impatience of man.
Pope Benedict XVI, April 24, 2005

The Passion of Christ

35   *Did Jesus have no friends left?*

**When Jesus' suffering began,
many of his friends left him.
When Jesus was crucified,
only a handful of followers were present:
his mother, a few other women,
and John.**

The disciples slept while Jesus
trembled in agony
before he was arrested.
Judas betrayed him for thirty silver coins.
Peter, the leader of the apostles,
pretended not to know
Jesus at all.

God's human resources policy

Why does Jesus make Peter, one of the weakest among his disciples, the leader of the apostles? All the Gospels tell the story of his failure. But that is not only the case with Peter. Why does a raving persecutor of Christians such as Paul become a great apostle to the nations? Apparently, Jesus is not looking for perfect heroes at all. Jesus has come "to seek and to save the lost" (Lk 19:10). And that applies to those whom Jesus gives a leading role. By the way, at times we all are weak, bad friends, cowards, and even traitors. But there is one source of comfort, Jesus, who told St. Paul: "My grace is sufficient for you, for my power is made perfect in weakness" (2 Cor 12:9). Paul responded, "I will all the more gladly boast of my weaknesses, that the power of Christ may rest upon me."

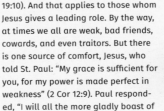

> Jesus remains faithful, he never betrays us: even when we [are] wrong.
> **Pope Francis, July 27, 2014**

Jesus' Passion (see Mk 14–15, Jn 18–19)

Jesus institutes the Eucharist

Jesus' agony in the garden

Jesus is betrayed by a kiss

Jesus is dragged before the judges

Jesus is denied by Peter

Jesus is scourged

Jesus is crowned with thorns

36 *Did Jesus really die on the Cross?*

Yes.

Jesus died on the eve of → Passover at around 3 P.M.
We call this day Good Friday.
The causes of his death were loss of blood
and suffocation.
When a soldier pierced Jesus' side with a lance,
blood and water poured out—
a sure sign of death.
His dead body was taken from the Cross,
wrapped in cloths,
and laid in an empty stone tomb.

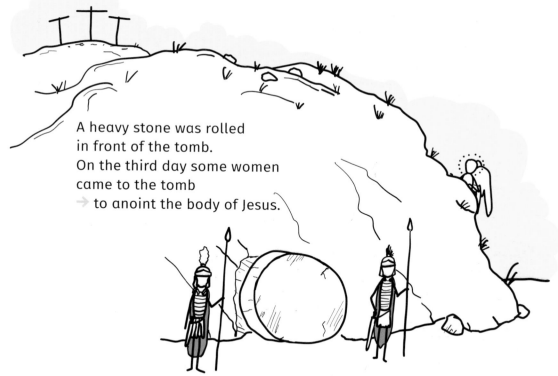

A heavy stone was rolled
in front of the tomb.
On the third day some women
came to the tomb
→ to anoint the body of Jesus.

And Jesus cried again with a loud voice and yielded up his spirit. And behold, the curtain of the temple was torn in two, from top to bottom; and the earth shook, and the rocks were split.
Mt 27:50

→ **Passover:** see p. 120.

→ **Anointing of the dead:** In the time of Jesus, the bodies of the dead were rubbed with a mixture of fragrant resins and oils.

Jesus gave his life for me, and it is an honor for me to do the same for him.
Mary Pierce (*1975), French tennis player

FACT 5 ... descended into hell; on the third day he rose again from the dead ...

Jesus Christ
went among the dead
and rose again
on the third day.
He lives.

37 Why do we celebrate Easter?

**Jesus' friends came to the tomb
and found it open and empty!
The women first thought that
someone had stolen the body of Jesus.
But his body
had not been stolen.
Jesus had risen from the dead,
just as he had foretold.**

The value of eyewitnesses

Jesus' Resurrection is no fairy tale; it was a concrete event, attested to by his disciples. The first eyewitnesses were women who discovered the empty tomb on Easter morning. If the Resurrection had been invented, women would never have been cited as eyewitnesses because in Judaism only the testimony of men was accepted as credible in court. See also:

Question 106: Are there proofs for the Resurrection of Jesus?

So they departed quickly from the tomb with fear and great joy, and ran to tell his disciples. And behold, Jesus met them and said, "Hail!" And they came up and took hold of his feet and worshiped him. Then Jesus said to them, "Do not be afraid."
Mt 28:8–10

38 — What does it mean to rise again from the dead?

To rise again from the dead means to receive new life from God after death.

Jesus rose again from the dead.
He showed himself, completely alive,
to his friends and many others.
He allowed his friends to touch him,
and he ate and drank with them.
The risen Jesus
lives forever.

**ℹ The Resurrection—
the apostles' hoax?**

Jesus' execution and burial took place in the middle of Jerusalem and was conducted by people who would have had no interest whatsoever in foolish rumors. The empty tomb was not contested by anyone, but some claimed that the apostles had stolen Jesus' body. But if that had been the case, the apostles would have known that they were liars, and yet almost all them accepted persecution, torture, and death for their faith. They would not have done that for a hoax they had invented. And Saul, the persecutor of Christians who later became St. Paul, would never have become a Christian and endured beatings, imprisonments, and death for the sake of Jesus if he had not encountered the risen Lord.

ℹ At Easter, Christians throughout the whole world celebrate the Resurrection of Jesus Christ, the Son of God. It is the most important Christian feast—even more important than Christmas. Beginning on Palm Sunday, the days leading up to Easter are called Holy Week, which includes Holy Thursday, Good Friday, and Holy Saturday. From the evening of Holy Thursday to the evening of Easter Sunday is the →

→ **THIS IS THE BLESSED NIGHT,
WHEN CHRIST
BROKE THE CHAINS OF DEATH
AND ROSE FROM THE DEEP
VICTORIOUS.**

→ Easter Triduum. Though chronologically three days, they are liturgically one day unfolding for us the unity of Christ's Paschal Mystery.
They are the most solemn and moving ceremonies of the Church year.
See also p. 161.

The joy of the Easter Vigil

The highest service of all is the Easter Vigil, which begins on the night of Holy Saturday. While it is still dark, the Easter fire is lit outside the church. From the fire, the priest lights the tall Easter candle. This is the sign that Christ lives and has overcome for us the darkness of sin and death. As the Easter candle is carried into the dark church, the *Lumen Christi* (Light of Christ) sounds three times, each time in a higher pitch. Everyone answers, *Deo gratias* (Thanks be to God). One by one, people have their own individual candles lit from the candles of others. As the light spreads, so does a deep joy about the miracle of our redemption.

→ Excerpt from the "Exsultet", the great Easter proclamation that is chanted at the beginning of the Easter Vigil.

39 How did more and more people learn about the Resurrection?

**According to the oldest text of the Bible about the Resurrection,
Jesus "appeared to Cephas, then to the Twelve.
Then he appeared to more than five hundred brethren at one time,
most of whom are still alive,
though some have fallen asleep.
Then he appeared to James,
then to all the apostles"** (1 Cor 15:5–7).

The → evangelists reported several
encounters with the resurrected Jesus:
in the garden, by the lake, on the way to Emmaus,
in the upper room of a house. 📖
The encounters with the risen Christ
must have been staggering.
Many came to believe that Jesus
is the Son of God.

Jn 20:11—18

Rabbi!

> I wish for us all Easter eyes,
> which in death can see
> as far as life,
> in guilt, as far as forgiveness,
> in separation, as far as unity,
> in wounds, as far as healing.
> I wish for us all Easter eyes,
> which in human beings can see
> as far as God,
> in God, as far as human beings,
> in the I, as far as the you.
> And for that, I wish for each of us
> all Easter power and peace,
> all Easter light, hope, and faith,
> that life might be stronger than death.
> **Bishop Klaus Hemmerle** (1929–1994)

📖 If you would like to read
these appearances of the
risen Jesus to your child, you can
look up the following passages:
**Jn 20:11–18, Lk 24:13–53,
Jn 21:1–14, Jn 20:19–30**.

Lk 24:13—35

Jn 21:1—14

Jn 20:19—29

Question 107: Through his Resurrection, did Jesus return to the physical, corporeal state that he had during his earthly life?

→ The **evangelists** are the four authors of the Gospel: Mark, Matthew, Luke, and John

In the YOUCAT, you'll find further information here:

Question 105: How did the disciples come to believe that Jesus is risen?

For Christians, Jesus is not a dead person from antiquity, but someone who is alive. He is our Lord. He is here. You can speak with him. **Pope Benedict XVI** wrote, "Whether Jesus merely was or whether he also is—this depends on the Resurrection."

40 *Is there life after death for us, too?*

→ **Yes.**

We are sad
when a beloved person dies.
Some might think that he is gone forever.
We Christians believe that he lives.
God has created us
for eternal life with him.
That doesn't end with death.
We, too, are going to rise again.

→ See also **Question 58:** What
happens to me when I die?

> Christians are people
> who know that they
> never see one another for the
> last time.
> **Source unknown**

Now if Christ is preached as raised from the dead, how can some of you say that there is no resurrection of the dead? But if there is no resurrection of the dead, then Christ has not been raised; if Christ has not been raised, then our preaching is in vain and your faith is in vain.
1 Cor 15:12–14

Hope in eternal Life
This is what happened when Adolf Hitler had Hans and Sophie Scholl and Christoph Probst, young Christian members of the anti-Nazi resistance, executed on February 22, 1943. **Christoph Probst** had himself baptized as a Catholic shortly before the execution. His last words to his companions: "In a few minutes we'll see each other again in eternity."

FACT 6

... ascended into heaven, and is seated at the right hand of God the Father almighty ...

Jesus Christ returned to his Father in heaven so that he could be close to everyone.

41 What happened at Jesus' farewell?

Jesus gave his friends a → mission: "All authority in heaven and on earth has been given to me. Go therefore and make disciples of all nations baptizing them in the name of the Father and of the Son and of the Holy Spirit, teaching them to observe all that I have commanded you" (Mt 28:18–20a).

The disciples were afraid. For this reason, Jesus encouraged them: "I am with you always, to the close of the age" (Mt 28:20b).

→ **Mission** = charge, assignment (from Lat. *mittere* = to send) Jesus gives his disciples and us a mission—to tell others about God and to make him known through our lives so that they might become friends of Jesus, too.

Being a missionary
Pope Francis reminds us that "every generation is called to be a missionary. To bring what we have inside, what the Lord has given us, and do this from the start! … The first thing Andrew and John did was to be missionaries. They went to their brothers and friends: 'We have found the Lord, we have found the Messiah!'" November 22, 2014

42 *What does it mean to say that Jesus "ascended into heaven"?*

**The disciples saw Jesus after
his Resurrection for forty days.
Then Jesus returned to his Father.
In the presence of his disciples, he was lifted up,
and then he vanished from their sight.
We say that Jesus
ascended into heaven.**

Jesus did not
simply disappear or
embark on space travel.
"The departing Jesus does not make
his way to some distant star. ...
Because Jesus is with the Father,
he has not gone away but remains close to us.
Now he is no longer in one particular place
in the world as he had been before ...
he is present and accessible to all."
(Pope Benedict XVI)

God is not where
heaven is, but heaven
is where God is.
Gerhard Ebeling (1912–2001),
Lutheran theologian

The feast of the **Ascension** is held in many countries forty days after Easter Sunday and, therefore, on a Thursday. These forty days have their origin in a passage from the Acts of the Apostles by St. Luke: "To them he presented himself alive after his passion by many proofs, appearing to them during forty days, and speaking of the kingdom of God" (Acts 1:3). Thus, the Ascension marks the end of the special appearances of the risen Jesus—but not his disappearance from our lives.

43   *Why did Jesus not stay on earth forever?*

**Jesus wanted to be close
to all people, all the time.
From heaven, Jesus
can be present
always and everywhere
to everyone.**

The disciples were afraid of losing Jesus.
Jesus comforted them and said,
"Let not your hearts be troubled" (Jn 14:1).
He said he was going to prepare
a place for them in heaven.
Then "I will come again and will take you to myself,
that where I am you may be also" (14:3).

Jesus gave them another promise:
"I will ask the Father,
and he will give you another Counselor,
to be with you for ever" (Jn 14:16).
He has kept his word.
Jesus has sent the Holy Spirit.
Until Jesus comes again,
the Holy Spirit is our teacher,
helper, and comforter.

In my Father's house are
many rooms; if it were not
so, would I have told you that I go to
prepare a place for you?
Jn 14:2

Heaven
"Heaven does not indicate a place
above the stars but something far more
daring and sublime: it indicates Christ
himself, the divine Person who welcomes
humanity fully and for ever, the One in
whom God and man are inseparably
united for ever. Man's being in God,
this is Heaven. And we draw close to
Heaven, indeed, we enter Heaven to the
extent that we draw close to Jesus and
enter into communion with him." **Pope
Benedict XVI**, May 24, 2009

Question 52:
What is heaven?

... from there
he will come to judge
the living
and the dead.

Jesus Christ will
come again at the end of the world.
He will judge
all the living
and the dead.

Is our world really going to come to an end?

**Yes. Our world has
a beginning and an**  **end.
But God was there before the beginning
and God will also be there
when our world
comes to an end:
"And behold, I am with you always,
to the close of the age"** (Mt 28:20).

You don't have to be
afraid of the end of the world.
God awaits us at the end of time,
because he loves us.

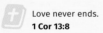 The **end of the world** is sometimes called the Last Day.

Love never ends.
1 Cor 13:8

Based on recent calculations, researchers guess that the earth will perish in 7.59 billion years, because then the earth will be consumed by fire; it will plunge into the fire of the dying sun. However, man could destroy the earth himself. Even if the world is going to end one day, God does not end, and we, too, are made for eternity.

 Hope is nothing but trust that God's love knows no end.
Blessed Charles de Foucauld

45 *How is Jesus Christ going to judge the living and the dead?*

**Only goodness can dwell with God.
To be with God, we must let go of all our sins—
pride, greed, anger, envy, hatred, violence.
Through the power of God's love and mercy,
we shall be made perfect.**

God's judgment sorts
the good from the bad.
But God does not want
to condemn anyone.
God invites everyone
to turn away from sin
and enter heaven,
where he wipes away every tear
and heals every wound (see Rev 21:1).

At the evening of your life, you will be examined in love.
St. John of the Cross (1542–1591)

The philosopher **Robert Spaemann** (*1927) tells the following parable: "Imagine a painter with infinite creative capacities. He starts to draft a huge painting. Someone who wants to spoil the painting is sitting next to him. Again and again, he splatters a thick blob of paint on the painting, defacing it. The painter incorporates each of these blobs into his painting and even

 makes something better out of them. At the end, there is a wonderful image."

46 Will God be a strict judge?

God will be a just, merciful, and forgiving judge.

When God judges,
we do not have to be afraid that he will be mean.
In every moment,
God is love and mercy.
"He judges us" means that
he wants to make us righteous and good.
But whoever does not want to be righteous and good,
whoever chooses evil, even up to the very last moment
of his life,
will not go to heaven.
Because in heaven there is no place for evil.
Everyone who is sorry for his sins
will be forgiven.
God longs to show his mercy.

Justice and Love

Ancient philosophy and later also **St. Thomas Aquinas** (1225–1274), the great philosopher and theologian of the Middle Ages, defined justice as "to each his own"—he didn't say "to each the same". Jesus was not equally "nice" to everyone. When necessary, he could be very strict: "Whoever causes one of these little ones who believe in me to sin, it would be better for him if a great millstone were hung around his neck and he were thrown into the sea" (Mk 9:42). It is often said that the Gospels are good news, not threatening news, and that is true. But Jesus did warn us that our actions have consequences—good actions have good consequences, and bad actions have bad ones. Our sins do real harm to ourselves and others. If we do not turn away from them and make amends for them, we can find ourselves far from God.

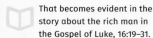

That becomes evident in the story about the rich man in the Gospel of Luke, 16:19–31.

The Holy Spirit
is, together with the Father
and the Son,
the one God.
The Holy Spirit
is the love of God
himself.
He is the giver of life.

47 *Who is the Holy Spirit?*

**The Holy Spirit is God,
just as the Father is God
and the Son is God.
He is the love between
the Father and the Son.**

The Holy Spirit
has filled creation from its beginning.
The Holy Spirit
has spoken through the prophets. 📖
Through the Holy Spirit
Mary became the Mother of Jesus.
The Holy Spirit
came down on Jesus at his Baptism in the Jordan.
The Holy Spirit
freed the disciples from their fear at Pentecost.
The Holy Spirit
brings divine life into the Church. 📖
The Holy Spirit
makes me into a dwelling place for God.

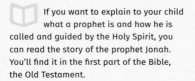
📖 If you want to explain to your child what a prophet is and how he is called and guided by the Holy Spirit, you can read the story of the prophet Jonah. You'll find it in the first part of the Bible, the Old Testament.

📖 An exemplary story about the working of the Holy Spirit in the New Testament is the encounter between Philip and the Ethiopian court official. The Spirit moved Philip to explain the Scriptures to the official, who was moved by the Spirit to recognize the truth of God's word and to ask for Baptism. You can read this story in Acts 8:26–40.

48 What does the Holy Spirit look like?

**We cannot see the Holy Spirit.
But we can see the results of his presence.
The Bible describes him
in many powerful images.
He is mighty like fire,
gentle as a dove,
thrilling like a storm,
and tender as a soft whisper.**

The Fruits of the Holy Spirit
- Love ● Joy ● Peace
- Patience ● Kindness
- Goodness ● Faithfulness
- Gentleness ● Self-Control
(see **Gal 5:22–23**)

Question 311: What are the fruits of the Holy Spirit?

And behold, the LORD passed by, and a great and strong wind tore the mountains, and broke in pieces the rocks before the LORD, but the LORD was not in the wind; and after the wind an earthquake, but the LORD was not in the earthquake; and after the earthquake a fire, but the LORD was not in the fire; and after the fire a still small voice.
1 Kings 19:11–12

49 How do we know that the Holy Spirit is within us?

**You can experience the working of the Holy Spirit
in the joy, the courage, and the power he gives you.
The Holy Spirit gives us good ideas
and urges us to carry them out.**

On Pentecost, the Holy Spirit filled the Church.
The disciples had hidden themselves out of fear.
Suddenly, the Holy Spirit came down on them
like flames of fire. The fear was gone!
A great joy filled them, and they praised God
in other languages.
A crowd gathered outside the house,
and each person heard them speaking in his own language.
This was stunning to the people in Jerusalem, and
about 3,000 came to believe in Jesus that day (see Acts 2:1–42).

To this day, the Spirit of God
brings a holy restlessness into the Church.
He does not cease to work miracles
and to spread his → gifts around the world.

At times he is like a flame that sets us on fire to do good.
At times we hear him in our conscience:
"Do something! Help that person!"

At times he is like a quiet guest,
living in our → soul,
changing us from the inside
and making us into better people.

Confirmation is the sacrament of the Holy Spirit. See also **Questions 70** and **71.**

→ **Soul:** see page 98

→ **The seven gifts of the Holy Spirit: wisdom, understanding, knowledge, counsel, fortitude, piety, and fear of the Lord** (see Is 11:1–2). St. Paul writes about the gifts of the Holy Spirit: "To each is given the manifestation of the Spirit for the common good. To one is given through the Spirit the utterance of wisdom, and to another the utterance of knowledge according to the same Spirit, to another faith by the same Spirit, to another gifts of healing by the one Spirit, to another the working of miracles, to another prophecy, to another the ability to distinguish between spirits, to another various kinds of tongues, to another the interpretation of tongues. All these are inspired by one and the same Spirit, who apportions to each one individually as he wills" (1 Cor 12:7–11).

The Church is the
community of all those
who belong to Christ.
The Church is holy,
because the holy God dwells in her.
The Church is catholic,
which means universal,
and open to everyone.
And she is apostolic,
because she is built on
the foundation of the apostles.

50 ***What does the word "Church" mean?***

**The word "Church" comes from the Greek word *Kyriaké*.
It means "belonging to the Lord (= *Kyrios*)".**

Jesus is our Lord. We are his body—
an international body, from every country,
every race, and every language group.
That is called catholic (= universal).
It doesn't matter where we come from;
the Lord has called us to be his Church
and to take care of the world—
as students, politicians, teachers, police, health care workers …
But you can also use your talents
in the parish or at Mass:
for example, as a → catechist or an altar server.
Everyone should work for a better world
with all his might.
There are special leadership roles within the Church,
such as pope, bishop, priest, and deacon,
so that the faithful can continue
the saving work of Jesus in his name.

All the baptized belong to Jesus
Christ. That is why the members of
other denominations are our brothers
and sisters. They are called Christians
with good reason. More on ecumenism
→ **Question 53**

→ **Catechist:** teacher of faith

" You can do things that
I cannot do. I can do
things that you cannot do.

Together, we can
do great things.
**St. Teresa of
Calcutta**

" The Church is not a welfare,
cultural, or political association
but a living body that walks and acts in
history.
Pope Francis, June 19, 2013

51 How did this community of the Church come about?

Jesus gathered disciples (= friends) around him.
From among these friends
he chose twelve as apostles.
He made Peter the leader:
"You are Peter, and on this rock
I will build my Church" (Mt 16:18).
The Church is forever built
on the foundation of these apostles. That's why
we call the Church "apostolic".
The bishops are the successors of the apostles.

The word "apostle"
comes from Greek
and means "messenger".
"And he [Jesus] appointed twelve,
to be with him,
and to be sent out to preach" (Mk 3:14).
All Christians are messengers of Jesus
and are, in that sense, apostles, too.

PETRUS =

---

i **The Church is still growing**
Jesus started out with two disciples. Today, there are more than two billion Christians in the world. Christianity is the largest religion on earth. Every third person is a Christian. In the past 100 years, the number of Christians has tripled.

When professional soccer player **Miroslav Klose** (*1978) was a child, he served as an altar boy and sang in the Christmas pageant at his parish. "Just like my entire family," he said, "I am a believing Catholic."

52 *What does it mean to go to church?*

**The church is not just a building
that people walk in and out of.
"Going to church" means
more than entering a building. It means
meeting Jesus himself.**

When we enter a Catholic church,
Jesus is present there.
When we go to Mass, we meet Jesus
by listening to his words
and receiving Holy Communion.
We also meet Jesus in the other members
of his body, our brothers and sisters in Christ.
After Mass, we all bring Jesus
with us into the world.

"Whoever thinks he is a Christian just because he goes to church, deceives himself. One doesn't become a car, either, just because one goes to a garage.
Albert Schweitzer (1875–1965), French-German physician, philosopher, and Lutheran theologian

i **Joining and leaving the Church**
The sacrament of Baptism joins a person to Christ, making him part of his Body, the Church. A baptized person always belongs to Jesus even if he stops going to Mass. Whenever we hear a person say that he has left the Church, let us pray that he will discover that Jesus has not left him and never stops offering him his love and mercy.

All the things a Catholic church contains

If you enter a Catholic church anywhere in the world, you can find certain objects that are used at Mass.

Perhaps you can discover them here!

Every church looks a little different, and these objects, too, can look a little different.

If you know what these objects are and how they are used, you already know a lot about the Mass.

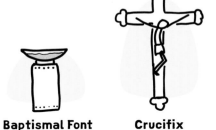

Baptismal Font   **Crucifix**

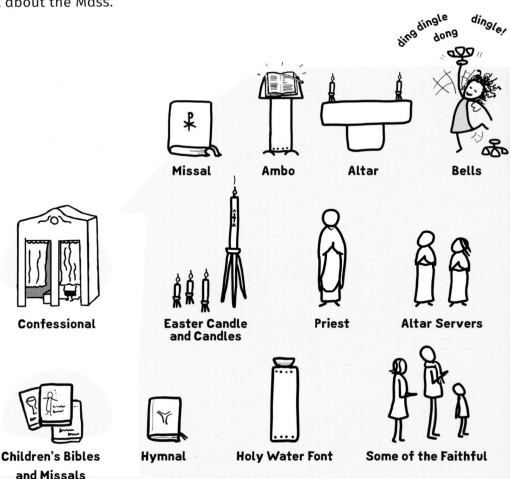

Missal   **Ambo**   **Altar**   **Bells**

Confessional   **Easter Candle and Candles**   **Priest**   **Altar Servers**

Children's Bibles and Missals   **Hymnal**   **Holy Water Font**   **Some of the Faithful**

ding dingle dong   dingle!

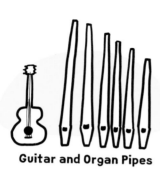

Guitar and Organ Pipes

Church Bells

Tabernacle

Sanctuary Light

Monstrance

Stained-Glass Window

Wine   **Water**

Kneelers

Paten

Chalice

sniff sniff

Statues of Saints

Church Mouse

Collection Basket   **Incense**

53 To whom does the Church belong?

The Church belongs to the baptized.

Being baptized means
belonging to Jesus Christ
in the way that
body and head
belong together.
Christ is the Head, and
all the baptized together
are the Body of Christ, the Church.
Perhaps you are his ear,
his hand, his foot, his mouth.
Whoever asks for Baptism says,
"Here I am, Lord. I want to be a
living part of your Body
forever!"

Ecumenism is the striving for unity among Christians. Jesus wants his Body to "be one" (Jn 17:21). St. Paul described Christians as having "one Lord, one faith, one baptism" (Eph 4:5). None of us today can be blamed for the old divisions in the Church. Nevertheless, we must not accept this state of brokenness. Christians know that they are connected through Baptism—that they are brothers and sisters in Christ. There is a great blessing whenever Christians take the first steps toward unity through prayer to our common Lord and acts of service.

What is the Church?
In addition to the Body of Christ, Holy Scripture has other beautiful images for the Church. Thus, the baptized are the People of God, made up of many nations, at whose center God himself lives. This image can speak to a world →

54 *Why is the Church holy?*

Only God is completely holy.
The Church is holy because
the holy God dwells within her and
works through her.

There are holy places,
for example, churches,
monasteries, and shrines.

There are holy occasions,
for example, when we receive Baptism
and Holy Communion
or when a couple is married in the Church.

There are holy people
who bring so much love into the world
that others see that
their love is from God.

The Church is holy only because of God.
The people in the Church
are a work in progress.
As they let Jesus help them
to become like him,
they gradually
become more and more holy.

→ marked by divisions. Another
image for the Church is the Bride
of Christ. For his Bride—and that
means for us—Christ gave up his
life. His love toward us is faithful
even when we are unfaithful.

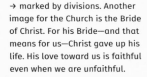

Saints are ...
- windows, through which God's light shines through into our world;
- the sun: they shine far beyond their own lives;
- bridges to heaven;
- trees that are rooted deep in God's mystery;
- reflectors on a bike: they shine God's light into the dark world;
- living road signs pointing the way to God; and,
- letters from the past that help us to change the present.

God can and will
forgive our sins.

55 *What is sin?*

**Sin is freely choosing
to do an evil action
while knowing
that one shouldn't do it.
Refusing to do a good action
while knowing that one
should do it, is also sin.**

I am a sinner. ... I am a sinner whom the Lord has looked upon.

This is what **Pope Francis** replied to a journalist who asked, "Who is Jorge Mario Bergoglio?" (Pope Francis' former name)

56 *What does sin do to us?*

**Every sin distances us from God,
from one another, and from ourselves.
Some sins are worse than others.**

Some sins are so serious that
they must be confessed to a priest
before receiving Communion.
Going to confession often
helps us to avoid sinning.

Everyone sins

All people have a dark side, and children do, too: "If we say we have no sin, we deceive ourselves, and the truth is not in us" (1 Jn 1:8). God asks us to be honest about our sins so that he can enter even our darkest corners and transform them into the pure light of his love. This is difficult to do, especially in a society that denies the reality of sin. **John Paul I** (1912–1978; "the smiling pope") adopted a serious tone when he said, "Banish God from the hearts of people; tell the children that sin is just a fairy tale, invented by their grandparents to make them meek as lambs; publish textbooks where God is not mentioned and his authority is mocked, but don't be surprised at the consequences."

57 *How does God deal with sin?*

**God hates sin,
but he loves sinners.**

He hates your sins
because they harm you
and others.
But God loves you so much
that he suffered and died for your sins.
Nothing can stop him from
loving you and offering you
his forgiveness.
But you need to accept it.

Confession: You'll find information about sin and confession in **Questions 81–87**. Also:

Questions 150–151, 224–239

At the end of the day
Before going to bed at night, think about the day with your child. Encourage your child to ask himself: What was good about the day? What did I do or not do? Together, thank God for all the good things that happened, and tell God that you are sorry for the ways you might have turned away from him. Ask for his help to do better tomorrow. His forgiveness helps both you and your child to fall asleep peacefully.

Η ΑΝΑCTACIC

... the resurrection of the body ...

Death is
not the end.
God is going to raise
all the dead.

58   *What happens to me when I die?*

When I die, my body decays,
but my → soul goes to meet God.
I can hope for heaven,
for a new life
that never ends.

After death, God himself
awaits us
with numberless angels
and saints and wonders
we can't imagine.
Heaven is eternal life with God.
It is unending joy,
because God himself is love.

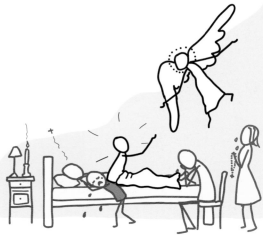

→ **Soul**
My soul is what is innermost to me, what
gives me my personality and my ability to
think and to choose. With it I encounter God.

Question 62: What is the Soul?

In the Mass for
the dead (requi-
em), there is this very
beautiful prayer:

May the Angels lead you into paradise;
may the martyrs welcome you at your
arrival, and lead you into the holy city, Jerusalem. May the choirs of Angels welcome you and
like Lazarus, who once was a poor man, may
you have eternal rest.

59 *Will we have bodies in heaven?*

**On the Last Day, at the end of the world,
God will give us back our bodies.
They will be like the body of Jesus
after his Resurrection.
We will be totally with God,
and we will no longer suffer from
sadness, pain, or death.**

After Jesus rose from the dead,
he showed himself to the disciples.
Jesus was not a ghost. He had a body.
He even ate with the apostles;
they were able to touch him.
We, too, will have an immortal body.
We will be as perfect and whole
as we always wanted to be.
We will be the way
God has always intended.

If you are particularly interested in the "last things":

Question 154: What happens to us when we die?

Question 157: Will we be brought to judgment after death?

Question 163: What is the Last Judgment?

Question 164: How will the world come to an end?

FACT
12 ... and life everlasting.

God wants me
to be with him completely.
There is a place for me in heaven.
With God, there is joy
without end.

60 *What is heaven like?*

**Heaven is
more beautiful
than any place
in the whole world.**

Sometimes people will say
that a certain place or moment
is so beautiful and peaceful that
it is "heaven on earth".
Think of a sunset, a rainbow,
a mother's hug, or a baby's smile.
These are glimpses of heaven.

And yet the heaven that awaits us
will be so much more than these signs
of God's love. God promises that he will
"wipe away every tear" from our eyes,
"and death shall be no more, neither shall
there be mourning nor crying
nor pain any more" (Rev 21:4).

Heaven

The fact that heaven awaits us is no cheap consolation; on the contrary, it is the greatest source of strength for Christians. We know that nothing we do now—no helpful deed, no tender gesture, no loving word—is in vain. We can begin good efforts even knowing that they will never be brought to completion in this life. We don't have to squeeze everything out of each opportunity. Thus, we peacefully work on making ourselves and the world better even though we know that perfection will become a reality only in heaven. By the way, it is exactly because of the mystery of evil that we should hope in heaven. Deep down we long for wrongdoing to be punished, goodness to be rewarded, illness and infirmity to disappear, and wars to end. But in this fallen world, this longing is never totally fulfilled. Only in heaven will everything be as it should be and suffering come to an end.

Being a good actor or a good producer: that's not going to ... get me into heaven. The most important thing ... is to be a good father, a good husband, and a good human being—a man who helps his fellow man and raises his kids to be good human beings too.
Mark Wahlberg
(*1971), American actor

61　*Will we be perfectly happy in heaven?*

Yes.

We long for happiness.
Many seek happiness in a loving family.
Some wish they could see a departed loved one again.
Some people dream of doing great things;
others of having lots of caring friends.
The sick want to be well,
while the hungry want more to eat.
Those suffering from injustice hope to see it end.

When you die, God will fulfill
your desires in *his own* way,
in a greater and more beautiful way
than you can even imagine.
God himself is the source of everything good,
and he will be your greatest joy.

Alfred Delp (1907–1945), Catholic priest, Jesuit, and resistance fighter against Hitler, asked on his way to his execution, "What's the news from the frontline?" His surprised companion was speechless. "Oh well," said Father Delp, "in half an hour I'll know more than you do!"

Your place in heaven will seem to be made for you, and you alone, because you were made for it.
C. S. Lewis

62 Who goes to heaven?

**All those who say yes to God's
mercy go to heaven;
those who say no do not.
Only God knows who is who.**

God's mercy is boundless.
He wants everyone to go to heaven,
and he gives everyone the
chance to accept his forgiveness.

After people accept God's mercy,
they still need to let his love free them
from the harm their sins have left behind,
such as bad habits or hardness of heart.
Sometimes after they die they need
to pass through → purgatory on their way to God.
We pray for the souls in purgatory,
that they will soon be in heaven.

→ **Purgatory**
Our image of purgatory as the purifying fire of God's love comes from the "burning pain" that overcomes us when we, for example, remember how we have let down a kind person. We could be in the same spot when we meet Christ. "Yet in the pain of this encounter, when the impurity and sickness of our lives becomes evident to us, there lies salvation. His gaze, the touch of his heart heals us through an undeniably painful transformation 'as through fire'." **Pope Benedict XVI,** Encyclical Letter *Spe Salvi*, November 30, 2007

 Every one who calls upon the name of the Lord will be saved.
Rom 10:13

63 What is the shortest summary of the faith?

**The shortest summary
of the faith is the Sign of the Cross:
In the name of the Father, and of the Son, and of the Holy Spirit.**

1

The Sign of the Cross starts with the right hand **up on your forehead**, with the Father in heaven. He created the world.

2

Your hand then goes **down, in the direction of the earth**, because Jesus Christ, the Son of God, became man. He shares the joy and the pain of this world with us.

3

Your hand first goes to your **left, to your heart**, where God's Holy Spirit dwells ...

4

... and then to your **right**, as a sign that God's liberating love embraces the whole world and doesn't leave out anything or anyone.

Amen!

> When an adult becomes a Catholic, in a special ceremony he is marked several times with the cross:

> Receive the cross on your forehead. It is Christ himself who now strengthens you with this sign of his love. Learn to know him and follow him.
> Receive the Sign of the Cross on your ears, that you may hear the voice of the Lord.
> Receive the Sign of the Cross on your eyes, that you may see the glory of God.
> Receive the Sign of the Cross on your lips, that you may respond to the word of God.
> Receive the Sign of the Cross over your heart, that Christ may dwell there by faith.
> Receive the Sign of the Cross on your shoulders, that you may bear the gentle yoke of Christ.
> Receive Sign of the Cross on your hands, that Christ may be known in the work that you do.
> Receive the Sign of the Cross on your feet, that you may walk in the way of Christ

Setting an example!

The Jamaican **Usain Bolt** (*1986) is probably the best sprinter who has ever lived. He has never hidden the fact that he is a Christian: "I thank God for everything that he has done for me."

"Brothers, before you begin your work, you must not neglect to make the Sign of the Cross, and you should not imitate the people who have no religion and who do not dare to do so because they are in company.

Through it, you will have the good fortune to call down the blessing of heaven on yourself and on everything you do.

St. Jean-Marie Vianney (1786–1859), parish priest of Ars, France

Part 2

CELEBRATING NEW LIFE IN CHRIST
THE
SACRAMENTS

7 Meetings
with God

How Jesus
makes us friends of God.
How he meets us
in the seven sacraments.
How we celebrate the sacraments correctly.
What exactly happens in them.

**Questions
64–109**

64 *What are sacraments?*

The → sacraments
are seven meetings with God.
God himself is present,
offering you his gifts
and guiding you deeper
into the community of the Church.

Some sacraments happen only once
and shape your entire life,
while others are received
repeatedly.

Baptism
The sacrament where Christ
welcomes you into new life
with him and you become
a member of his Body,
the Church; you become a
Christian.

Penance
The sacrament
where you confess
your sins and God
forgives you.

Eucharist
The sacrament where Christ
gives himself to you as
nourishment: you receive
the Body of Christ, and you
grow to be more and more
like him.

Confirmation
The sacrament where
God the Holy Spirit
makes you strong to
serve in the kingdom
of God.

Marriage
The sacrament where
God joins a baptized
man and a baptized
woman in his love.

 Recurring
Sacraments

Once-only
Sacraments

Holy orders
The sacrament where God
equips a man with his power and authority to serve
the Church in his name.

Anointing of the Sick
The sacrament where God
strengthens the sick and those
close to death.

→ **Sacraments** are holy signs of God's
action instituted by Christ. Through
them, God gives us his divine life,

which we call grace. Their words,
symbols, and gestures signify what
they bring about.

More on this:
Question 173: Why do we need
sacraments in the first place?

Baptism

Baptism is the sacrament
where Christ welcomes you
into new life with him
and you become a member
of his Body, the Church.
You become a Christian.

65 *How is Baptism administered?*

At Baptism, the person to be baptized
is immersed in water three times
or water is poured over the head three times.
While this is happening, the baptismal words,
which Jesus has instructed us to say, are said:

> → **N., I baptize you**
> **in the name of the Father**
> **and of the Son**
> **and of the Holy Spirit.**

Other symbols at Baptism are
the anointing with chrism, a blessed oil;
the clothing in a white garment;
and the lighting of a baptismal candle.

Parents, siblings, godparents, and guests
sing and pray for the person being baptized.
Everyone is happy.

→ N. stands for the
name of the person
to be baptized.

Baptism is our birth as children of Holy
Mother Church. I would like to ask you a
question: Who among you knows
the day you were baptized? So
few, so few … now, here is your
homework!
Pope Francis, October 4, 2013

Nick watched the christening of a
ship with a champagne bottle on
television. When a newborn cousin was
about to be baptized, he asked his mother,
"But how can you do that with a baby,
when his head is so fragile?"

66 *What does Baptism do for me?*

Water gives life.
You emerge from the baptismal water
as a newborn Christian!
You have risen with Christ.
Now you belong to him.

Water cleanses.
In the sign of the water,
God washes away sin,
including → original sin.

From now on, you are under the protection
of the Father, the Son, and the Holy Spirit.
You have been received
into the family of God, the Church.

Chrism shows how important you are to God,
because only priests, kings, and prophets
were anointed with this blessed oil.
Being anointed is also like being rubbed with
the strength and the protection of God—
like a baby to prevent rashes or
a wrestler to make him unbeatable.

The white garment says that God clothes you in his love,
which makes you pure and beautiful.
"For as many of you as were baptized into Christ
have put on Christ" (Gal 3:27).

The baptismal candle says that
you are now the "light of the world" (Mt 5:14).

→ On the topic of original sin:
   see also **Question 22**

> Can a person baptize him
> or herself? No one can be
self-baptized! No one. We can ask
for it, desire it, but we always need
someone else to confer this Sacrament in the name of the Lord. For
Baptism is a gift which is bestowed
in a context of care and fraternal sharing. Throughout history, one baptizes
another ... it is a chain.
Pope Francis, January
8, 2014

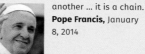

67 *Who may administer Baptism?*

Normally a → priest or a deacon baptizes.
When someone is in danger of death, anyone
may baptize.

This is the simplest form of Baptism:
water is poured over the head
of the person to be baptized,
and the baptismal formula is said.

 68 *Why are babies baptized, when they can't*
make their decisions themselves?

Baptism is a gift from God.
Faithful parents accept this gift
because they want the best for their child.

That is why they have
said yes to God and to Baptism
in your name.
Today, you can
say yes to God yourself.

You can be sure that
before you choose God,
he has already
chosen you.

→ See **Question 95**

ℹ A true story about the value of Baptism: Recently, in Mali, a priest was preparing forty people for Baptism. In the last few weeks before Easter, they lived close to the church in order to prepare for Baptism together. That didn't go unnoticed. At night, the pastor received threatening phone calls: If these people are baptized, anything might happen. The priest told the people about it and said, "I won't be angry with you if you leave, because I know that you have families!" None of the forty went away. One of them said, "We want to be baptized—with water or with blood." They were baptized—with water. Fortunately, to this day, nothing bad has been done to them.

ℹ Children sometimes ask: **Why is that kid in my class not baptized?** For one thing, the child might not be from a Christian family that baptizes very young children. But sometimes even Catholic parents have not given the gift of Baptism to their children. Perhaps they are not practicing their faith, or they think it would be better for their children to decide the matter for themselves. We know that God loves these parents and their children. Let us pray that they discover God's love and decide to draw closer to him.

69 What is a godparent?

A godparent is a believing, confirmed Catholic who helps his godchild to become a faithful Christian.

When a child is named for a saint, that person becomes the child's special friend in heaven.
If you do not have a saint's name, you can ask your favorite saint to be your patron.

In prayer, you can ask your patron saint for help.
On your patron saint's feast day, you can celebrate with your family and friends!

Quiz!

Who is this saint?
He is a very well-known saint and the patron saint of children. Another well-known man, who makes his appearance in December, is named after him. Well? → Do you know the answer?

---

i Sharing the faith
The faith passes from generation to generation and from heart to heart. Pope Francis said, "We cannot spread the Gospel of Jesus without the concrete witness of our lives." In order to pass along the faith to the next generation, parents and godparents must strive to practice it themselves. As St. John wrote, "That ... which we have heard, which we have seen with our eyes, which we have looked upon and touched with our hands, concerning the word of life—[we] testify to it, and proclaim to you the eternal life" (1 Jn 1:1–2).

i Actions speak louder than words. Thus the French Catholic author **Paul Claudel** (1868–1955) once said,

"Speak about Christianity when you are asked. But live so that people ask about Christ."

→ Solution to the Quiz on page 232.

Confirmation
is the sacrament where
God the Holy Spirit
makes you strong to serve
in the kingdom of God.
You can serve God
right now, right where you are.

70 *How is Confirmation celebrated?*

**The bishop places his hands
over the person to be confirmed
and calls down the → Holy Spirit.
Then he anoints
the person with chrism,
drawing the Sign of the Cross
on his forehead.
He calls the person by name
and says,**

The sponsor stands behind the person as he is confirmed,
with his hand gently placed upon the person's shoulder.

Sealed with the Holy Spirit?
In the past, an author of an important letter or document sealed it with a drop of hot beeswax or resin, which he impressed with a mark that confirmed his identity. When a person is confirmed, he is sealed with the gift of the Holy Spirit. This "mark" shows that he identifies with Christ, belongs to him, and is under his protection as he enters his service.

→ See also **Question 47:** Who is the Holy Spirit?, **Question 48:** What does the Holy Spirit look like? and **Question 49:** How do we know that the Holy Spirit is within us?

71 *What does Confirmation do for me?*

**Confirmation fills you with the Holy Spirit.
He becomes your source of strength
and your interior guide.
The Holy Spirit continues
the saving work he began at your Baptism.**

The word "confirmation" comes from *firmare,*
the Latin word meaning "to strengthen".
The Holy Spirit strengthens you in your faith.
He helps you to know God
and to do what is right.
He gives you the ability
to stay true to Christ
and to tell others about him.
You need his help for that.
If you listen to him,
the Holy Spirit is like
an interior navigation system
that shows you the way through life.

" The Holy Spirit is first
incredibly tender and sweet.
He does not force anything, he does
not impose himself. He is rather like
someone who courts you and invites
you. For example, he invites you to
get to know Jesus better. He invites
you to pray, which means, to learn to be
in conversation with Jesus. He also invites
you simply to be good to
the people around you.
Bishop Stefan Oster (*1965)
in a Confirmation homily

" What you wish to
ignite in others
must first burn within
yourself.
St. Augustine

Who administers Confirmation?

The bishop, the successor of the apostles, administers Confirmation.

But a bishop can commission a priest to administer Confirmation in his place.

 What is a Confirmation sponsor?

A Confirmation sponsor is a believing, confirmed Catholic who helps the person being confirmed to be a → convicted and convincing Christian.

Godparents do the same thing, so they may be chosen as Confirmation sponsors. But you also may choose a new sponsor.

→ **What characterizes a convicted Christian?**
1. He knows the faith.
2. He practices the faith.
3. He shares the faith with others.

i **Testimony of Faith:** The inter-generational contract is not about whether or not today's teenagers will one day be in a position to feed tomorrow's elderly, but about whether or not the

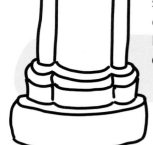 adults have sufficiently nourished the teenagers with the contents of the faith.
Manfred Kock (*1936), Lutheran theologian and bishop

" Live what you have understood from the Gospels. Even if it is very little. But live it.
Brother Roger Schutz (1915–2005),

 founder and prior of Taizé, an ecumenical Christian monastic fraternity in France.

The Eucharist
is the sacrament
where Christ gives himself
to you as nourishment:
you receive Christ,
and you grow to be
more and more like him.

74 *What is the Eucharist?*

**The Eucharist
is the sacrament where
Jesus Christ gives us
his Body and Blood
under the signs of
bread and wine.
In this way we are united
with him and his Church.**

Because Jesus is in everyone
who receives him,
they belong together
like brothers and sisters in
a big family.
The new life in Christ,
begun at Baptism,
is nourished by the Eucharist.
The members of the Church
grow together in Christ.

> Let nothing be put be-
> fore the work of God.
> **Rule of St. Benedict**

Sunday and the Eucharist

The origin of the Church is not a few Christians getting together to do something. The origin of the Church is Jesus, who invites us to receive him in the Eucharist, especially on Sundays. By eating the Body of Christ, we become the Body of Christ, which is the Church. "Our participation in the Body and Blood of Christ aspires to nothing other than to become what we receive" (Pope Leo I, around 400–461). That is why the Eucharist is the "source and summit of the Christian life" (Second Vatican Council) and nothing else can replace it.

75 *What happens in Holy Mass?*

**Holy Mass is a miracle:
it makes present to us the saving
death and Resurrection of Jesus.
With Jesus, our risen Lord,
we celebrate his feast of → thanksgiving.**

On the night before Jesus died,
he celebrated the → Passover
with his disciples.
This meal was his Last Supper.
He took → bread and wine,
gave thanks, and
said these incredible words:

This is my bod[y]

→ The word **"Eucharist"** comes from the Greek word for **"thanksgiving"**. At the Last Supper with his disciples, Jesus gave thanks to God.

→ **Passover** is the great Jewish feast that celebrates the time when God freed his people from slavery in Egypt. You can read about the first Passover in chapter 12 of the Book of Exodus.

→ The small pieces of bread used at Mass are called **hosts**. The word "host" comes from the Latin word *hostia* (= victim, offering). Jesus takes on the appearance of bread in order to re-present his sacrifice to God on our behalf. Then he offers himself to us.

Holy Mass
When **St. Bonaventure** (1221–1274) was asked to explain the Holy Mass, he said it is Jesus saying to us, "I gave myself to you, give yourself to me!" The Eucharist is like marriage. Jesus, the Bridegroom, gives his life for his Bride, the Church. We accept his love and love him in return.

In every Mass, the priest repeats
the words of Jesus over bread and wine.
Through the Holy Spirit, bread and wine
become the Body and Blood of Jesus.

In every Holy Mass,
Jesus' death and Resurrection
become present to us: we meet
the crucified and risen Lord
and unite ourselves with him
by going to → Communion.

It is not like TV,
where we see for the hundredth time
a rerun of an old movie.
Through Holy Mass,
we are truly present at
the death and Resurrection of Jesus.

This is my blood.

→ **Communion** comes from Latin *communio* (= union, community). When we receive the Body and Blood of Christ in Communion, we become one with Jesus Christ and with our sisters and brothers in union with him.

There are days when Mass becomes difficult for you. Offer your body up to *him* then, since your presence is already a sign of your desire to praise your Lord, which you are unable to put into effect at that moment. Believe in the presence of Christ in you, even if you don't feel it.
Brother Roger Schutz

76 *How is Holy Mass celebrated?*

God holds a feast for us. As you enter his house, the church, make the Sign of the Cross with holy water and think about your Baptism, which was the door you entered to become a Christian. Notice the red light next to the tabernacle. It is the sign that Jesus is present and waiting for you. As you pass by, greet him by genuflecting.

First Part of Holy Mass: The Liturgy of the Word

The bells ring; the music starts. The priest and the altar servers process to the altar. They are wearing special clothes because they are doing divine things now. Together, we greet God with a song.

At the beginning of every Holy Mass we **confess our sins.** If we are truly sorry for them, God says, "Forgiven and forgotten!" (Very serious sins, however, must be confessed to a priest before receiving Communion.) We call out: **Lord, have mercy** (or in Greek, *Kyrie eleison*).

Now we can do something for others: pray along with the **intercessions** from the bottom of your heart. You can also quietly tell God your own prayer intentions for your family members and friends. God hears you.

The **Creed,** the profession of faith, comes after the homily. We stand with all the courageous and faithful believers down through the ages and throughout the world and say, "This is true. We believe it."

Gloria!!

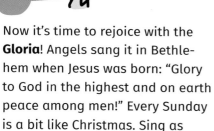

Now it's time to rejoice with the **Gloria**! Angels sang it in Bethlehem when Jesus was born: "Glory to God in the highest and on earth peace among men!" Every Sunday is a bit like Christmas. Sing as loudly as you can!

Now we may sit down. Perk up your ears! Something is being read to us. Don't worry, the **readings** from the Bible are not supposed to put you to sleep! "The word of God is living and active, sharper than any two-edged sword" (Heb 4:12). God wants to tell us something, perhaps console us, encourage us, or challenge us.

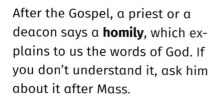

After the Gospel, a priest or a deacon says a **homily**, which explains to us the words of God. If you don't understand it, ask him about it after Mass.

Now, the **Gospel** is proclaimed: Jesus himself speaks to us. Alleluia! That's why everyone stands up. Listen closely! Imagine you are a few yards from Jesus—like Zacchaeus, who climbed a tree to see the Lord better—and Jesus calls out to you and says: "Come to me. I want to dine with you today."

The Second Part of Holy Mass: The Liturgy of the Eucharist

When the priest goes to the altar, the second part of the Mass begins. It is the **gift-giving** part: God gives himself to us. We give ourselves to God.

We bring the **gifts** of bread and wine to the altar. With these offerings, we bring ourselves, our good will, our dreams, our worries … "Lord, take everything and make the best of it!" Now we stand up. Because Holy Mass is nearing its peak.

The body of Christ. Amen.

The moments after Jesus has come to you belong to you and him. At the end of Holy Mass, there is a **blessing** and the **dismissal**: "Go forth in peace!" After Holy Mass, we have every reason to look more cheerful than we did before.

Now it's time for **Communion**! How am I, a small human being, supposed to receive our great God? We say: "Lord, I am not worthy that you should enter under my roof; but only say the word, and my soul shall be healed!" (see the words of the Roman centurion in Lk 7:6).

Holy!

Peace be with you

Our Father who art in heaven...

The **Eucharistic Prayer** begins with the **Sanctus**: "Holy, holy, holy ..." About 2,700 years ago, the prophet Isaiah had a vision of God and his angels. He heard the angels singing this beautiful song. Now with the angels and the saints, we sing the same song. Our loved ones already in heaven are singing it, too.

Heaven and earth are united at the **Consecration**, when bread and wine become the Body and Blood of Christ. The crucified and risen Lord is made present. While this is happening, we kneel, full of reverence, in humble awe before this miracle.

Jesus gives us the gift of his peace, which we pass on to each other in the **Sign of Peace**.
In the **Agnus Dei** (Latin for "Lamb of God"), we thank Jesus, who like an innocent lamb let himself be killed on the Cross to give us the gift of forgiveness and peace.

After the great **Amen**, we stand to pray the **Our Father** together. We are happy that big and small, tall and short, old and young may call God their Father. We all are children of the one Father.

77 How does Jesus come to us in bread and wine?

**Through the power of his words
and the working of his Holy Spirit,
Jesus is made present.
At the Last Supper, Jesus took bread
and said, "This is my body!"
He took wine and said, "This is my blood!"**

**Jesus keeps his promises.
That is why the priest takes
bread and wine just as Jesus did
at the Last Supper
and says the words of Jesus over them.
Then bread is no longer bread,
but the Body of Christ.
The wine is no longer wine,
but the Blood of Christ.**

What we eat looks like bread,
but it is Jesus who comes to us.
What we drink looks like wine,
but again, it is Jesus.
God comes to us
and gives us his eternal life.

For more than 2,000 years
the Church has been repeating and believing
the words of Jesus at Holy Mass.

 I am the living bread which came down from heaven; if any one eats of this bread, he will live for ever; and the bread which I shall give for the life of the world is my flesh.
Jn 6:51

Real Presence
In the Gospel of John, when Jesus called himself the "bread of life", which must be eaten to have eternal life, many of his disciples were shocked: "This is a hard saying; who can listen to it?" (6:60). In fact, "many of his disciples drew back and no longer walked with him" (6:66). Jesus said to his twelve apostles, "Will you also go away?" Peter answered for them and for all believers down to the present day: "Lord, to whom shall we go? You have the words of eternal life" (6:67–68).

Whoever receives the Holy Eucharist loses himself in God like a drop of water in the ocean. The two can no longer be divided. If after Communion someone surprised us with the question: "What are you carrying home with you?", we could answer:

 "We are carrying heaven with us."
St. Jean-Marie Vianney
(1786–1859), parish priest of Ars, France

78 *What is Communion?*

**"Communion" is from a Latin word
that means "community".
When we receive the Body of the Lord,
a holy community is created
between him and us.**

Our great God makes himself very small—
and you very big!
The one whom
the universe cannot contain
enters your mouth and your heart.
That is Communion, and it
brings about a community between us and Jesus,
and between us and all the other people
who receive him.

He who eats my flesh and drinks my blood abides in me, and I in him. As the living Father sent me, and I live because of the Father, so he who eats me will live because of me
Jn 6:56

Prepare to receive Holy Communion with a prayer like this:
Yes, Lord,
come to me!
Enter my heart!
Come and make me strong—
strong, loving, courageous, and loyal.
Lord, I am ready
to receive you.

Friends leave behind a sign, perhaps a ring, but Christ leaves us his Body and his Blood, his Soul and his Divinity, himself, without holding back anything.
St. Bernardino of Siena
(1380–1404)

79 *What do I do when Jesus the Lord comes to me in Holy Mass?*

**Receive the Lord
by preparing yourself
inside and out.
Show him that you are looking
forward to meeting him
by dressing up in nice clothes
and, if necessary, by going to confession.
Also, be respectful during Mass
with a prayerful heart.**

Things that don't belong in a church:

Olalalaaa Laleeeeelalaaa!

> The day of my First Holy Communion was one of the most beautiful days of my life.... Not only because of our nice clothes or the gifts we receive, nor because of the parties! It is above all because, that day, we receive Jesus Christ for the first time.... I should welcome him with love and listen closely to him. In the depths of my heart, I can tell him, for example, "Jesus, I know that you love me.... I give you all my joys, my troubles, and my future."
> **Pope Benedict XVI**, November 19, 2011

Genuflection
Bending one's knee before the presence of Christ in the tabernacle is a sign of reverence. Here is a beautiful prayer for this moment—and not only for children:
"Jesus, I greet you.
But you bless me!"

This is how Jesus enters your heart

Imagine that Jesus arranges a meeting with you.
With you, of all people!

Before Communion

Tell Jesus how happy you are that he is coming to you:
he, whom wind and waves, animals and people,
sickness, and even death obey;
he, the great God, who makes himself very small;
he who enters under your roof
and remains in your heart.

After Communion

Go back to your place and kneel.
Close your eyes. Look at him. He is looking at you.
Thank him for entering your heart.
Tell him what is important to you, what is beautiful,
what is difficult, what is sad.
Bring people to him in prayer,
especially the sick and all those who are in need.
Ask him to help you to keep your good resolutions.
Finally, thank him for all that is good in your life.

80 *Why do Catholics go to Mass on Sunday?*

Sunday is the day of Jesus' Resurrection.
Since the time of the apostles,
Christians have gathered on that day
to thank and worship God.
We celebrate Holy Mass
to meet Jesus in his words
and in Holy Communion.

If you go to Mass every Sunday,
Jesus will help you
to grow into a real Christian.
You might not feel it right away,
but that's the case with growing.
You don't notice it; then suddenly
your shoes are too small for you.
Sometimes it seems that nothing is happening
when you pray or go to Mass,
but slowly your faith grows.
Little by little, you become a strong Christian.

A girl once asked **Pope Benedict XVI** about what she could say to her parents so that they would take her to Mass on Sunday. He answered, "With a daughter's respect and love, you could say to them: 'Dear Mommy, dear Daddy, it is so important for us all, even for you, to meet Jesus. ... Let's find a little time together, we can find an opportunity." October 15, 2005

Let us consider how to stir up one another to love and good works, not neglecting to meet together, as is the habit of some, but encouraging one another. **Heb 10:24–25**

SACRAMENT 4 Penance

The sacrament of Penance,
confession,
is where God forgives
all your sins
and reconciles you
with the community.

81 *What's so bad about sin?*

**Sin separates us from
God and others.
It leads us away
from goodness and love.
Every sin causes harm.
It injures not only the person
who sins but everyone else, too.**

A small sin is a minor and
thoughtless action done
out of laziness, cowardice, anger,
envy, jealousy,
or other bad habits.

A grave, or serious, sin
is a very bad action
that is freely
and knowingly chosen.

Someone who has committed
a grave sin must confess it
before receiving Communion.
It helps us to confess
small sins, too.

Sin and mistakes

Sin, which is a freely chosen act of the will, must not be downplayed by calling it a mistake. Mistakes and sins are two different things. A mistake is not a sin, but an error, like adding numbers incorrectly or forgetting to send someone a birthday card. Jesus didn't come to correct our mistakes; he came to die for our sins and to give us the gift of forgiveness.

Can we learn from our sins?

We say that we learn from our mistakes. Do we also learn from our sins? Look at the story Jesus told of the Prodigal Son (see Lk 15:11–32). After the young man goes astray and wastes all of his money on behaving badly, he finds that he is miserable. He comes to his senses and returns home to his father, sorry for his sins. His father gladly welcomes him and forgives him everything. We can safely suppose that the young man has learned an important lesson the hard way.

82 *Do our sins hurt God?*

**God loves everything he has created.
That's why with every sin,
it's as if it were done to God himself.**

God lovingly empathizes
with every human being.
Jesus says: "As you did it
to one of the least of these my brethren,
you did it to me" (Mt 25:40).

Whenever you are mean, tell a lie,
steal, or cheat, for example,
you are hurting God's children:
yourself and your brothers and sisters,
and this offends God.

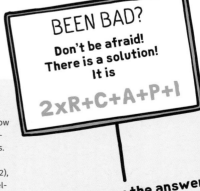

BEEN BAD?
Don't be afraid!
There is a solution!
It is

$2 \times R + C + A + P + I$

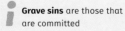 **Grave sins** are those that are committed
- knowingly,
- deliberately,
- and against God's will in a serious matter.

Question 315: What is a sin in the first place?

" God loves us the way we are. But he loves us too much to leave us that way.
Leighton Ford (*1931), Canadian Presbyterian minister and author

" We shall never learn to know ourselves except by endeavoring to know God: for, beholding His greatness, we realize our littleness.
 St. Teresa of Avila (1515–1582), Spanish Carmelite and mystic

You don't know the answer?
The solution is on the following page!

The solution—quite simply: **2xR+C+A+P+I = <u>Confession!!</u>**

  83 *How do you make a good confession?*

Reflection and **R**epentance

Confession starts
with reflection,
with an examination of conscience.

You think about
the bad things you have done
and the good things
you have not done.

You are sorry,
and you resolve
never to commit
these sins again.
This turning away from sin
is repentance.
You can write down
your sins on a piece of paper
so that you will remember
to confess them.

Confession

You go to the priest
and ask for forgiveness.
As the priest blesses you,
you make the Sign of the Cross.
Say when your last confession was.
List your sins—you can read from
your piece of paper, if you like.
Say when you are finished.
Say that you are sorry.

GRRRRRRR!!

Absolution

Now, it's the priest's turn.
He talks to you.
He might ask you a question or two.
He gives you a task, a penance,
to do afterward.
This is a prayer or an action that
can help you undo the harm done
by your sins.
Then he says by the power of Jesus:

Penance and Improvement

Go and do the penance
the priest gave you as soon
as you can.
Take with you the firm
resolution to do better.
Ask God to be the source
of your improvement.

.... I absolve you
from your sins
in the name of the Father,
and of the Son,
and of the Holy Spirit.

You are free!
God has forgiven you everything.
Between you and God, it is as if
you had never done anything bad.
Now you can begin
again.

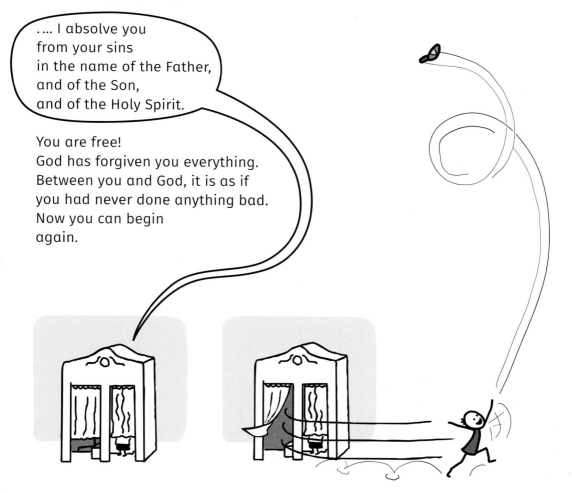

84   *Is the priest allowed to tell what he has heard in confession?*

Never! Under no circumstance! Absolutely not!

It is a very strict rule
that priests may never tell
what they have heard in confession.
That is called the seal of confession.
Some priests have allowed themselves to be killed
rather than violate the seal of confession.

You can absolutely rely on
the priest to keep the seal of confession.
He may not even tell the police
about a murder
that was confessed to him.

ST. JONN OF NEPOMUK

---

i Seal of confession
There is a whole list of priests who preferred to accept death as a martyr rather than break the seal of confession. St. John of Nepomuk (1340–1393), the patron saint of confessors, is said to have been executed because he didn't want to tell the king what the queen had confessed to him. According to legend, King Wenceslaus had him drowned in the river Vltava. In remembrance of his loyalty to the seal of confession and the manner of his death, there are statues of him on many bridges.

i Absolute duty to remain silent
The seal of confession is in canon law, as a sort of "oldest data security regulation in the history of law." John F. Jungclaussen, (*1970), historian and journalist

85 *What does confession do for me?*

**Confession
reconciles you with God
and the community of the Church
and gives you the gift of
a new beginning.**

It is freeing for me
to say openly and honestly
what I have done wrong.
It is even more freeing
to hear with my own ears
that God has forgiven me.

99 All who are frequent in
confessing and take great
value in this matter, indeed are
praiseworthy.

Maimonides
(1135–1204), Jewish
philosopher

99 Confession is like a broom
which sweeps away the dirt
and leaves the surface brighter and
clearer.

Mahatma Gandhi (1869–
1948), Hindu leader
who led the nonviolent
Indian independence
movement

99 In confession there occurs a
breakthrough to new life. The
break with the past is made when sin
is hated, confessed, and forgiven.

Dietrich Bonhoeffer
(1906–1945), German
Lutheran pastor who
resisted Nazism

86 *Why should I confess to a priest?*

**Jesus, who knows what is good for us,
said to the apostles:
"If you forgive the sins of any,
they are forgiven;
if you retain the sins of any,
they are retained" (Jn 20:23).
Today, this task that belonged to the apostles
now belongs to priests.**

Even if it is difficult for us—
it is good to look closely at and to confess
what weighs on our conscience.

After all, we don't actually confess
to a priest, but to God.
The priest is God's representative.
He lends God his ear and his voice.
He also stands for the Church,
which we have weakened
with our sin.

God alone can forgive
sins, but he chooses to
do so through his priests.

 Some people say, "I have done too much evil, God can't forgive me." That's grave blasphemy. It means to impose a limit on God's mercy. But it doesn't have one: it is limitless. Nothing insults God as much as doubting his mercy.
St. Jean-Marie Vianney (1786–1859), parish priest of Ars, France

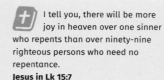 I tell you, there will be more joy in heaven over one sinner who repents than over ninety-nine righteous persons who need no repentance.
Jesus in Lk 15:7

87 *Is it a sin if I feel like doing something forbidden?*

No.
It is only a temptation.
Resisting a temptation
is a great achievement.
It causes great joy in heaven.
You can be happy about it, too.

It is a temptation
to want to take
the ball that doesn't belong to you.
It is a temptation
to want to watch a forbidden video in secret.
It is a temptation
to want to embarrass
the know-it-all in your class.
If you don't do the evil you are tempted to do,
you are a conqueror of evil.
Just like Jesus in the desert.

Read with your children the story of Jesus' temptation in the desert: **Lk 4:1–13**

Be watchful, stand firm in your faith, be courageous, be strong.
1 Cor 16:13

" Temptations usually comes in through a door that has deliberately been left open.
Arnold H. Glasow (1905-1998), American businessman and humorist

" All men can be criminals, if tempted; all men can be heroes, if inspired.
G.K. Chesterton (1874–1936), English writer and journalist

Anointing of the Sick

The Anointing of the Sick
is the sacrament
where God, with his power,
comes to the aid
of the sick and those
close to death.

88 *What does the Anointing of the Sick do for me?*

**The Anointing of the Sick gives you the gift of
consolation, peace, and strength.
You meet Jesus, who strengthens you.
Sometimes sick people
are healed by this sacrament.**

The Anointing of the Sick
is for those who are very sick or
in danger of death from illness or old age.
Those who are about to leave this life
should confess their sins
and receive the Eucharist
as *viaticum*, which is Latin for
"provision for the journey".

This sacrament helps the sick person
to bear the hardship of suffering.
It helps the dying person to pass from this life in peace.
Jesus is the only one
who can accompany us in dying
and guide us through death to heavenly life.

> May God accompany you on
> your way; may he give you
> strength when you are ill, may he
> console you when you are sad, and
> may he rejoice with you when you
> are doing well.
> **Irish blessing**

> I think that illnesses are keys that
> can open certain doors to us. I be-
> lieve that there are certain
> doors that only an illness
> can open.
> **André Gide** (1869–1951),
> French writer

And they cast out many
demons, and anointed
with oil many that were sick and
healed them.
Mk 6:13

89 *How is the Anointing of the Sick celebrated?*

**The priest anoints the forehead and the hands
of the sick person with holy oil.
While doing so, he speaks the words:**

> **Through this holy anointing
> may the Lord in his love and mercy
> help you with the grace of the Holy Spirit.
> May the Lord who frees you from sin
> save you and raise you up.**

The Gospels show that
Jesus cared especially for
the sick. He made many people
whole in body and soul.
Jesus continues to heal people today
through his Church.
In the person of the priest,
Jesus gives his strength to the
sick and the dying.

 Jesus went about all the cities and villages,
teaching in their synagogues and preaching
the gospel of the kingdom, and healing every disease
and every infirmity. When he saw the crowds, he had
compassion for them, because they were harassed and
helpless, like sheep without a shepherd.
Mt 9:35–36

90 *Who administers the Anointing of the Sick?*

**The Anointing of the Sick
is administered by
bishops and priests.**

91 *How often may one receive the Anointing of the Sick?*

As often as one needs it.

The Anointing of the Sick may be received
when one is seriously ill,
especially when one's condition becomes worse.
It doesn't matter if one is young or old.
When suffering from a serious illness
or infirmity and before operations, people
may ask for the Anointing of the Sick.

 There is a very beautiful
prayer for sick people by
Karl Rahner (1904–1984) which
children are also
able to understand,
especially if some-
one in the family is
seriously ill:

"Do not let me grow bitter
but mature, patient, selfless, mild, and full of longing
for that land where there is no suffering
and for that day when you will wipe away every tear
from the eyes of those who have loved you
and in pain have believed in your love
and at night have believed in your light."

 Is any among
you sick? Let him
call for the elders of the
Church, and let them pray
over him, anointing him
with oil in the name of the
Lord.
Jas 5:14

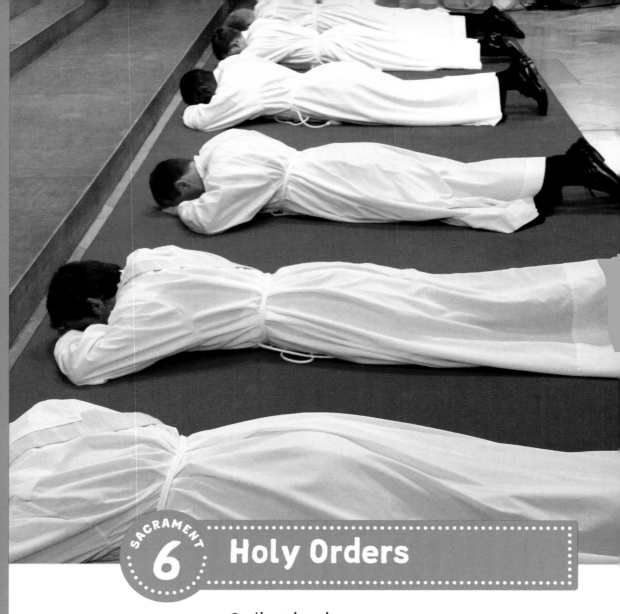

Holy Orders

Ordination is
the sacrament
where God
equips men, as he did his apostles,
with full power and authority
to serve the Church in his name.

92 *What happens in the sacrament of Holy Orders?*

**At ordination, men
who have been called by Christ
and his Church are given full authority
to serve the community of believers
on behalf of Jesus.**

They do so as bishops,
priests, or deacons.

93 *What is a bishop?*

**A bishop is a successor of the apostles
and Jesus' representative
in his → local area.
The pope is a bishop, too,
the bishop of the diocese of Rome.
One has to be a priest
before he can become a bishop.**

Just as Jesus taught people, guided them,
and helped them to become holy,
the bishop teaches, leads,
and sanctifies his people.
The priests and deacons
are his helpers.

→ The **local area** of a
bishop is called a
diocese.

 The ministers of the Gospel must be people
who can warm the hearts of the people, who
walk through the dark night with them, who know
how to dialogue and to descend themselves into their
people's night, into the darkness, but
without getting lost. The people of God
want pastors, not clergy acting like
bureaucrats or government officials.
Pope Francis, August 19, 2013

And they prayed and said,
"Lord, you know the hearts of
all men, show which one of these two
you have chosen to take the place in
this ministry and apostleship from
which Judas turned aside."
Acts 1:24–25a

94 What is a → pope?

**The pope is the successor
of St. Peter. Jesus said to him,
"You are Peter, and on this rock
I will build my Church. ...
I will give you the keys to the kingdom of heaven;
and whatever you bind on earth
shall be bound in heaven,
and whatever you loose on earth
shall be loosed in heaven"** (Mt 16:18–19).
**That is why he is first among all bishops
and Christ's representative on earth.**

→ The word **"pope"** comes from Greek *papas* (= father).

" Anyone can become a pope. Look at me!
St. John XXIII (1881–1963)

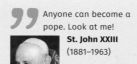

How many popes have there been up to today? In Rome, in the Basilica of St. Paul Outside the Walls, there is a long row of pictures—from the first pope (St. Peter) all the way to his 266th successor: Pope Francis.

95 *What are priests?*

**Priests are men
called by Jesus for a very
special role in the Church:
to bring God closer to his people
and his people closer to God.**

Jesus gives us the gift of himself
through the priest in the Eucharist.
Jesus forgives us our sins through the priest.
Jesus anoints and strengthens the sick
through the priest.

Perhaps a priest is no better at driving a car,
cooking, thinking, or speaking than other people.
But in very special moments,
namely, when he administers the sacraments,
every priest is a representative of God:
Jesus acts through him.

When I think of the parish priests who knew the names of their parishioners, who went to visit them; even as one of them told me: "I know the name of each family's dog." ... What could be more beautiful than this?
Pope Francis, October 4, 2015

The priest is a monstrance: his role is to show Jesus. He himself must disappear and allow only Jesus to be seen.
Blessed Charles de Foucauld

i Because of the greatness of their vocation and the special trust people place in priests, every abuse of this trust is an especially grave sin.

96 *Who can become a priest?*

**Every baptized and confirmed man
can become a priest
if God calls him and the Church
commissions and consecrates him.**

God has a plan for each of us.
If God calls a man to be a priest,
he makes this calling known in his heart.
Some already hear it as children.
Many experience their calling
as young adults.
Some are called by God's voice
from out of the midst of their professional lives
into the service of God
and his people.

97 *What is a → deacon?*

**Deacons help bishops
and priests with their service.
Some deacons
care for
the poor, the sick,
or those in prison.
Some teach the faith
and assist at Mass.**

→ **Deacon** means "servant" (from the Greek word *diakonia*, "service"). An ancient Syrian book describes the deacon as the "bishop's eyes, mouth, heart, and soul."

✝ In these days when the disciples were increasing in number, the Hellenists murmured against the Hebrews because their widows were neglected in the daily distribution. And the Twelve summoned the body of the disciples and said, "It is not right that we should give up preaching the word of God to serve tables. Therefore, brethren, pick out from among you seven men of good repute, full of the Spirit and of wisdom, whom we may appoint to this duty. But we will devote ourselves to prayer and to the ministry of the word." And what they said pleased the whole multitude, and they chose Stephen, a man full of faith and of the Holy Spirit, and Philip, and Prochorus, and Nicanor, and Timon, and Parmenas, and Nicolaus, a proselyte of Antioch. These they set before the apostles, and they prayed and laid their hands upon them. And the word of God increased; and the number of the disciples multiplied greatly in Jerusalem, and a great many of the priests were obedient to the faith. **Acts 6:1–7**

98 *Why don't priests and bishops marry?*

Bishops and priests are called to live like Jesus:
Jesus was not married.
He lived only for God
in order to save us.
Jesus was available to everyone.

Giving up marriage and family
is a strong sign that
God is greater than everything.
That is called living in → celibacy.

99 *What are religious?*

Religious are people
who give their lives to God
by promising to live by
poverty, chastity, and obedience.

These are the evangelical counsels, so called
because in the Gospels Jesus repeatedly
counsels certain people to live his way of life.
Through poverty, chastity, and obedience,
religious show that they love God more than anything
and want to help all people
to know God's love.

→ The word "**celibacy**" comes from Latin *caelebs* (= alone, unmarried). This word by itself is not enough to express the fact that priests are "married" to God. Their love belongs to God alone in order to serve his people, the Church, in an undivided way. That's the reason they do not marry.

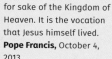

" Family life is the vocation that God inscribed into the nature of man and woman, and there is another vocation which is complementary to marriage: the call to celibacy and virginity for sake of the Kingdom of Heaven. It is the vocation that Jesus himself lived. **Pope Francis,** October 4, 2013

" As soon as I believed that there was a God, I understood that I could live only for him. **Blessed Charles de Foucauld**

100 Can women be priests?

**No. Because Jesus called only men to be apostles,
from the Church's beginning,
only men can be consecrated as priests.
But women were part of
Jesus' closest circle of friends.
Men and women are equal
in his eyes.**

**Mary carries Jesus in
her womb and rejoices
with her pregnant cousin,
Elizabeth.**
(see Lk 1:39–56)

**Jesus mourns with Mary and Martha,
two sisters, the death of their brother,
Lazarus.**
(see Jn 11:1–46)

**At Jacob's well, Jesus has an amazing conversation
with a woman from Samaria.**
(see Jn 4:1–42)

**Four women
stay with
Jesus as he
dies.**
(see Jn 19:25)

The risen Jesus appears first to Mary Magdalene.
(see Jn 20:11–18)

The Old Testament honors many strong women. Eve is the "mother of all living"; Sarah, Rebecca, Rachel, and Leah are the names of the great mothers of the people of Israel. Deborah, Jael, Esther, and Judith saved the people from impending annihilation by their courage and their vigor. Women also figure as prophetesses, such as Miriam, Hannah, Abigail, and Huldah. Three books of Holy Scripture bear the name of a woman and tell her story: Ruth, Judith, and Esther.

101 *What role do women have in the life of Jesus?*

A major role.

God entered the world through a woman.
Mary gave birth to Jesus
and accompanied him all the way to the Cross.
In Jesus' time, many women
were treated like children.
But Jesus took women seriously.
He gave them the gift of his friendship.
Some women became his disciples
and walked with him.
After his Resurrection, Jesus
first appeared to a woman,
Mary Magdalene. She was to
tell the apostles: Jesus lives! That's why
she is also called "apostle to the apostles".

Just as Jesus needed Mary and other women back then,
he needs women in his Church today, too.
Without them, it would be as if the Church
were paralyzed on one side.

 Mary was more important than the Apostles, than the bishops and deacons and priests.
Pope Francis, July 28, 2013

 By birth, I am Albanian, I am an Indian citizen; I am a Catholic nun. In what I do, I belong to the whole world, but my heart belongs entirely to Jesus.
St. Teresa of Calcutta

Oh ... I have the vocation of the Apostle ... I would want to preach the Gospel on all the five continents simultaneously, ... I would be a missionary, not for a few years only, but from the beginning of creation until the consummation of the ages.
St. Thérèse of Lisieux (1873–1897)

Matrimony

Matrimony
is the sacrament
where God unites
a baptized man and
a baptized woman
in his love.

102 *What is beautiful about the love between a man and a woman?*

**What is beautiful about the love
between man and woman
is that God created them for each other.
He made them different
so that they would long for one another,
complement, and be there for one another.
They find each other physically attractive
and find joy in one another.
What is also beautiful about their love is
that it creates new life.**

When your mom and dad became parents,
together with God
they brought into the world
something completely new and unique
that hadn't existed before:
you!

" To love someone is to see a miracle invisible to others.
François Mauriac (1885–1970), French writer

✠ You have ravished my heart, my sister, my bride, you have ravished my heart with a glance of your eyes, with one jewel of your necklace. How sweet is your love, my sister, my bride! How much better is your love than wine, and the fragrance of your oils than any spice!
Song 4:9–10

" To be able to find joy in another's joy—that is the secret of happiness.
Georges Bernanos (1888–1948), French writer

103 *What does getting married in the Catholic Church mean?*

**Getting married in the Catholic Church
means a baptized man
and a baptized woman decide
to love each other for the rest of their lives,
in good times and bad times.
They make this promise before God,
their family, their friends,
and the whole Church.**

 Set me as a seal upon your heart, as a seal upon your arm; for love is strong as death. ... Many waters cannot quench love, neither can floods drown it. If a man offered for love all the wealth of his house, it would be utterly scorned.
Song 8:6–7

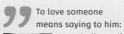 To love someone means saying to him: You shall not die.
Gabriel Marcel (1889–1973), French philosopher

 If I speak in the tongues of men and of angels, but have not love ... if I have all faith, so as to remove mountains, but have not love, I am nothing. ... Love bears all things, believes all things, hopes all things, endures all things. Love never ends.
1 Cor 13:1–2; 7–8

104 *What happens at a Catholic wedding?*

**Bride and groom
make their marriage vows before a priest:
"Before God, I take you, → N.,
to be my wife/my husband.
I promise to be true to you
in good times and in bad,
in sickness and in health, until
death do us part.
I will love you and honor you
all the days of my life."**

They put a ring on each other's fingers
as a sign of their love and loyalty.
They promise to accept from God's hands
the children that he will give them.
God binds them together.
Then they are no longer two,
but one.

→ Here the bride or the groom's
first name is said.

 Be renewed in the spirit
of your minds, and put on
the new man, created after the
likeness of God in true righteousness and holiness.
Eph 4:23–24

**A humane law from the Old
Testament:**
When a man is newly married, he
shall not go out with the army or
be charged with any business; he
shall be free at home one year, to
be happy with his wife whom he has
taken.
Deut 24:5

 The great things in this
world—life, love, God—
cannot be made; they can only be
received as a gift.
Pope Benedict XVI

Question 262: What is necessary for a
Christian, sacramental marriage?

105 *What does the sacrament of Matrimony do for a married couple?*

With his divine love, God
enters the newlywed couple's human love.
A Christian marriage is
a covenant between three partners:
the wife, the husband, and God.
A couple that marries in the Church
has God to help them.
He guides them and goes through
thick and thin with them.

Have you not read that he who made them from the beginning made them male and female, and said, "For this reason a man shall leave his father and mother and be joined to his wife, and the two shall become one"? So they are no longer two but one. What therefore God has joined together, let no man put asunder.
Jesus in Mt 19:4–6

Valid marriage
Jesus rejects divorce by referring to the will of the Creator (see left). True to Jesus, the Church believes that marriage is for life, but she knows that without the full and free consent of both bride and groom, a valid marriage does not take place.

More on this:

Question 263: Why is marriage indissoluble?

Question 416: What are the essential elements of Christian marriage?

When we think of weddings, we often think of
flowers, music, dancing, beautiful clothes,
good food, and many friends and relatives.
But the most important part happens in a church:
the moment when both bride and groom
promise to marry each other before God.
God blesses them and binds them together
with his love, so that they
have the strength
to remain true to each other
in his love for a lifetime
and to accept children as the fruit of their love.

106 **Why can't men marry men or women
marry women in the Catholic Church?**

**Marriage can exist only between a man and a woman,
because only a union of male and female
can create new life.**

Two people of the same sex
caring for each other
or living with each other
is not the same thing as marriage.

> Marriage is also an everyday task, I could say a craftsman's task, a goldsmith's work, because the husband has the duty of making the wife more of a woman, and the wife has the duty of making the husband more of a man. ... And the children will have the inheritance of having a father and a mother who grew together, by making each other—one another—more of a man and more of a woman!
>
> **Pope Francis** addressing young couples, February 14, 2014

107 How can love grow in the family?

**If parents and children
seek the help of God daily,
their love for each other can grow,
even in difficult times.**

Seeking God's help
is like going to the gas station.
We can "refuel" with God's love in three ways.

Through **prayer**:
Mother Teresa said, "A family
who prays together, stays together."

Through **reconciliation**:
The Bible recommends,
"Do not let the sun go down
on your anger" (Eph 4:26).

EXCLUSIVE OFFER!
HERE ONLY!!
Super-Fuel
for your
Marriage

> You become responsible,
> forever, for what you
> have tamed.

**Antoine de
Saint-Exupéry**
(1900–1944), French
writer and pilot

Sacrament of Matrimony
The Austrian writer **Gertrud Fuss-
enegger** (1912–2009) wrote that "a broken
marriage is a broken world." If Jesus
stresses the indissolubility of marriage,
he doesn't do it to impose a commandment on people that puts them in shack-
les; rather, he frees them to expect great

love not only from one another, but from
him. The following sentence is only true
with God: "Love never ends" (1 Cor 13:8).

Through **Holy Communion**:
Jesus says, "Abide in me,
and I in you" (Jn 15:4).
With God's help we can
love as he does.

  108 *What if spouses separate?*

Only God is perfect.
We, on the other hand, can and do fail,
even at marriage.
The special thing about God is
that he doesn't leave us,
even if we have failed.

No child can be blamed
for his parents' separation.
Even if father and mother
no longer live together,
most of them want to be good parents
because they love their children.

Not being able to live with
both parents
is very sad.
But even in the most difficult situations,
our hearts can be healed.
Burdens can become easier to carry,
and we can become better people
if we let God into our hardships.

In the evening of our life, it is by love that we will be judged, the love, that we have allowed gradually to grow and unfold itself in us, in compassion for every person in the Church and in the world.
Brother Roger Schutz

Pope Francis said, "Living together is an art." He added that it has three rules, which can be summarized in three phrases: please, thank you, and I'm sorry.

May you find rest when the day comes to a close and your thoughts once again seek out the places where you have experienced good things. May their memories warm you, and may good dreams accompany your sleep.
Old Irish blessing

109 *What are sacramentals?*

**Sacramentals are
sacred objects, gestures, and prayers
that remind us of God's love
and give us the gift of God's blessing.**

The entire Church year
is characterized by sacramentals:
on Ash Wednesday, our foreheads are signed
with ashes to make a cross;
on Holy Thursday, the washing of the feet takes place;
at Epiphany we write a house blessing
above our doors with blessed chalk;
and there is the blessing of throats on the feast of Saint Blaise.
Processions are held on some feast days,
and people take pilgrimages to holy places.

Holy water, candles, crosses, icons,
images and statues of saints,
medals, and rosaries
are sacramentals.

Sacred signs
In the Catholic Church we show reverence
for gestures, objects, and places that have been
touched by God. These sacred signs remind us of
God's presence in our lives.

> Throughout the liturgical year, ... the Lord walks
beside us and explains the Scriptures to us,
makes us understand this mystery: everything speaks of
him. And this should also make our hearts burn within us,
so that our eyes too may be opened (Lk 24:32). The Lord is
with us, he shows us the true path.
Pope Benedict XVI, March 26, 2008

The Liturgical Year: An Entire Year with God

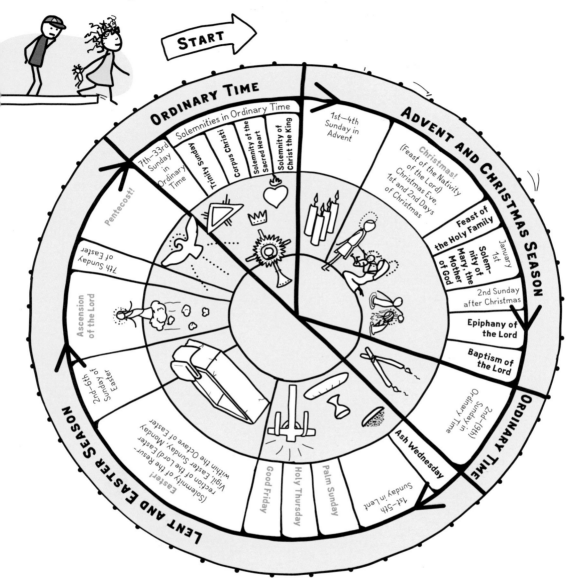

START

ORDINARY TIME

Solemnities in Ordinary Time

7th–33rd Sunday in Ordinary Time

Trinity Sunday

Corpus Christi

Solemnity of the Sacred Heart

Solemnity of Christ the King

1st–4th Sunday in Advent

ADVENT AND CHRISTMAS SEASON

Christmas! (Feast of the Nativity of the Lord) Christmas Eve, 1st and 2nd Days of Christmas

Feast of the Holy Family

January 1st Solemnity of Mary, the Mother of God

2nd Sunday after Christmas

Epiphany of the Lord

Baptism of the Lord

ORDINARY TIME

2nd–9th Sunday in Ordinary Time

Pentecost!

7th Sunday of Easter

Ascension of the Lord

2nd–6th Sunday of Easter

LENT AND EASTER SEASON

Easter! (Solemnity of the Resurrection of the Lord) Easter Vigil, Easter Sunday, Monday within the Octave of Easter

Good Friday

Holy Thursday

Palm Sunday

1st–5th Sunday in Lent

Ash Wednesday

Liturgical year

In the liturgical year, the Church repeats the core of Jesus' life, more or less in rhythm with the calendar year. Celebrating the liturgical year with the Church means participating in Jesus' life—from his becoming man (= Advent), through his birth (= Christmas), his last time with the disciples (= Holy Thursday), his death (= Good Friday), his Resurrection from the dead (= Easter), all the way to the sending of the Holy Spirit (= Pentecost). Two periods of preparation, each taking several weeks, lead up to the high points in the liturgical year: Advent prepares our hearts for the arrival of God made man; the Lenten season teaches us to repent, so that we will have new life at Easter. The saints' feast days also lead us to Jesus. Every day of the year, the Church places before us passages from Holy Scripture and offers us the "bread of life". To participate in the liturgical year is not only a beautiful experience—it is the express lane to Jesus and leads into the heart of the Church.

Part 3

DOING GOOD

THE COMMANDMENTS

God's 10 Rules for Life

How we learn step by step
to live really well and happily.
What the TEN COMMANDMENTS
mean exactly,
and how through them
we can walk in the ways
of God.

Questions
110–137

110 *Why is it important to God how I live?*

**God wants you to be happy
and for everyone else to be happy, too.
Sometimes being happy is difficult.
God shows you how.
His commandments help us to live well
by doing good. God's commandments are helpful,
like the rules of a game.**

Just as you can play soccer well
only if you know the rules,
you can live well only
if you know the rules for life.
Being stingy, lying, cheating,
and bullying—
these are like fouls in soccer.
They spoil the game for everyone.

There are even worse offenses—
theft, murder, betrayal.
These destroy the happiness
and lives of others.
Obeying God's commandments protects us
from harming others.

It protects us from
harming ourselves, too.

Where did the Ten Commandments come from?

God created us with free will. But freedom needs order. That is why he gave his people the Ten Commandments after he rescued them from slavery in Egypt. They are the foundation of our social order to this day.

He has showed you, O man, what is good; and what does the LORD require of you but to do justice, and to love kindness, and to walk humbly with your God? **Mic 6:8**

111 *Which commandments has God given us?*

God gave the people of Israel the Ten Commandments.
They are rules for living together well.
Jesus summarized all these commandments
in a single sentence:
"You shall love the Lord your God with all your heart,
and with all your soul, and with all your strength,
and with all your mind;
and your neighbor as yourself" (Lk 10:27).

Jesus also wants us to love our enemies:
"Love your enemies,
do good to those who hate you,
bless those who curse you,
pray for those who abuse you.
To him who strikes you on the cheek,
offer the other also;
and from him who takes away your cloak
do not withhold your coat as well" (Lk 6:27–29).

Don't be afraid to love until it hurts. It is the way Jesus loved.
St. Teresa of Calcutta

Whoever comes to his neighbor's aid in his suffering, this man has done more than he who builds a cathedral at every milestone from Cologne to Rome, so that there might be praying and singing in it until the Last Day. For thus speaks the Son of God: "I did not suffer death for the purpose of a cathedral, nor for the sake of singing and praying, but for the sake of man."

St. Albert the Great (ca. 1200–1280)

112 *What are the → Ten Commandments?*

THE TEN COMMANDMENTS

1. I am the Lord your God. You shall have no other gods before me.

2. You shall not take the name of the Lord in vain.

3. Remember the Sabbath day—keep it holy.

4. Honor your father and your mother.

5. You shall not kill.

6. You shall not commit adultery.

7. You shall not steal.

8. You shall not lie.

9. You shall not covet your neighbor's wife.

10. You shall not covet your neighbor's house or anything that belongs to your neighbor.

The Ten Rules for Life

Can you list the Ten Commandments
in your own words?
Try it!
Use these to help you:

1. God makes everything.
   He decides how things work.
   No one is more important
   than he is.

2. Don't make silly jokes about God.
   Don't use his name to say bad
   things.

→ The **Ten Commandments** are in the Old Testament in two places: **Ex 20:2–17** and **Deut 5:6–21.**

i **Ten Commandments for freedom**
In order to understand the Ten Commandments correctly, one needs to read the sentence that introduces them in the Book of Exodus: "I am the LORD your God, who brought you out of the land of Egypt, out of the house of bondage" (Ex 20:2). God provides rules that protect them for a life beyond slavery, so that the People of God never fall back into a wrong way of life again.

3. Chill with God!

4. Respect your parents. Without them, you wouldn't be here.

5. Don't mess with anyone! Don't kill anyone! Don't hit anyone! Don't hit back!

6. If you are married, keep your promise!

7. Don't steal anything! No illegal downloads!

8. Don't lie! Don't be a show off!

9 & 10. You can't have everything, okay?!

113 *How do I know if I am doing something good or bad?*

**You have an inner voice
that tells you if something is good or bad.
We hear the echo of God's voice
in our conscience.**

When I tell the truth,
even when I have difficulty doing so,
I have a good conscience.
When I take something
that belongs to someone else,
even though I know God's commandment,
"You shall not steal", and I feel bad,
that too is a sign of a good conscience.

My conscience guides me
to do good and protects me
from doing evil.
So do the voices of my parents
and my teachers
and the Church.

i **Conscience:** Everyone wants to act in accordance with the good or wants to be able to think that his actions are good. That is why, today, we like to refer to our personal conscience when we knowingly decide against keeping a commandment. However, a well-formed conscience (i.e., one that understands the commandments)

is needed for clear moral thinking, because we tend to make decisions to our own advantage.

If you would like to read more on the topic of conscience, read:

Y **Questions**
295–298

99 Conscience—there are two ways of regarding conscience; one as a mere sort of sense of propriety, a taste teaching us to do this or that, the other as the echo of God's voice. Now all depends on the distinction—the first way is not of faith, and the second is of faith.
Blessed John Henry Newman

114 *What does it mean to say: "You shall have no other → gods before me"?*

FIRST COMMANDMENT

"You shall have no other gods before me."

The first rule for life is this: there is only one God. God is more important than anything else.

God is more important
than making a lot of money.
God is more important
than being famous
and having a lot of fans.
God is even more important than I am.
God gives me the gift of my life;
he is my joy,
my happiness.

→ **Many gods?**
Of course there is only one God—and not many gods. Sometimes, though, we make objects or other people our gods; we treat them as if they were so important a thing that we are willing to disobey God in order to have them or to please them. Thus, they become false gods, or idols.

ℹ **Putting God first**
Living well means setting priorities. What is most important comes first, what is less important comes next, and the things that are good, but which might as well be left alone, too, come last. A Christian knows: God must have the first place in his heart, otherwise something is not right.

However, that can also mean that I might not be able to go to Mass one Sunday because I have to look after my sick children at home. For God is love, and love demands that I look after my children.

115   What does the First Commandment protect us from?

The First Commandment protects us from false gods, or idols. There are many false lords that would rule over us if we let them.

If we do not worship God above everything else, we let our desire for wealth, ambition for power, or longing for popularity take over our lives. We can become hooked on sweets, movies, computer games, or social media. Next thing we know, we have lost our freedom. God loves us and wants us to be free.

> Worshipping God means learning to be with him, stripping ourselves of our secret idols, and choosing him as the center of our lives.
>
> **Pope Francis**

False idols

The word "idol" (from the Greek word for "image", "picture") reminds us of the Old Testament. The golden calf (Ex 32:1–35) is perhaps the most famous idol. People still dance around the golden calf, just as they did then, thinking that their wealth can save them. It harms people to serve false gods, as the Bible points out: "Those who choose another god multiply their sorrows" (Ps 16:4).

All kinds of idolatry

Sports are great, but it is idolatry when the father of a family squanders all of his time and money watching his favorite teams. When the television in the living room is the family altar, and parents and children spend most of their free time in front of it, that too is idolatry. Smartphones, celebrities, designer clothes, fancy cars—these can become idols, too.

116 *What does "You shall not take the name of the Lord in vain" mean?*

SECOND COMMANDMENT

"You shall not take the name of the Lord in vain."

**God has entrusted us with his holy name.
We should never misuse it.
We may call him by his name,
like a father or a friend.
That's how we pray.**

The fact that God has told us his name
shows his great trust in us.
Whoever knows his name
has the key to his heart.
That's why one mustn't mock
or make jokes with sacred words
such as "God", "Father in heaven",
"Jesus Christ", or "Holy Spirit".
Swearing an oath falsely and
using God's name in curses
are grave sins.

The name of God is so holy to the people of Israel that it mustn't even be pronounced. But in the burning bush (Ex 3:14), God revealed his name: *Yahweh* = "I AM." God is, and he is here with us. When parents want to comfort their children after a bad dream, they often say: "Don't be afraid, it's me. I'm here!" That's what God wants to tell us with his name.

One of the most powerful passages in the Bible about the power of God's name is in the Letter to the Romans: "Every one who calls upon the name of the Lord will be saved." **Rom 10:13**

117 What does the Second Commandment protect us from?

The second commandment protects us from a lack of respect for God.

Not taking God seriously means
to say his name
as if he couldn't hear it,
entering a church
as if he weren't there,
speaking about God in a hurtful
and unloving way,
as if he were deaf,
laughing at people and their prayers
as if God didn't exist.

One of the key passages in the Old Testament is God's revelation in the burning bush (Ex 3). Man is confronted with the unfathomably holy. "Then [the Lord] said: 'Do not come near; put off your shoes from your feet, for the place on which you are standing is holy ground' " (Ex 3:5).

Reverence is the way we show respect and veneration for the mystery of divine presence. Genuflecting is a sign of reverence, the body language of humility before the greatness of God.

The fear of the LORD is the beginning of wisdom; a good understanding have all those who practice it.
Ps 111:10

118 *What does "Remember the Sabbath day—keep it holy" mean?*

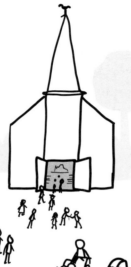

"Remember the Sabbath day— keep it holy."

For us Christians, Sunday is the Lord's Day. On this day, we celebrate the Resurrection of Jesus. This day should be different from all the other days in the week.

Even though people are more and more under pressure, Sunday is not the time for professional activities, everyday junk, and business. Normally, it is not for homework, either, or even tutoring. We should rest on Sunday, eat and play with one another, take time for our family. The most important appointment on Sunday is Holy Mass—time for God.

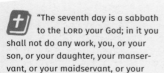

"The seventh day is a sabbath to the LORD your God; in it you shall not do any work, you, or your son, or your daughter, your manservant, or your maidservant, or your cattle, or the sojourner who is within your gates" (Ex 20:10). Exciting point: children, slaves, foreigners, and even animals were granted this divine break!

119 Why do we rest on Sunday?

**To take a break one day a week
and to rest in God—
that's God's desire for us.
For Jews, the day of rest is Saturday.
For Christians, it is Sunday.**

God gave his people Israel
a day of rest
as a gift.
It's called the Sabbath.
Christians have adopted this day of rest,
but they transferred it from Saturday to Sunday
because that's the day Jesus
rose from the dead.

 For the first Christians, the **gathering on Sunday** was the central event in their week. The Church Father **Justin Martyr** (100–165) describes the things that happened then: "On the day we call the day of the sun, all gathering in the ... same place. The memoirs of the apostles or the writings of the prophets are read, as much as time permits. ... Then someone brings bread and a cup of water and wine. ... The presider ... takes them and offers praise and glory to the Father of the universe, through the name of the Son and of the Holy Spirit and for a considerable time he gives thanks (in Greek: *eucharistia*) that we have been judged worthy of these gifts."

120 *What does the Third Commandment protect us from?*

It protects us from two great threats:
forgetting God
and becoming workaholics
who work themselves to exhaustion.

In some non-Christian countries,
people have very few holidays.
They have to work hard every day.
Sundays are going to disappear in our country, too,
if we Christians don't really celebrate them.
God has not made us to be
robots that
work hard until they drop.
That's why there is no
school on Sundays. Isn't that brilliant?

Things that were forbidden in ancient Israel on the Sabbath
Sowing, ploughing, harvesting, bundling sheaves, threshing, sorting, selecting, grinding, sifting, kneading, baking; shearing wool, cleaning, combing, dyeing, spinning, stretching threads, making bows, weaving threads, separating threads, making knots, opening knots, sewing, tearing; catching, butchering, skinning, curing, tanning, scraping, cutting, writing, dousing, building, tearing down, extinguishing a fire, lighting a fire, hammering, carrying something from one place to another.

Exceptions
The commandment about Sunday rest does not apply to professions that are necessary for the upkeep of the common good day and night, all seven days a week, e.g., doctors, nurses, and police.

121 *How do Christians celebrate Sunday?*

**Sunday is a feast day with God.
Just like the first Christians,
the friends of Jesus meet on
the Lord's Day.
Catholics go to church and celebrate
Holy Mass together.
There they encounter Jesus, the Lord.**

Sunday is also a day
for dressing nicely to honor God
and sharing a special meal with family and friends.
You may do what makes you and others happy
that isn't work—like playing in the park.
Parents and children should spend
time together.

Martyrs for Sunday
In the year 304 in Abitene, 49 Christians were caught celebrating the Eucharist one Sunday. The cruel emperor Diocletian had forbidden it under penalty of death. The 49 were arrested, brought to Carthage, and interrogated there. Even though they knew that it would cost them their lives, they told the judge to his face: "We cannot live without Sunday."

Sunday culture
There is nothing children long for more than for their parents to take plenty of time for them on Sunday. This very human longing has a deep religious foundation in the Sunday commandment. Taking time for each other and being good to one another—that is Sunday, and it reflects God's way of being.

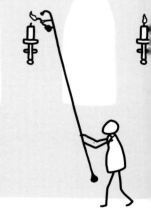

Be a living expression of God's kindness: kindness in your face, kindness in your eyes, kindness in your smile.
St. Teresa of Calcutta

Some Enjoyable Things you can do on

SUNDAY

Celebrating Holy Mass with others
hiking
playing ball games
playing with other kids
visiting grandparents
cooking with one another
reading a story
lighting a candle and having quiet time
going swimming
painting
making music
visiting the sick
playing with animals
picking flowers for your home
going on a boat ride
making phone calls
observing nature
making a pilgrimage
watching movies and looking at pictures
dreaming
making plans
stargazing ...

**Make your own list
with your friends!**

122 *What does "Honor your father and your mother" mean?*

**Everyone has a father and a mother
to thank for his life.
God wants us to
love, respect, and honor our parents
and to thank them
for the good they have done for us.**

> "Honor
> your father and
> your mother."

To have loving parents
is a great blessing.
You can learn from them so much that is
good and important.
And if there are times when
you don't understand Mom and Dad, you can
still thank them for the fact that you exist.
Try to forgive them
their weaknesses and mistakes.

When they are old,
don't leave them alone, but be
loving and patient with them instead.

God will one day ask
your parents and godparents
whether they have honored
their children.

i **The Fourth Commandment** was often used in the past to teach children unconditional obedience and to treat them as immature human beings for as long as possible. But that is not how the Bible sees it. The Fourth Commandment is preceded by the First Commandment. Rabbi **Marc Stern** (1956–2005) said,

"If God is our one Lord according to the First Commandment, no one has the right to be lord over another human being, neither fathers over mothers and children, nor older people over the young."

✝ Listen to your father who begot you, and do not despise your mother when she is old.
Prov 23:22

❞ The family is the cradle of humaneness.
Blessed Adolph Kolping
(1813–1865)

123 *What does the Fourth Commandment protect us from?*

The Fourth Commandment protects the family from breaking apart.

The Fourth Commandment
wants to keep us from
letting one another down
or giving up on one another.
It wants to help us
to support each other and to make
each other strong.

If a family
lives in ➔ God's good order,
it is warm and beautiful.
It gives a person security and strength
to love.

> *We did have to live very frugally and simply, for which I am very grateful. For thereby joys are made possible that one cannot have in wealth. I often think back on how wonderful it was that we could be happy over the smallest things and how we also tried to do things for one another.*
>
> **Pope Benedict XVI**

➔ Such a family has attentive-
ness, warmth, dependable
relationships, but also prayer
in the morning and at night.
With God, a calm security
and joy come into a family's
life, and it does both children
and adults good.

i The meaning of
the word **Family:** FATHER
AND
MOTHER
I
LOVE
YOU

124 *What does "You shall not → kill" mean?*

**No person may
take his own or
another person's life.
Every human life is precious
to God and beloved by him.
I must not hate anyone or treat anyone
with contempt or violence.**

> **"You shall not kill."**

God is the author of life.
The end of life, too, is in God's hands.
God is Lord over life and death.
God made man in his own image;
therefore human life is sacred.
Knowingly taking the life of
an innocent human being is murder.
Murder is a grave sin.

→ Killing or murdering?
The Fifth Commandment is often translated from Hebrew as "You shall not kill." But the original word, *ratsah*, means "murder". The commandment does not forbid justified killing (of animals, for example, when they are slaughtered for food), but taking the life of an innocent human being.

Y Question 379: What sorts of attacks on human life are forbidden by the Fifth Commandment?

125 *What does the Fifth Commandment protect us from?*

**The Fifth Commandment
protects the life
of every human being.**

We must not take the lives of other people.
We must not even put other people's lives in danger
by rash or reckless behavior.

If someone kills a person in self-defense,
he is not guilty of murder.
Soldiers and police are not sinning
when they use force to defend people
against the violence of others.

God wants every child to be able to be born,
even if he has a disability.
He doesn't want sick people, disabled people,
or those close to death
to be killed, even if
they are suffering. We must comfort
those in pain, not end their lives.
Whoever denies help to the suffering
sins against the Fifth Commandment, too.

He who causes fights, bullies others,
or harasses people on the Internet
is causing serious injury to others.

We must not do needless harm
or cause needless pain to anyone,
not even to animals.

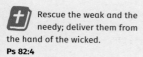 Rescue the weak and the
needy; deliver them from
the hand of the wicked.
Ps 82:4

Question 383: Why is abortion
unacceptable?
Question 382: Is it permisssible to
offer assistance to the dying?

" Never torture an
animal in vain,
because, like you, it feels
the pain.
German proverb

126 *What does "You shall not commit adultery" mean?*

**If you are married,
you shall keep your marriage vows.**

> "You shall not commit adultery."

When a man and a woman
make their marriage vows
before God, they give themselves away:
the man gives himself to the woman,
and the woman gives herself to the man.
And God gives them to each other.
But one never asks for a present to be given back.
Committing ➜ adultery means taking something back
that one has already given away.
To leave a spouse
because one would like to have someone else
is a grave sin. God wants
us to be loyal to one another.
Loyalty is practiced
in good friendships.

➜ **Adultery** is a grave sin. But only God can judge a person. Jesus said, "Judge not, that you be not judged" (Mt 7:1). He defended a woman caught in the act of adultery: "Let him who is without sin among you be the first to throw a stone at her" (Jn 8:7). But he said to the woman, "Go, and do not sin again" (Jn 8:11).

ℹ **The nature of marriage**
Christian marriage is more like a covenant than a contract. In a contract, two parties arrange what it is they may expect of each other. If the service is no longer rendered, the contract can be ended. A covenant between two people, however, is based on love; it is entered without a right of termination, without conditions, and without a service in return; instead, it is entered with God.

127 · What does the Sixth Commandment protect us from?

**The Sixth Commandment
protects the greatest and most beautiful thing
between a man and a woman,
namely, married love.**

When a man and a woman fall in love,
they feel physically attracted to each other.
They want to be very close to each other
and to become one.

Sex is a wonderful gift.
But this gift loses its value
and beauty if it is not protected.

Precious things need protection.
Just as a valuable gift is carefully wrapped
so that it doesn't break, our hearts, too,
need protection. Marriage is this protection.

When a man and a woman promise
to be together until death, they
can surrender themselves completely and
give themselves to each other physically.
Their bodies say the same thing
as their words:
"I will love you forever!"
That promise connects them deeply
for the rest of their lives.

i **The sense of shame** has a valuable protective function. Especially children have a right to privacy and not to be burdened with things too early that would overwhelm them. Artificially breaking through thresholds of shame in sex education (for example, in order to steel children against abuse), often makes children more vulnerable to those who would exploit them.

i **Protecting children** In lots of media, children are targeted by sexual predators. Parents must be vigilant about protecting their children from vicious people on the Internet.

i **Pornography and the danger of addiction** An abundance of research proves that pornography is consumed at increasingly younger ages. Today it is a key addiction with young teenagers. Parents have to consider very carefully when they allow their children to have a mobile phone with Internet access. **Tabea Freitag** (Office for Media Addiction, Hanover, Germany) said, "Every year that a child doesn't yet have one is a win."

128 *What does "You shall not steal" mean?*

If you take something that doesn't belong to you, you are stealing; you are a thief.

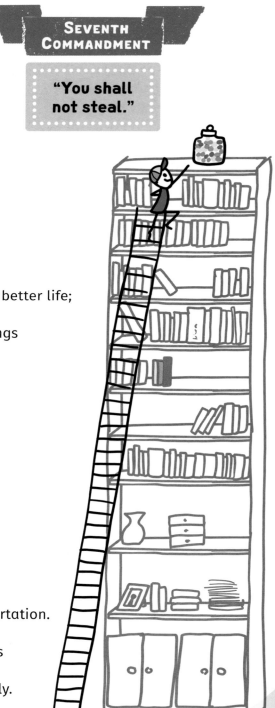

SEVENTH COMMANDMENT

"You shall not steal."

The Seventh Commandment speaks about things that belong to you or to other people.

God has created us to take care of ourselves with things that we own. They make it possible for us to have a better life; they give us security and bring us joy. You should take good care of your things and protect them. With these things, you can bring joy to other people; you can share them, lend them, or give them away.

Many things are not for individual persons or societies to have entirely to themselves.

We must protect what is common and share it in a just way: air, water, soil, energy, raw materials, means of communication, and transportation.

We should take good care of the things that belong to everyone, just as if they belonged to us personally.

129 *What does the Seventh Commandment protect us from?*

**Through the Seventh Commandment,
God protects man's property.
He does not want the world
to fall into the hands of thieves and robbers.
Wherever there is no Seventh Commandment,
the stronger person takes everything
that he can get.**

- Don't even take away small things that belong to another person.
- Take good care of things that have been lent to you, and return them without being asked.
- If you have broken things, repair them or replace them.
- Don't use anything that doesn't belong to you without asking first.
- Don't just keep things that you have found; bring them to your parents or to the school office.

- Don't waste energy.
- Treat things well that belong to everyone (e.g., seats on a bus or computers at school).
- Don't copy or download music, films, and computer games illegally.

Property
The philosopher **Aristotle** (384–322 B.C.) said something about the topic of property that is important to children, too: "Wherever there is no property, there is also no joy of giving; no one can have the pleasure of helping friends, wayfarers, and the suffering in their need." The Church has always emphasized man's right to property; at the same time, however, she has also highlighted the owner's social obligations: whoever has much should give much and do so readily.

> Giving does not make one poor. Stealing does not make one rich. And wealth does not make one smart.
> **An English saying**

130 What does "You shall not lie" mean?

EIGHTH
COMMANDMENT

"You shall
not lie."

**You shall not say anything
that is not true.
God is truth.
He doesn't deceive us and wants
us to be honest with each other.**

Lying often starts out small—
with an excuse
or a small deception—
and it often ends in great chaos.

If you lie,
you can't be trusted anymore.
Lying is a poison
that destroys every friendship.

There is an old saying: "Another good thing about telling the truth is that you don't have to remember what you say to everyone."

A priest once said in a sermon: "Next week, I'd like to preach about the sin of lying. I'd like to ask you all to read the 17th chapter of the evangelist Mark until then, so that you might better understand the homily." On the following Sunday, the priest asked: "Who has read Mark 17?" All hands went up. The priest smiled: "Interesting! Mark only has 16 chapters. Let me start my homily about lying."

131 *What does the Eighth Commandment protect us from?*

The Eighth Commandment protects us from being lied to and being cheated. It also protects us from becoming false, dishonest people whom no one can trust.

An honest person does not exaggerate.
He doesn't make himself more important than he is.
He doesn't judge others or
belittle them. He doesn't gossip.
He doesn't spread falsehoods about others.
Whoever follows God's commandment,
receives more and more courage
to tell the → truth,
even when it's difficult to do so.

One should hold out the truth to another person like a coat, so he can put it on—not like a wet towel to hit him with. **Max Frisch** (1911–1991), Swiss author and architect

→ Truth
Jesus said: "For this I was born, and for this I have come into the world, to bear witness to the truth. Every one who is of the truth hears my voice" (Jn 18:37). Christians, who name themselves after Christ, must take the truth seriously. Lies destroy trust between people and make communication pointless. Going along with falsehoods in order to be liked by others is also a form of lying.

132 *What are white lies?*

White lies are lies.
In most cases, white lies are
needless cheap apologies and excuses
because we are afraid to say the truth.

Sometimes we lie because we are ashamed.
Other times we are afraid of
being laughed at,
being punished,
or of no longer being popular.
Sometimes we lie because
it is easier than telling the truth.
But we mustn't lie for these reasons.

One may, in very rare cases,
to protect against evil,
conceal the truth.
Thus, someone who
is hiding an innocent person
from people with evil intentions
is not required to give away
his hiding place.

Oh, God, how glorious: one person, or two, who speaks the truth can do more than many others together can! Through them, the blind gradually rediscover the way, and God gives them joy in it and emboldens them.
St. Teresa of Avila

133 *What do "You shall not covet your neighbor's wife" and "You shall not covet your neighbor's property" mean?*

NINTH AND

AND

TENTH COMMANDMENT

**The Ninth and the Tenth Commandments
tell us to be content
with the things we have.
We must not want the family members
or the belongings of others.**

**"You shall not covet
your neighbor's
wife."
and
"You shall not covet
your neighbor's
property."**

We have strong desires.
God made us this way,
and that is good.

But sometimes our desires
are for something
we can't have,
such as when it belongs to someone else.
Envy or jealousy can consume our hearts
and tempt us to take someone or something
away from someone else. For example:

● when a man wants the wife
of another man

● when a ruler wants a
neighboring country

● when a girl wants her
classmate's fancy markers

● when a boy wants his
friend's cell phone

134 What do the Ninth and Tenth Commandments protect us from?

**With the Ninth and Tenth commandments,
God protects us from
being greedy.**

God has made us in such a way
that we can be happy
even when we don't have
all that we want.

Your mercy, O LORD, extends to the heavens, your faithfulness to the clouds.
Your righteousness is like the mountains of God, your judgments are like the great deep;
man and beast you save, O LORD.
How precious is your mercy, O God! The children of men take refuge in the shadow of your wings.
They feast on the abundance of your house,
and you give them drink from the river of your delights. For with you is the fountain of life;
in your light do we see light.
Ps 36:5–9

135 What are the five precepts of the Church?

The precepts of the Church are the basic duties that Catholics owe to God and one another.

- You shall worship God on Sundays and → holy days of obligation by going to Mass and resting from unnecessary work.

- You shall confess your sins at least once a year.

- You shall receive Holy Communion during the Easter Season.

- You shall observe the Church's → days of fasting and abstinence.

- You shall help to provide for the needs of the Church.

→ For example, All Saints' Day and Christmas. See the **Liturgical Year, pp. 160–161**

→ All Fridays during Lent are days of abstinence (no meat). Ash Wednesday and Good Friday are days of fasting (only one regular meal) and abstinence (no meat). See the **Liturgical Year, p. 161**

ℹ Thinking and living with the Church St. Ignatius of Loyola (1491–1556) lived at a time when the Church was being torn apart. Martin Luther and other Protestants were forming their own churches. St. Ignatius formed a group of priests (the Society of Jesus, called Jesuits) to renew the Catholic faith and to win souls back to the Catholic Church. His book of spiritual exercises was a great contribution, and it included eighteen instructions for conforming one's mind and heart to the Church (*Sentire cum Ecclesia*). One must love the Church and be united with her wholeheartedly no matter how disfigured she is by sin, St. Ignatius wrote, because Jesus sought community with us sinners and trusted Peter after his betrayal. "The first fruit of baptism is that you belong to the Church," Pope Francis said, "to the people of God." "The Church is not a cultural or religious organization," he also said, but "the family of Jesus!" A passive membership in the Church is as nonsensical as a passive membership in a family.

136 What does Jesus say about happiness?

**Jesus wants all people to be happy
by being in the kingdom of God.**
**You do not need to be healthy, famous,
beautiful, rich, strong, or brilliant
to be in God's kingdom.**
**Jesus shows us the way to the kingdom
in the Beatitudes:**

The Beatitudes say that those who are humble,
sad, and meek are close to God.
So are the pure of heart, the merciful,
and those who strive for justice and peace.
To such people Jesus says,
"I am your joy!
Here and now, and in heaven!"

> Let no one ever come to
> you without leaving better
> and happier.
> **St. Teresa of Calcutta**

A king was once presented
with a judge's verdict, which
he was supposed to sign. The judge's
verdict read: "Mercy impossible, to
be left in prison!" The king was a just
and good man. The verdict seemed
too harsh to him. Thus, he changed it:
"Mercy, impossible to be left in prison!" The man was freed by shifting
a comma.
Source unknown

The Beatitudes

Blessed are the poor in spirit,
for theirs is the kingdom of heaven.
Blessed are those who mourn,
for they shall be comforted.
Blessed are the meek,
for they shall inherit the earth.
Blessed are those who hunger and
thirst for righteousness,
for they shall be satisfied.
Blessed are the merciful,
for they shall obtain mercy.
Blessed are the pure in heart,

for they shall see God.
Blessed are the peacemakers,
for they shall be called sons of God.
Blessed are those who are persecuted
for righteousness' sake,
for theirs is the kingdom of heaven.
Blessed are you when men revile you
and persecute you and utter all kinds of evil
against you falsely on my account.
Rejoice and be glad,
for your reward is great in heaven.

Mt 5:3–12

137 *How can we be the joy of Jesus to others?*

We can share what we have with others.
We can fight injustice,
comfort the sad, and feed the hungry.
We can work for peace among those who are fighting.
We can visit the sick and the imprisoned.
We can forgive people who offend us.
We can shelter the homeless and welcome refugees.

You can share your lunch.
You can defend someone
who is bullied in your class.
You can speak English patiently and slowly
with refugee children at school.
You can hug someone who is crying.
You can give the gift of your time to a lonely person.
You can offer a sandwich or a blanket
to a homeless person.
You can make Christmas cards
for people in prison or nursing homes
and others who are often forgotten.

Part 4

STAYING IN TOUCH

PRAYER

God Always
Has Time

God is always reachable,
for all people in all countries.
How we can come into contact with God
and speak with him directly.
How we learn to pray with Jesus.
How happy God is when we are happy.
How he listens to us
when we are afraid.
How he comforts us
when we are sad.

Questions
138–159

138 *Why do people pray?*

**Because God exists.
Deep within, people have
a longing for God.
And God longs for them.
That's why people from all
cultures and religions pray.**

**As Christians, we pray
to the heavenly Father
through Christ, our Lord.
The Holy Spirit
gives us the words to say.**

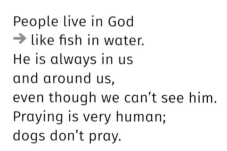

People live in God
➜ like fish in water.
He is always in us
and around us,
even though we can't see him.
Praying is very human;
dogs don't pray.

➜**Fish in water**
See the bottom of **page 13!**

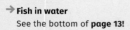
God never
leaves us alone.
Pope Benedict XVI

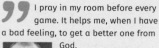
I pray in my room before every
game. It helps me, when I have
a bad feeling, to get a better one from
God.
Wesley Sneijder (*1984),
Dutch soccer player

Rrrrrring! Rrring!

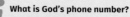
What is God's phone number?
It's very simple, everyone can remember this number: 333! Jeremiah 33:3
can be translated as: "Call to me and I
will answer you." So, one can call God.
He is available 24 hours a day!

139 *What is prayer?*

Praying is talking to God.
Praying is being with God with one's heart.
Praying is becoming quiet
to listen to God.
Praying is thanking him.
Praying is asking him for what you need
and telling him every worry, every fear,
everything that weighs on your conscience,
everything that makes you happy.
Praying is also
accepting what is sad
and asking God to be with you
in your hardships.

Our Father in heaven
is very close to us.
He sees you, he hears you,
and he really knows you.
He is interested in you
even more than your own mom is.
He has time for you, and over the years
he will give you things more beautiful
than you can imagine.

> I don't think there is anyone who needs God's help and grace as much as I do. Sometimes I feel so helpless and weak. I think that is why God uses me. Because I cannot depend on my own strength, I rely on him 24 hours a day. My secret is simple: I pray. I love to pray. The urge to pray is always in me. Prayer enlarges the heart until it is ready to receive God's gift of himself. We so much want to pray correctly, but then we fail. If you want to pray better, pray more. If we want to be capable of love, we must pray.
> **St. Teresa of Calcutta**

> To the person who stops praying, God becomes a nobody.
> **Cardinal Carlo Maria Martini** (1927–2012)

140 *How can I hear God?*

**You can't hear God the same way
you hear people or sounds around you.
God speaks within you very quietly
because he doesn't want to scare you.
He speaks in the depths of the heart.**

Sometimes you can hear his voice inside you,
sometimes through words in the Bible, sometimes through coincidences.
Sometimes he speaks to you through other people.

God says:

"Everything will be okay!"

Sometimes he says this through your mom when she is comforting you.

God says:

"Help!"

Sometimes he says this through the tears of a child who is being teased.

God says:

"Can you see how beautiful this is?"

Sometimes he says this when the sun is shining and the flowers are blooming.

God says:

Sometimes he says this when you are listening to your favorite music.

God says:

Sometimes he says this through the eyes of your dad, who is proud of you.

God says:

Sometimes he says this through a word in Holy Scripture.

God says:

Sometimes he says this at night, when you are in bed and all is quiet.

141 How can I speak with God?

**When your heart is with God,
it doesn't matter whether
you are speaking or
whether you are quiet.
God hears you when you talk to him
in a prayer
that you know by heart.
And he hears you
when you simply tell him
what is on your mind
in your own words.**

Praise and bless God,
because he has made the stars
and the cute kitties, too.
Tell him your most secret wishes
that you wouldn't tell anyone else.

Prayer has great power ...
It makes a bitter heart sweet, a cold soul ablaze.
a sad heart happy, It draws the great God down
a poor heart rich, into a small heart.
a foolish heart wise, It drives the hungry soul
a faltering heart bold, up to God's fullness.
a weak heart strong, **Mechthild of Magdeburg**
a blind heart sighted, (1207-1282)

A few nights before Michael's birthday,
he shouted loudly from his bed,
"God, please bring me a new bicycle for my
birthday!" His annoyed older brother said, "Be
quiet! You don't need to shout for God to hear
you." Michael replied, "No, but I need to shout
for Mom and Dad to hear me."

142 *How do we praise and adore God in prayer?*

**We can praise and adore God by saying,
"Praise be to you, God!
You alone have made everything.
You alone are the Lord.
You alone are holy.
I love you most of all."
No one but God
may be worshiped like this,
not even Mary and the saints.**

For many people,
prayer before the → Blessed Sacrament
in the → monstrance on the altar
is a beautiful way to adore God.

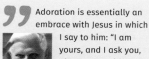

Jesus, who is present in the Host,
draws near to us. We can see
him and feel close to him.

→ The **Blessed Sacrament** is the bread that has been transformed into the Body of Christ during Holy Mass. In the Host, which is presented for adoration, the Lord says, "I, your God, am really here. I am close to you; come close to me."

→ The word "**monstrance**" comes from the Latin word *monstrare* = to show. The monstrance is a beautiful container used to hold the Blessed Sacrament.

Adoration is essentially an embrace with Jesus in which I say to him: "I am yours, and I ask you, please stay with me always."
Pope Benedict XVI

ℹ **Greeting God**
When you enter a Catholic church, especially when you are with children, it is important to show respect for God's presence. You do this by lowering your voice, blessing yourself with holy water, genuflecting before the tabernacle, and taking a minute to kneel in a pew and greet God in prayer. (For more on **genuflection**, see pp. 122, 128, 172)

143 Does God hear our petitions?

**God doesn't fail
to hear a single petition,
and he answers every single one.
Sometimes, he doesn't
fulfill our wishes in the way we want.
Sometimes he doesn't fulfill them immediately.
Sometimes he gives us something else
that is better for us,
which we recognize only in hindsight.** 📖

Jesus himself
encouraged people
in the Sermon on the Mount
to ask God for everything they need:
"Ask, and it will be given you;
seek, and you will find;
knock, and it will be opened to you. ...
What man of you,
if his son asks him for bread,
will give him a stone?" (Mt 7:7–9)

A true story
A man asked God to heal his seriously ill sister. God did not grant this request, but then the man learned that he also had a life-threatening illness and experienced a cure in a wonderful way. He recognized the reality of God, changed his life for the better, and became a Catholic deacon.

❞ We are not shy to ask God even for the most difficult things (such as the conversion of great sinners or of entire nations). Let's ask him, then, all the more, the more difficult they are, trusting that God loves us passionately and that one who loves passionately loves to give all the more, the greater the gift is.
Blessed Charles de Foucauld

❞ If God had granted all the silly prayers I've made in my life, where should I be now?
C. S. Lewis

144 *Do I have to pray even when I don't feel like it?*

**Those who pray only when they feel like it
are like fair-weather friends
who are not true friends,
but who only come around
when it's easy
or when they
want something from you.**

There is always and everywhere
time for a short prayer:
when you get up, when you have breakfast,
when you are walking down the street,
when you are on the bus,
when you are at school,
when you are playing sports,
when you are doing homework,
when you go to sleep.

A true story
A Catholic from one of these countries told me that they cannot pray together—it's forbidden! They can only pray alone and in hiding. If they want to celebrate the Eucharist, they organize a birthday party, they pretend to celebrate a birthday ... And if ... they see the police coming, they immediately hide everything and go on with the party. ... When these agents have left, they finish celebrating the Eucharist ... because it is forbidden to pray together.

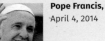
Pope Francis,
April 4, 2014

The great prayer of the people of Israel:
Hear, O Israel: The LORD our God is one LORD; and you shall love the LORD your God with all your heart, and with all your soul, and with all your might. And these words which I command you this day shall be upon your heart; and you shall teach them diligently to your children, and shall talk of them when you sit in your house, and when you walk by the way, and when you lie down, and when you rise.
Deut 6:4–7

145   *How can I pray?*

You can pray standing up, sitting down, kneeling, lying down. You can spread your arms or fold your hands. You can pray while you walk and by dancing.

Just try the various prayer positions for yourself, perhaps in your room. Feel what they "say". You'll see that your body is already praying before you have found the words. Sometimes even the cuddly blanket, under which you feel safe and secure, shows you how warm God's love is.

> The faithful kneel down, stand up, sit down, bow. Why should I stand up? Do I have to go through this eternal Up and Down, like a puppet? What is the point of that? Kneeling, for example, is the posture of one who is humble.

The innermost interior feelings must be in harmony with outward signs; otherwise the whole thing would just be a show.
Pope John Paul I

> When you bend the knee, let it not be a mere hasty, empty gesture. Give it a soul! But the soul of kneeling ... is the bowing down of the innermost heart in reverence and awe before God.
Romano Guardini (1885–1968), German priest

I can pray standing up.

"Lord, here I stand in reverence before you! I listen to your wishes. Tell me what I should do!"

I can pray sitting down.

"Lord, I take time for you; I listen to you. I want to understand you."

I can pray while kneeling.

"God, I am kneeling before you. You are great and I am small."

I can prostrate myself before God.

"Lord, I prostrate myself before you and worship you!" Or, "Lord, I worship you with my body and my soul!"

I can fold my hands.

"Lord, now I am completely with myself and completely with you."

I can spread my arms

"Lord, come to me. I am open to you."

146 *How do I pray when I get up?*

I say to God, "Good morning!"
I thank him for the night.
I think about everything
that the day will bring,
and I ask God for his blessing.

Suggestions for prayers in the morning:

Stay with me, good God,
all day today.
Guide me, protect me,
come what may.
Amen.

Thank you, God,
for this morning.
Thank you for being with me.
Thank you for good friends.
Thank you for never forgetting me.
Thank you for the time to play,
for the joy that you give,
and for thinking of me
especially on dark days.
Amen.

Dear Father in heaven,
another day where I am alone
with my child. Be a Father to him and help
me to do the right thing today. Take away
my worries and help me to be
a cheerful and wise mother.
Amen.

The Bedside Rule:
The bedside is a wonderful place to start the day with God and to end the day with God. That's equally important for parents and for children. Resolve not to get out of bed a single morning without saying a morning prayer. And in the same way, resolve to remain sitting on the edge of your bed at least for a little while each night, to speak with God and to be at peace.

How Jesus started the day

Jesus prayed in the morning, too. The evangelist Mark relates how one evening people had pressed in upon Jesus: "The whole city was gathered around about the door." It must have gotten late, for we read how Jesus started the next morning: "And in the morning, a great while before day, he rose and went out to a lonely place, and there he prayed" (Mk 1:33, 35).

147 *How does one pray before a meal?*

**We thank God for the food,
for the people who have made it,
and for everyone who is sitting at the table with us.**

Suggestions for prayers before meals:

> God is great and God is good.
> Let us thank him for our food.
> By his blessings we are fed.
> Give us Lord, our daily bread.
> Amen.

> Come, Lord Jesus, our guest to be
> and bless these gifts bestowed by thee.
> And bless our loved ones everywhere,
> and keep them in your loving care.
> Amen.

> Bless us, O Lord, and these thy gifts,
> which we are about to receive from
> thy bounty, through Christ, our Lord.
> Amen.

Prayer in the family

Many parents have discovered the importance of rituals: prayer at the beginning of the day, daily mealtime prayer, quiet time in the evening, and night prayer. These situations ask for nothing extravagant, but, rather, for tried and tested words and what comes from the heart and goes to the child's heart. One must guard against mindless habits. Children feel secure in a world where God plays a role. They learn to give thanks, to see what is beautiful in life, and to bear what is difficult with God's help. Thus, children grow up full of trust in a world that never falls out of God's hands.

> For me, prayer is an aspiration of the heart, it is a simple glance directed to heaven, it is a cry of gratitude and love in the midst of trial as well as joy.
> **St. Thérèse of Lisieux**

Thank you so much, Lord!

Help me!

Lord, bless me!

Don't leave me alone!

Be with me!

Let it turn out really well!

Please, please, please!

Be my friend!

QUICK PRAYERS

I can't go on!

How wonderful, O God!

Bless my friends!

I'm so sad!

Jesus, I need you!

I'm sorry, God, please forgive me!

Make things bright in me!

Where are you?

Don't let anything happen to me!

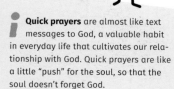

i **Quick prayers** are almost like text messages to God, a valuable habit in everyday life that cultivates our relationship with God. Quick prayers are like a little "push" for the soul, so that the soul doesn't forget God.
Sister Michaela Voss

" If the words "thank you" were the only prayer you ever spoke, they would be sufficient.
Meister Eckhart (1260–1328), theologian and philosopher

148 *How can I pray in the evening?*

Think about the past day.
Thank God for everything he has given you.
Ask his pardon for your sins.
Ask God for his blessing and say good night to him.

It is best if you speak with God
in your own words.
If you are too tired,
you can also say one
of the following prayers:

Now I lay me down to sleep.
I pray the Lord my soul to keep.
If I should die before I wake,
I pray to God my soul to take.
If I should live for other days,
I pray the Lord to guide my ways.
Father, unto you I pray,
You have guarded me all day;
Safe I am while in your sight,
Safely let me sleep tonight.
Bless my friends, the whole world bless;
Help me to learn helpfulness;
Keep me ever in your sight;
So to all I say good night.

Thank you, God, for a lovely day,
for sun and rain, for work and play.
For all my family and friends,
and for your love, which never ends.
Amen.

Praying with Sacred Scripture
Letting oneself be inspired by
Sacred Scripture is a good method of
prayer. For example, the
Lutheran pastor **Georg**
Christian Dieffenbach
(1822–1901) was moved
by a little scene in the

Gospel of Luke. The resurrected Jesus
was on his way to Emmaus with two
disciples. The disciples did not understand yet who was with them on
the way, but they asked the stranger,
"Stay with us, for it is toward evening
and the day is now far spent." So

Jesus went in to stay with them (Lk 24:29).
At this point in the story, Dieffenbach
continued praying, and he created an
evening prayer that is still loved and
prayed more than 150 years later: →

Jesus, tender Shepherd,
hear me:
Bless your little
child tonight;
Through the darkness be
you near me,
Keep me safe till
morning light.

All this day your hand has
led me,
And I thank you for
your care;
You have warmed me,
clothed me, fed me;
Listen to my evening prayer.

May my sins be all forgiven;
Bless the friends I love so well;
Take me, Lord, at last to heaven.
Happy there with you to dwell.

→ **"Abide with us, Lord,**
for it is toward evening and the day is far spent;
abide with us, and with your whole Church.
Abide with us in the evening of the day,
in the evening of life,
in the evening of the world.
Abide with us in your grace and mercy,
in holy Word and Sacrament,
in your comfort and your blessing.
Abide with us in the night of distress and fear,
in the night of doubt and temptation,
in the night of bitter death,
when these shall overtake us.
Abide with us and with all your faithful ones,
O Lord, in time and in eternity.
Amen."

149   Why do we pray the Our Father?

The → **Our Father**
is a very special prayer,
because it is the only prayer
that Jesus himself has taught us.
In seven great steps,
he shows us how we can
speak with God.

Our Father, who art in heaven,
hallowed be thy name.
Thy kingdom come.
Thy will be done
on earth, as it is in heaven.
Give us this day our daily bread,
and forgive us our trespasses
as we forgive those
who trespass against us,
and lead us not into temptation,
but deliver us from evil.
For thine is the kingdom, the power,
and the glory, forever and ever.
Amen.

→ You could spend an entire lifetime deepening your understanding of the **Our Father**, the most important prayer in the world. When parents want to introduce a child to the faith, they should talk about the Our Father with them again and again. Below you will find suggestions for explaining this prayer to your child.

● **Our Father** …
Jesus spoke Aramaic and says *Abba* to God, which means "dad" or "father". God is a good, just, loving, and strong father; we can feel completely safe with him. We have become his children through Baptism. That's why all Christians are our brothers and sisters.

● **… who art in heaven …**
You don't go to heaven on a plane. Heaven is where God is. Thus, there can be a bit of heaven in our midst, too. Where God is present, there is heaven. There is joy without end. Jesus has made room for us in heaven. That is why

we don't have to be afraid of dying. Our dear Father is waiting for each of us with outstretched arms.

● **… hallowed be thy name.**
God wants all people to know him, to love him, and to call to him. To that end, he has entrusted to us his mysterious name: *Yahweh* = "I am." This name tells us: Don't be afraid! I am here! Always! God wants us to know this, wants us to thank him for this, and wants us to treat his name reverently.

Even Jesus' best friends
didn't know in the beginning
how to pray well.
So, they asked Jesus:

"Lord, teach us to pray!" (Lk 11:1)

They saw that no one was as good
at prayer as Jesus.
Jesus knew the way to
to speak with God.

● **Thy kingdom come.**
May lies disappear from among us! May there be truthfulness among us! May hatred make way for love! May wars cease and peace increase! May fear disappear! May trust spread. With Jesus, the kingdom of God has dawned. It is in our midst. Help us to welcome it, Father in heaven!

● **Thy will be done on earth, as it is in heaven.**
Heaven is the world where God's will is always upheld. On earth, we put obstacles in God's way. Heaven is heavenly. There is a mess on earth, fighting and tears, because everyone wants his own way. We have to pray that we know and fulfill God's will on earth. Because if God's will prevails on earth, it is going to be heavenly, too.

● **Give us this day our daily bread, ...**
We should ask God for everything we need in order to live. The poor often understand that better than the rich. The problem is that people are often greedy, want everything for themselves, and let others starve.

● **... and forgive us our trespasses as we forgive those who trespass against us, ...**
We should pray that God forgives us when we have been bad. God wants to give us a new beginning. And we should do the same: forgive people who have been bad to us.

● **... and lead us not into temptation, but deliver us from evil.**
God does not set traps for us; he never has evil plans for us, but he allows temptations. That's why we pray that he will strengthen us in our temptations. Temptations are those thoughts and feelings that lure me toward evil and away from the good that I want to do but is hard to do. By the way, Jesus prayed in Aramaic; and translated from Aramaic, these words say, "Guide us, so that we don't fall into temptation!"

150 *Why do we turn to Mary in prayer?*

**We ask for Mary's intercession
because God became man through her.
Mary is the Mother of Jesus.
She is also our Mother.
Because on the Cross,
Jesus gave Mary to us as a mother.
Loving mothers help their children.
Mary does, too.**

Marian devotion

Many non-Catholic Christians have a hard time with Mary. Yet the role of Mary can be explained very easily to children by using the icon above. Mary is the Mother of Jesus. She is holding Jesus in her hands. She also holds us, his brothers and sisters. We, too, are her children. We can call on her.

When Jesus saw his mother, and the disciple whom he loved standing near, he said to his mother, "Woman, behold your son!" Then he said to the disciple, "Behold, your mother!" And from that hour the disciple took her to his own home.
Jn 19:26–27

151 *What is the → Hail Mary?*

Hail Mary,
full of grace, the Lord is with thee.
Blessed art thou among women,
and blessed is the fruit
of thy womb, Jesus.
Holy Mary, Mother of God,
pray for us sinners,
now and at the hour of our death. Amen.

The first half of this prayer is from the Bible.
The first sentence is the angel Gabriel's greeting.
He gave Mary the message that she
would bear the Son of God.
The second sentence repeats the joyful words
of her cousin Elizabeth:
"Blessed art thou among women...."
That is like saying,

"Mary,
you are the most
blessed woman
in the whole world!
Because God has chosen you
to be the Mother of our Savior."

The second part of the prayer,
"Holy Mary, Mother of God ...",
was added by the faithful who believed
that Mary can hear our prayers and help
us in the most important moments
of our lives: "Now ... and at the hour of our death."

Holy Mary, Mother of God, you have given the world its true light, Jesus, your Son.... Show us Jesus. Lead us to him. Teach us to know and love him, so that we too can become capable of true love and be fountains of living water in the midst of a thirsting world.
Pope Benedict XVI, Encyclical Letter *Deus Caritas Est,* December 25, 2005

→ **"Hail Mary"** in Latin is *Ave Maria.* That is why this prayer is often also called the Ave Maria.

152 *What is the Angelus?*

**The Angelus (Latin = angel) is a prayer
that consists of three Bible passages.
They are each followed by a Hail Mary.
It is a prayer of joy
about God becoming man.**

At 6 in the morning, 12 noon,
and 6 in the evening, in many places
the church bells ring.
They remind us of this prayer,
which many people like to pray:

Leader: The angel of the Lord declared to Mary:
All: ... and she conceived of the Holy Spirit.
Hail Mary...

Leader: Behold, the handmaid of the Lord:
All: ... be it done unto me according to thy word.
Hail Mary ...

Leader: And the Word was made flesh:
All: ... and dwelt among us.
Hail Mary ...

Leader: Pray for us, O Holy Mother of God,
All: ... that we may be made worthy of the promises of Christ.

Leader: Pour forth, we beseech thee, O Lord, thy grace into our
hearts that we, to whom the Incarnation of Christ, thy Son, was
made known through the message of an angel, may by his Passion
and Cross be brought to the glory of his Resurrection, through the
same Christ, our Lord.

All: Amen.

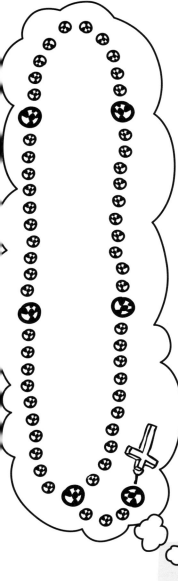

153 *What is the Rosary?*

**The Rosary is a prayer
by which, with Mary, we can gaze upon
the whole life of Jesus.
No one is closer
to Jesus than Mary.**

154 *How do I pray the Rosary?*

**You take the rosary beads in your hand,
you start at the cross, and
you go from bead to bead.**

On the cross, you say
the Creed (see Question 13).
On the first big bead, you say an Our Father,
then three Hail Marys on the small beads, and a Glory Be.
At each of the next five big beads,
you pray the Our Father;
at the following ten small ones, the Hail Mary.
At the end, you pray a Glory Be.
Each set of ten beads is called a "decade".
Before you begin each set, you recall
one of the main episodes in the life of Jesus.
These are called "mysteries".

(see next page)

Contemplation (from the Latin word *contemplatio*, "fixing one's gaze on something", "reflecting on something") is a form of prayer where one focuses on a mystery of the faith with love, time, and attention. The Rosary is probably the most widespread form of contemplative prayer. Whoever prays the Rosary daily (and thus, with Mary, turns his attention 50 times a day to the central mysteries of Jesus), meditates 350 times a week on the miracle of our salvation. This has effects deep down. No wonder that **St. Pope John Paul II** (1920–2005) declared the Rosary his "favorite prayer" and repeatedly made the case for it: "What actually is the Rosary? A compendium of the Gospel. It brings us back again and again to the most important scenes of Christ's life, almost as if to let us 'breathe' his mystery. The Rosary is the privileged path to contemplation. It is, so to speak, Mary's way. Is there anyone who knows and loves Christ better than she?" (October 7, 2003)

155 *What are the mysteries of the Rosary?*

There are four sets of mysteries of the Rosary:
the Joyful Mysteries,
the Sorrowful Mysteries,
the Glorious Mysteries,
and the Luminous Mysteries.

Some people pray certain Mysteries of the Rosary
on certain days:
Joyful Mysteries: Mondays and Saturdays
Sorrowful Mysteries: Tuesdays and Fridays
Glorious Mysteries: Wednesdays and Sundays
Luminous Mysteries: Thursdays

The *Joyful* Mysteries are
- The Annunciation
- The Visitation
- The Nativity of Our Lord
- The Presentation of Jesus at the Temple
- The Finding of Jesus at the Temple

The *Sorrowful* Mysteries are
- The Agony in the Garden
- The Scourging at the Pillar
- The Crowning with Thorns
- The Carrying of the Cross
- The Crucifixion

The *Glorious* Mysteries are
- The Resurrection
- The Ascension
- The Coming of the Holy Spirit
- The Assumption of Mary
- The Coronation of Mary

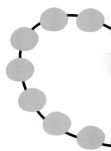

The *Luminous* Mysteries are
- The Baptism of Jesus
- The Wedding Feast at Cana
- The Proclamation of the Kingdom of God
- The Transfiguration of Jesus
- The Institution of the Eucharist

An additional prayer was added to the end of each decade of the Rosary, after the Glory Be. It was given to the children who saw the Blessed Mother at Fatima, Portugal, in 1917:

"Oh my Jesus, forgive us our sins,
save us from the fires of hell,
and lead all souls to heaven
especially those in most need of your mercy."

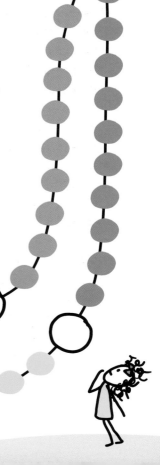

156 *What are the psalms?*

**The psalms are 150 songs that
the people of Israel have been praying to God
for thousands of years.**

Jesus, Mary, and the apostles prayed the psalms.
On the Cross, Jesus called to the Father with
words from a psalm. From the beginning,
Christians have been praying the psalms.
Catholics pray one at every Mass.

 The LORD is my shepherd,
    I shall not want;
he makes me lie down in green pastures.
He leads me beside still waters;
he restores my soul.
He leads me in paths of righteousness
for his name's sake.
Even though I walk through the valley
of the shadow of death, I fear no evil;
for you are with me;
your rod and your staff, they comfort me.
You prepare a table before me
in the presence of my enemies;
you anoint my head with oil, my cup overflows.
Surely goodness and mercy shall follow me
all the days of my life;
and I shall dwell in the house of the LORD
for ever.

Ps 23

Psalm 139 is also well suited for praying with children, contemplating it verse by verse. But the following psalms can also be explained to children and are good for praying together with them: **8, 16, 27, 34, 51, 57, 63, 91, 92, 95, 100, 103, 104, 113, 116, 121, 130, 150.**

The famous German writer **Arnold Stadler** (*1954) was an altar server at a funeral when he heard Psalm 130: "Out of the depths I cry to you, O LORD! ... my soul waits for the LORD more than watchmen for the morning." Stadler wrote, "For the first time in my life, I encountered the beauty of language.... I heard that there was a God who was approachable, even from the depths."

157 *How do you bless someone or something?*

**You make the Sign of the Cross
over the person or the object you
want to bless. You can also sprinkle holy water.
A blessing places someone or something
under God's special protection.**

The Latin word for blessing
is *benedicere*. The literal translation
is "to speak good things upon someone or something".
At Mass, it is the priest
who in the name and by the power of Christ
bestows the blessing.

Every Christian can bless people and things.
Parents can bless their children.
They can draw a cross on their child's forehead
and say "God bless you"
before he leaves for school in the morning,
before he falls asleep at night,
and before he takes a trip.
When parents bless their children,
they are saying to them,
 "You are my treasure and God's treasure!
You are under his protection!"
Children, ask your parents for a blessing.

Children, you can bless someone, too,
for example, your little brother or sister.
You can even bless your pet.

God said to Abraham, "You will be a blessing"
Gen 12:2

Blessing for everyone
Jews and Christians see in their forefather Abraham the first person who believed in the one and only God. To the man who put his entire trust in him, God offered a covenant that contained a blessing for all mankind.

The LORD said to Moses, "Say to Aaron and his sons, Thus you shall bless the sons of Israel: you shall say to them, The LORD bless you and keep you: The LORD make his face to shine upon you, and be gracious to you: The LORD lift up his countenance upon you, and give you peace."
Num 6:22–26

158 *Why do we pray the Glory Be?*

**The one and only God
has shown us that he is the Father,
the Son, and the Holy Spirit.
That is the deepest mystery of the faith:
that the one God in himself
is a community of three Persons.**

Thus Christians often end their prayers
with a Glory Be:

**"Glory be to the Father and to the Son
and to the Holy Spirit.
As it was in the beginning,
is now, and ever shall be,
world without end."**

> You hear wonderful music: Will you praise the notes—instead of the composer who has joined them to make a symphony? You are invited to a delicious feast: Will you praise the pots—instead of the cook whose artistry made the dishes? You look at the magnificent cathedral: Will you praise the stones—instead of the architect who has devised its form that strives toward the heavens? So it is with God, too. He is the master of all masters; it is he who has created everything, who sustains everything, and completes everything in divine love. Will you admire the transient traces of his creation—or him, the Creator, to whom all honor is due in heaven and on earth?
> **Luc Serafin** (*1953), German journalist

159   *Why do we end all prayers with "Amen"?*

**Saying Amen means
agreeing with your whole heart.**

Amen is a Hebrew word
and literally means
"May it be so!"
Amen must never become an empty word.
It has to sound
as if you were saying:
Great! Absolutely! Yes!

Amen!"

 Let what you say be simply 'Yes' or 'No'; anything more than this comes from the Evil One. **Jesus in Mt 5:37**

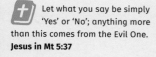 **Amen**
In the Old Testament, the word "Amen" occurs 30 times; in the New Testament, 152 times. Christians say "Amen" after a prayer. Jesus also often says "Amen" before an especially important statement: "Amen, amen, I say to you, whoever believes has eternal life" (Jn 6:47; NABRE). With that, Jesus wants to say: What I'm saying now is absolutely certain; you can rely on it one hundred percent.

A special "Amen" is expected of us when we receive Communion; the priest shows us the Host, Christ's Body, and the chalice with Christ's Blood and says: "The Body of Christ … the Blood of Christ." Before we commune, we should affirm our faith in this mystery and wholeheartedly say "Amen" to it.

Index of Key Words

Index of Bible Passages

Abbreviations of the Biblical Books

Old Testament
Gen Genesis
Ex Exodus
Lev Leviticus
Num Numbers
Deut Deuteronomy
Josh Joshua
Judg Judges
Ruth Ruth
1 Sam 1 Samuel
2 Sam 2 Samuel
1 Kings 1 Kings
2 Kings 2 Kings
1 Chron 1 Chronicles
2 Chron 2 Chronicles
Ezra Ezra
Neh Nehemiah
Tob Tobit
Jud Judith

Esther Esther
Job Job
Ps Psalms
Prov Proverbs
Eccles Ecclesiastes
Song Song of Solomon
Wis Wisdom
Sir Sirach
Is Isaiah
Jer Jeremiah
Lam Lamentations
Bar Baruch
Ezek Ezekiel
Dan Daniel
Hos Hosea
Joel Joel
Amos Amos
Obad Obadiah
Jon Jonah

Mic Micah
Nahum Nahum
Hab Habakkuk
Zeph Zephaniah
Hag Haggai
Zech Zechariah
Mal Malachi
1 Mac 1 Maccabees
2 Mac 2 Maccabees

New Testament
Mt Matthew
Mk Mark
Lk Luke
Jn John
Acts Acts of the Apostles
Rom Romans
1 Cor 1 Corinthians
2 Cor 2 Corinthians

Gal Galatians
Eph Ephesians
Phil Philippians
Col Colossians
1 Thess 1 Thessalonians
2 Thess 2 Thessalonians
1 Tim 1 Timothy
2 Tim 2 Timothy
Tit Titus
Philem Philemon
Heb Hebrews
Jas James
1 Pet 1 Peter
2 Pet 2 Peter
1 Jn 1 John
2 Jn 2 John
3 Jn 3 John
Jude Jude
Rev Revelation

Index of Names

→ Solution to the Quiz on page 113:
It is St. Nicholas of Myra! He lived in the 4th century in present-day Turkey. The name Santa Claus is from the Dutch version of his name: Sinterklaas.

Picture Credits

Front matter and back matter
Martine Boutros; Charles Costantine; Thomas Crouzier; Ildikó von Ketteler; Mattia Mohr; Father Jude Thaddeus Langeh; Alexander von Lengerke; Pixabay, licensed CCo 1.0; Albus Pioquinto; Peter Rydzon; Jodi Stauffer

12, 44, 102, 202: Arthur P. Strong/Ingrid Franzon; 26: PeopleImages (Stock-Fotografie); 106: travnikov-studio (Stock-Fotografie); 109: Birgit Korber (Stock-Fotografie); 194: Aldo Murillo (Stock-Fotografie); 70: S. Chiara Audiovisivi Soc. Coop. a.r.l.; 72: Gedenkstätte Deutscher Widerstand; 83: Amador Alvarez; 86: Erich Lessing; 97: Martin Kornas; 114: Loretto (Gianna Mohr, Lucia Berktold); 116: Pressestelle Bistum Augsburg; 132: Martine Boutros; 131: Father Jude Thaddeus Langeh; 152: Alexander von Lengerke; 140: Philipp Werner/Stefanie Bross; 144: Richard Hörmann; 168: CNS/Crosiers; 196: Football Tribe Asia

Creative Commons-License by-sa.2.0:
5, 6, 32: Korean Culture and Information Service (Jeon Han); 21, 62, 95, 170: Agamitsudo; 17, 31, 34, 37, 45, 61, 71, 76, 103, 112, 128, 130, 155, 160, 179, 196f., 201, 215: Flickr; 42, 87, 151, 158, 165, 176, 192, 197: Túrelio; 65, 95, 101, 117, 121, 159, 204, Wikimedia Commons; 220: Blaues Sofa

Creative Commons-License by-sa.3.0:
16, 22, 89, 137, 178 Deutsches Bundesarchiv (146-1987-074-16, 183-W0409-300, Rolf Unterberg/ 3B145-00014770, 46-1983-098-20); 60: RPP-Institut 102, 143, 158, 178: Wikimedia Commons; 105: Fernando Frazão/Agência Brasil; 117: Dietmar Jendreyzik; 154: Beeldbank Nationaal Archief

Creative Commons-License by-sa.4.0:
33, 79: Wikimedia Commons; 88: Michael Kranewitter; 187: ETH-Bibliothek

Creative Commons Public Domain
14, 116: Sandro Botticelli; 35, 168: John Everett Millais; 41: St. Catherine's Monastery, Sinai (Egypt)/K. Weitzmann; 42, 43, 44, 75, 78, 79, 146, 147, 149, 153, 165, 181, 191, 200, 202, 204, 209, 217, 241: Unknown; 43: Stefan Bernd; 80: National Gallery London; 113: Library of Congress; 137: Alamy Stock Photos, Ramban Institute; 139: Ernest Herbert Mills; 181: Johann Schäfer; 185: Jastrow; 186: USA International Trade Administration; 141: Nobel Foundation; 23, 60, 163, 204, 241: Pixabay, lizensiert CC0 1.0; 118: Demetrio (Cathopic); 35, 45, 50, 74, 87, 110, 113, 145, 147, 149, 151, 157, 159, 191, 203: Luis Ángel Espinosa (Cathopic); 24, 89, 105, 126, 127, 133, 138, 151, 188, 208: Heiligenlexikon; 221: Abraham Lilien

Art in the YOUCAT for Kids

Master Bertram of Minden
(1345–1415)
Creation of the Animals
Page 29

Anonymous Artist from Lombardy
(15th Century)
Study for the Last Supper
Page 40

Fra Angelico
(1395–1455)
The Annunciation
Page 47

Giotto di Bondone
(1266/67–1337)
Last Judgment
Page 77

Konrad von Soest
(1370–1422)
Altar in Wildung,
Pentecost
Page 81

Jaume Ferrer Bassa
(ca. 1285–1348)
Pentecost
Page 83

Gaudenzio Ferrari
(1475–1546)
The Resurrection of Christ from the Tomb
Page 66

Mihály Munkácsy
(1844–1900)
Ecce Homo
Page 58

Benvenuto Tisi Garofalo
(1481–1559)
Ascension of Christ
Page 73

Eugène Burnand
(1850–1921)
Peter and John Rushing to the Tomb
Page 86

Albrecht Altdorfer
(1480–1538)
The Battle of Alexander at Issus
Page 100

Rembrandt van Rijn
(1606–1669)
The Return of the Prodigal Son
Page 94

ONLINE BONUS MATERIAL
for Kids

You can find free bonus material to go along with specific topics on the official YOUCAT for Kids website, **www.youcat.org/y4k**. Short videos and games for going deeper, finding inspiration, and illuminating the material.

www.youcat.org/y4k

YOUCAT for Kids

Inspiration

Material

Games

Videos

www.youcat.org/y4k